EVERYTHING

YOU NEED TO KNOW ABOUT...

Low Fat
Cooking

EVERYTHING

YOU NEED TO KNOW ABOUT...

Low Fat Cooking

LISA SHAW

D&C

David and Charles

A DAVID & CHARLES BOOK
David & Charles is a subsidiary of F+W (UK) Ltd.,
an F+W Publications Inc. company.

First published in the UK in 2005
First published in the USA by Adams Media, an F+W Publications Inc. company,
as The Everything® Low-Fat High-Flavor Cookbook in 1998

Project Manager Ian Kearey
Cover Design Ali Myer

A catalogue record for this book is available from the British Library.

ISBN 0 7153 2225 7

Printed in Great Britain by CPI Bath
for David & Charles
Brunel House   Newton Abbot   Devon

Visit our website at www.davidandcharles.co.uk

David & Charles books are available from all good bookshops;
alternatively you can contact our Orderline on (0)1626 334555 or
write to us at FREEPOST EX2110, David & Charles Direct,
Newton Abbot, TQ12 4ZZ (no stamp required UK mainland).

Everything You Need to Know About Low Fat Cooking is intended as a reference
book only. While author and publisher have made every attempt
to offer accurate and reliable information to the best of their
knowledge and belief, it is presented without any guarantee.
The author and publisher therefore disclaim any liability incurred
in connection with the information contained in this book.

Contents

398 Recipes

DELICIOUS, EASY, LOW-FAT RECIPES

Introduction

OK, you've decided that it's time – time to start looking after your health, time to start eating healthier foods that are lower in fat. In other words, it's time to start thinking about *you*. So you've picked up *this book* to kickstart your plans and to give you some new ideas. Congratulations!

No matter how strong your resolve, if you're like most people, there's a tiny part of you that is saying, yes, you want to eat healthier foods and probably lose some weight in the process, and all this is very well and good. But what it still comes down to is that you're taking these steps because they are good for you, and not because you think you'll enjoy it.

I'm telling you to stop thinking that way right now. Eating a low-fat diet is not the same thing as going on a low-calorie diet where carrot sticks and hard-boiled eggs – and no enjoyment – are the order of the day. On the contrary, eating a low-fat diet is a wonderful adventure where, once the sensation of 'missing' your usual dose of greasy chips and burgers wears off – and it will, sooner than you think – you'll discover that you're able to experience the variety of tastes, textures and temperatures that eating freshly prepared low-fat food delivers – an experience that is never possible with a diet of fat-laden foods.

For instance, you'll discover the true sweetness and crispy crunch of a red pepper, the nuttiness and tang of a spoonful of brown rice that's been sprinkled with spring onions and freshly ground black pepper, or the salty bite that comes with a forkful of fresh fish that's been simply prepared with lemon and spices and perhaps a touch of fruity olive oil. If these same foods were buried under ladlefuls of fatty salad dressing, loads of butter or a deep-fried coating, you would be missing these taste sensations.

In fact, following a low-fat diet is easier than you think. As with anything new, old habits initially die hard, but a recent study suggests that in time, you may learn to like and even prefer – gasp! – dishes that contain little or no fat.

A study conducted at Philadelphia's Monell Chemical Senses Center in the USA involved 18 men and women who ate low-fat diets. Some were extremely low in fat, while others were just moderately low in fat. After six months on the diets, the researchers found that the people who were following the diet lowest in fat actually came to prefer low-fat foods to fatty foods.

Like many people, I grew up eating a typical Western diet, high in fat and sodium, while avoiding anything green and fresh whenever possible. Today, unfortunately, many children follow the same pattern, which is especially disheartening given all the information we now know about how an excess of fat in the diet can affect health, both in the short-term and decades down the road. If you are a member of today's average British family, where everyone is running

around from work to home to appointments to chores, you need to cut corners on time. One easy way is by opting for takeaway and restaurant dishes that tend to be high in fat.

The good news about the recipes in this book is that the majority of them take less than 15 minutes to assemble. During the time the dish is cooking, you can get other things done or just relax and put your feet up. In addition, once you find a number of dishes that turn out to be your favourites, you can double or even triple the amount you make and place the extras in the freezer for future meals.

It's a good idea to use each recipe as a guideline, not as gospel. For instance, I love garlic and have used it liberally in the recipes where I think the dish would be enhanced by the 'stinking rose'. I know that not everyone feels the same way, however. So you can cut down on the use of garlic – or any other spice or seasoning – in the recipes here, or even eliminate it completely. If you're a fan of rosemary or tarragon, or any other herb or spice, then by all means go ahead and use it.

At the same time, you shouldn't transform yourself into such a virtuous creature that you never indulge in a rich dessert. Humans are so single-minded that frequently we get off on one track – in this case, the low-fat track – and we refuse to allow anything to divert us from our goal. Then, suddenly, a craving for a piece of chocolate – or anything else considered to be a 'bad' food – derails us.

After that first bite of heaven, all hell breaks loose, and we think that since we've fallen off the wagon, we might as well go all the way. Days or weeks later, after eating so much 'bad' food that we're actually sick of it, we return to our roots and get started on the 'right track' again.

The good thing about following a low-fat diet and not a low-calorie diet is that these extremes can easily be tempered. If you eat a low-fat salad for lunch, you can allow yourself a bit of a rich dessert and be satisfied. Experiment with the point at which you feel satisfied, and learn to recognize when you've crossed over the line. Keep these parameters in mind for the next time and consciously stop short of that line. It may make you feel a bit anxious at the time you're doing it, but I guarantee you'll forget all about it an hour later.

Indeed, if you completely forego the kinds of foods you have come to view as forbidden, the world can sometimes seem like a much harsher place, no matter what your circumstances are or where you live. A sense of balance – eating a low-fat diet but remembering to occasionally treat yourself – will go a long way towards helping you to feel better about your life.

As you leaf through this book, you may wonder how to choose a particular dish for a meal you're planning for friends and family, or for one you're just throwing together in minutes. My opinion? The best way to select a recipe from the 300-plus in the pages that follow is to use your own instinct. What catches your eye? What are you in the mood for at this moment? Of course, the time of year will also influence your choices: in the summer, you probably won't want to heat up your kitchen by preparing a long-cooking oven dish.

And remember that you don't always have to follow your mother's advice. Don't feel as though it's absolutely necessary to make sure that the main course you choose 'matches' the vegetables and the salad. Wine connoisseurs agree that it's acceptable to serve white wine with beef and red wine with fish, so you have my permission to mix and match as you see fit. If you cook with love and spirit, it's a good bet that no matter what you serve – a creamy dessert to follow a rich main course, or a light dessert that follows a salad – people will clean their plates.

Why Low Fat?

In the 1960s and 1970s, weight-conscious men and women became concerned with the calorie content of the food they were eating. Diet doctors-turned-book-writers at the time suggested that eating a combination of high-fat foods with high-protein foods – in addition to drinking a gallon of water to wash it all down – but almost no carbohydrates, was enough to cause weight to melt away effortlessly. And melt away they did…at least for a few weeks. After a steady diet of fatty meat and a gallon of water, people were too nauseated to eat much more, and therefore started to eat as little as possible, making it easy to drop 9kg (20lb) or more over the course of a month.

The decade of the 1980s saw the entry of high-carbohydrate diets, mainly to coincide with the running boom and marathoners' need to load up on as much pasta and bread as they could choke down before hitting the race circuit. Again, people who followed this high-carb programme lost weight for a while.

For most of the 1990s, low-fat eating was extolled as a sane way of life and perhaps the first diet programme in years that didn't promise that you'd lose 3–5kg (7–10lb) during the first couple of weeks. At first, people balked at the idea of a low-fat diet. But as the truth about decades of unrealistic crash diets began to sink in, the low-fat lifestyle started to make a lot of sense. For one, it didn't ask that you give up anything, just to eat everything in moderation. Plus, if you follow a low-fat lifestyle, it means that you are able to eat lots of food, since many low-fat foods, such as wholemeal breads, fruits and vegetables, have bulk, therefore fewer calories per spoonful, slice or serving.

What Is Low Fat?

Opinion is greatly divided among the experts who regularly dish out statistics and prescriptions to tell us how we can live healthier lives.

The ultra-low-fat proponents, such as those of the Pritikin Diet that was popular in the early 1980s, believe that getting 5 per cent of our daily allotment of calories from fat is the number to strive for. One thing about this goal, however: since most food contains at least some fat – including most vegetables, cereals and even fish – getting 5 per cent of our daily calories from fat means cutting out at least some of these foods that we already think of as low-fat. Fat is what provides us with satiety and that feeling of fullness after a meal; without at least 10 per cent fat, well, you may

be eating loads of vegetables and fruits every day, but it's doubtful that you'll ever feel really full.

Fat is a nutrient that contains 9 calories per gram. Carbohydrates and protein contain only 4 calories per gram. You can use this information to calculate the percentage of fat calories that a particular food contains, once you know the number of fat grams.

For instance, say that the ingredient panel for a frozen chicken dinner says that the chicken contains 4 grams of fat per 30g (1oz). This sounds OK, until you work out that a serving equals 90g (3oz) and contains 270 calories in all. (A table-spoon of vegetable oil, even though the label will scream that it contains *no cholesterol*, is still not a heart-healthy food, since it contains anywhere from 11 to 13 grams of fat.) There are a total of 12 grams of fat per serving, which translates to 108 calories that are pure fat. This means that the chicken is 40 per cent fat, which in no way trans-lates to a low-fat food. (By the way, experts esti-mate that most people who follow the conventional meat-and-potatoes diet consume a diet that gets 40 per cent of its calories from fat.)

Low-Fat Health Benefits You Didn't Expect

Everyone knows that following a low-fat diet can help you to reduce the chances of getting heart disease and some types of cancer. Here are a few other unexpected benefits:

- A high-fat diet can cause heart disease, but according to Irwin Goldstein, MD, Professor of Urology at Boston University School of Medicine, USA, the same kind of circulatory problems responsible for causing heart disease can also cause impotence. 'In fact', he says, 'impotence can be the first indication of cardiovascular disease.'
- A diet that's high in fat generally increases your chances of developing atherosclerosis, a disease where fatty deposits known as plaque build up on the inside of the walls of your blood vessels, which narrows arteries and restricts the flow of blood. When plaque forms in the arteries that carry blood to the spine, the supply of oxygen and nutrients to the spine is decreased, sometimes significantly. This can result in disk degeneration, which causes chronic back pain.
- A recent two-year study discovered that when patients with skin cancer ate a low-fat diet with 20 per cent of calories from fat, they developed 70 per cent fewer precancerous lesions than those patients who stuck to their regular high-fat diet with an average of 40 per cent of calo-ries from fat.

How These Recipes Were Selected

In a world where high-fat everything reigns, some-times it's difficult to find tasty low-fat recipes. Indeed, it took some time to scout out recipes that were truly low in fat and still tasted delicious.

Many of the recipes were modified from the original high-fat version. Others were created by combining low-fat foods that would work well

together and still be enticing enough to make a hungry diner choose the dish without knowing it was deliberately low in fat.

Use these recipes as a springboard for your own culinary imagination. If an item of produce is out of season, substitute another fruit or vegetable that you and your family enjoy. And use some of the suggestions in the introduction to further reduce the fat content of the recipes. Sometimes this is as easy as just adding more of a food that is naturally low in fat, so that the fat – and calorie – content of the entire recipe is reduced. For instance, in a chicken and vegetable stir-fry, cut the amount of meat you use by a third, while doubling the amount of vegetables, which is really how people in most Asian countries prepare stir-fry dishes. Then cut the amount of oil by a half and substitute an equal amount of low-fat chicken stock.

Once you become familiar with the ingredients and cooking methods that a low-fat recipe entails, you can experiment with reducing the fat in your own high-fat recipes.

In the meantime, bear these tips in mind when you're cooking at home or eating out to make sure that a low-fat diet will turn into a habit that is easy to follow – and delicious enough to keep you following it.

Meat, Seafood and Poultry

- Choose the leanest cuts and remove as much fat as possible before cooking.
- Bake or grill instead of frying.

Low-Fat Questions and Answers

Q: Does red meat include pork and ham? What's the leanest red meat available?

A: The category of red meat includes beef, pork, lamb and veal.

A lean cut of meat is one that has less than 10 grams of fat and 4.5 grams or less of saturated fat in a cooked 90g (3oz) serving. The eye of the loin and fillet are the leanest cuts of beef. Veal shoulder, minced veal, cutlets or sirloin are low in fat. Pork tenderloin, sirloin and top loin are low in fat.

- Poach poultry or fish in seasoned stock or stock diluted with wine.

Vegetables

- Steam vegetables rather than stir-fry them.
- Use vegetable oils rather than butter and sour cream for cooking and flavouring.
- Substitute low-fat versions of sour cream and yogurt for full-fat versions.

Milk and Cheese

- Substitute low-fat milk for heavy cream and skimmed milk for whole milk.
- Use low-fat cheese in pasta salads and other recipes.
- Use Parmesan cheese sparingly.

Sauces

- Mix flour with low-fat milk, skimmed milk or stock.
- Increase the stock and reduce the oil in recipes.
- Use cornflour, dissolved in liquid, to thicken stir-fry sauces quickly.
- Purée semi-skimmed ricotta cheese or low-fat sour cream to enrich a cream sauce.

Easy Low-Fat Cooking Tips

- Pancakes are lighter and fluffier when you substitute soda water for milk in the batter.

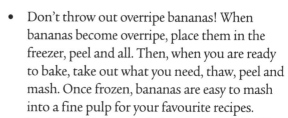

- Don't throw out overripe bananas! When bananas become overripe, place them in the freezer, peel and all. Then, when you are ready to bake, take out what you need, thaw, peel and mash. Once frozen, bananas are easy to mash into a fine pulp for your favourite recipes.
- For high-rising, rounded tops on muffins like the ones you see in bakers' shops, preheat your oven to 250°C (500°F), gas mark 9. As soon as you put the muffins into the oven, decrease the temperature to whatever the recipe indicates. Remember to decrease the baking time. This may take a bit of watching and practice, but the results will be worth it. The increased temperature causes the muffins to rise quickly, giving them that nice dome-shaped top.
- To make lighter, fluffier mashed potatoes, add a pinch or two of baking powder to the potatoes before whipping.
- When greasing and flouring cake pans for baking chocolate cakes, use cocoa powder instead of flour. The cake will have a rich dark colour. This is especially great for cakes that don't need icing.
- To make perfect hard-boiled eggs, poke a hole, using a needle, in the rounder end of each egg. Bring a saucepan of water to the boil, then remove from the heat. Add the eggs and return the pan with boiling water to boil gently for 9 to 10 minutes. Pour out the water and shake the eggs in the pan to crack them. Drop the eggs into a bowl of water and ice. Remove the shell under water for easier peeling, then place the

peeled egg back in the water. This will prevent green-tinged egg yolks and a sulphur smell.

- Use good nonstick baking tins. They will help reduce the amount of oil needed in cooking.
- Coat your baking tins with flour or cornmeal to prevent sticking. You won't have the added fat and calories of lard or oil.
- In recipes calling for multiple eggs, replace some of the whole eggs called for with 2 egg whites. Each egg replaced with 2 egg whites will save 5 grams of fat. It's usually a good idea to keep at least 1 or 2 whole eggs to maintain the correct taste and consistency. For example, replace 3 whole eggs with 1 whole egg and 4 egg whites. You'll save 10 grams of fat.
- When baking a cake, bake at 170°C (325°F), gas mark 3, for a moist cake every time.
- To remove salt from over-salty gravies and sauces, add a peeled potato to the sauce and cook; discard when finished.
- For easier removal of muffins and cup cakes, spray the paper liners with nonstick cooking spray.
- Drain all crispy fried foods on the inside of brown-paper grocery bags. They will help the food retain more crispiness and eliminate more fat than by draining on paper towels, which tend to make the food soggy.
- To remove the core from iceberg lettuce, whack the head of the lettuce, core side down, on the worktop.
- The most efficient way to remove fat from soups, stews and gravies is to refrigerate the dish when cool. When the fat congeals, it will rise to the top and you can spoon if off easily.

Alternatively, place thin strips of paper towels on the top of the dish while it is still hot. They will soak up grease.

- You can reduce the amount of fat in baked products by a quarter to a third. For example, if a biscuit, shortbread or muffin recipe calls for 250ml (8fl oz) oil, use 160ml (5fl oz) instead. (Do not use this method for yeast breads and pie crusts.)
- Crumble dried herbs in your hands before using to release their oils and flavour.
- Peel broccoli stems instead of discarding them. Slice on the diagonal for stir-fries or soups.
- To remove salt from over-salty sauces, add a dash (no more, or the taste of the dish will be dramatically changed) of vinegar to the sauce. This works particularly well for tomato-based sauces.
- When measuring flour, stir it first to loosen and aerate it. Carefully spoon the flour into a measuring cup – never scoop. To level, use the flat side of a knife.
- When measuring liquids, use a measuring cup specifically for liquids. When measuring dry ingredients, use a measuring cup specifically for dry ingredients.
- To restore crystallized honey, microwave just to add a bit of warmth to melt the crystals, then stir.
- Store flour in the freezer to avoid insects.
- Never store onions with potatoes. Onions give off gasses that make potatoes turn bad quickly.

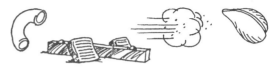

- Don't store carrots in the same refrigerator bin as apples. The carrots will become bitter.
- Soak strong-smelling fish in milk for 30 to 40 minutes to freshen it.
- When buying sun-dried tomatoes packed in oil, drain them and rinse thoroughly. Use the reddest tomatoes. Avoid the dark brown ones.
- Avocados and tomatoes ripen more quickly when placed in brown paper bags and put into a cupboard.
- Place a piece of white bread in with hardened brown sugar to soften it.
- Make sure your pan is hot before adding oil when frying. You'll use less oil and you'll also have no problem with food sticking.
- Use low-fat salad dressings to marinate meat, poultry and fish before baking or grilling.
- To remove a garlic smell from your hands, wash with soap and cold water, then, before drying, run them along your stainless-steel tap (if you have one).
- Never marinate meat or poultry in metal containers. The acids in the marinade may pit the container and ruin the taste of the marinade.
- Store unpopped popcorn in your freezer to retain freshness.
- A low-calorie solution for high-fat frying of corn tortillas is to place them in the oven, directly on the rack. Bake at 180°C (350°F), gas mark 4, to desired crispness. The tortillas will automatically fold over into taco-shell form with just a little positioning help.

Low-Fat Substitutions

Original ingredient	Substitution	Use for
180ml (6fl oz) double cream	2 egg whites	Mousse
250ml (8fl oz) double cream	180ml (6fl oz) nonfat yogurt + 60ml (2fl oz) milk	Baking
250ml (8fl oz) whole milk	250ml (8fl oz) buttermilk	Baking
250g (8oz) cream cheese	250g (8oz) semi--skimmed ricotta cheese	Cheesecakes
125ml (4fl oz) sour cream	125ml (4fl oz) plain low-fat yogurt	Baking
3 whole eggs	3 egg whites + 1 egg yolk	Cakes, custards

Cooking Method Substitutions

- Bake instead of deep-fry.
- Grill or griddle instead of pan-fry.
- Griddle instead of pan-fry to brown meat, fish and poultry.
- Stock-soften instead of fry. Use stock instead of fat, which is required in many Mexican dishes, such as refried beans.
- Griddle-roasting or toasting is a standard Mexican cooking method that intensifies flavours in foods. Tortillas are dry-toasted on a griddle; many people grease the griddle with a bit of oil first, which is unnecessary.
- As a substitute for sautéing or poaching, fresh vegetables with a high moisture content, such as tomatoes, can be placed on a griddle over high heat and turned frequently until surfaces are charred.

How to Achieve 30 Per Cent or Less Fat in Your Diet

Experts recommend that you get no more than 30 per cent of your total calories from fat. This applies to all the food you eat in a day or week.

The following is based on a 2,000-calorie-a-day eating plan: multiply the total calories by 0.30 (30 per cent) to get the allowable calories from fat. Then divide the calories from fat by 9 (1 gram of fat = 9 calories) to get the allowable grams of fat per day. Therefore, 2,000 calories per day x 0.30 = 600 calories from fat, and 600 ÷ 9 = 67 grams of fat. So no more than 67 grams of fat per day.

This is meant to be a guideline for your overall eating. If you go slightly over the 30-per-cent line once in a while, go easy on yourself: pull back on the next meal.

To figure out the percentage of calories of fat for an individual recipe, first multiply the grams of fat by 9, which will give you the total number of calories from fat. Then divide that number by the number of calories in the recipe to get the percentage.

Always look at the number of grams of fat in a food item or recipe, as well as the percentage of calories from fat. A given recipe might list 45 per cent of calories from fat. But on closer look, it may list only 7 grams of fat and 145 calories. When the calories are low, the chances are that the percentage will be misleadingly high.

Modifying Recipes to Reduce Fat

- To compensate for removing fat, increase the use of extracts, spices and condiments such as mustard, vinegar, garlic, lemon juice and fresh ginger.
- Use an equal amount of skimmed milk in soups or sauces that call for cream or half-and-half.
- If you reduce the amount of oil, replace the liquid with an equal amount of milk, water, stock or fruit juice.
- Sprinkle nuts and cheese on top of food rather than mixing them throughout.
- Replace up to half the fat in muffins and other baked goods with apple sauce or puréed fruit.

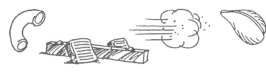

- Cook onions used for seasoning in water, stock or wine.
- Substitute water for up to a third of the oil called for in salad dressings.
- For baking recipes calling for buttermilk, substitute nonfat yogurt to provide some added moistness.
- Use no more than 1 to 2 tablespoons of oil or butter per 250g (8oz) flour when baking muffins and shortbreads.

Reducing Fat in Baked Goods

Ingredients high in fat, such as margarine, butter, lard, oil, double cream, cream cheese, sour cream and chocolate add flavour to recipes but also add calories and grams of fat to our diet. In addition to enhancing the taste, fat makes pastry flaky, cakes moist and tender, and biscuits crisp. Decreasing fat in a baked item can create a drier, coarser, denser texture and reduce the overall flavour. If you would like to try reducing the fat in baking recipes, here are some suggestions:

- Reduce the amount of margarine, butter, lard or oil in a recipe by a quarter to a third.
- Substitute nonfat milk for low-fat milk (2%) or whole milk.
- Substitute low-fat versions of yogurt, sour cream and cream cheese in place of the regular products. Although nonfat counterparts are readily available, they are not always as successful in baking recipes.
- Use skimmed milk instead of double cream in dessert sauces.

- Substitute or add flavourings and/or seasonings to replace the flavour lost from fat. For example, add chocolate and rum flavouring to a cocoa sauce for a more intense taste.
- Serve low-fat baked items such as muffins and coffee cakes warm from the oven. The texture change is not as noticeable when they're eaten warm.

Replacing Fats and Oils

- In place of 125ml (4fl oz) oil, margarine or butter in baking, use 125ml (4fl oz) apple sauce or 60ml (2fl oz) apple sauce and 60ml (2fl oz) buttermilk.
- In place of 125ml (4fl oz oil for marinades and salad dressings, use 125ml (4fl oz) stock or unsweetened pineapple juice.
- In place of 2 tablespoons oil for sautéing, use 2 tablespoons of stock, unsweetened pineapple juice or dry wine.

How to Cook Lean Meat

- Trim off all visible fat from meat before cooking. This significantly reduces the total fat and cholesterol in the cooked portion.
- Choose lean cooking techniques such as griddling, grilling, pan broiling, poaching or roasting.
- Remember to roast and grill meats on a rack so that fat drips away during cooking.
- Discard dripping instead of making it into gravy.

- Limit additional fats or, better still, refrain from using them in meat recipes.
- Use nonstick cooking spray instead of oil for browning.
- Use low-fat ingredients whenever possible.
- For juicier results, cook lean meats to no more than medium-done. Lean meats that are cooked until well-done may have less taste and may be dry and tough. Not overcooking is especially important for top-quality beef cuts.

Lower Fat, Lighter Muffins and Breads

Sometimes low-fat cooking and baking methods can change the texture from what we're used to in their high-fat cousins. Here are some suggestions that will help make the low-fat versions indistinguishable from the high-fat varieties.

- Rubbery or tough textured:
  Usually fat is used to coat flour particles so that the gluten will not develop during mixing. By eliminating the fat, you will eliminate this. To solve this problem, add a small amount of grated apple to the batter. This will add moistness and compensate for the tough texture, or add some fat back into the recipe (you may have taken out too much). You can also add chopped dried fruits and nuts to the batter to add another texture to the baked product.

- Not enough body:
  Using a fat-free liquid substitute, such as nonfat milk, fruit juice or water, which is much less viscous than oil, can cause this problem. Use buttermilk as the liquid in the batter, or add a small amount of grated apple.

- Wet texture:
  Different kinds of flours absorb different amounts of moisture from doughs and batters. Plain flour absorbs less water than wholemeal flour. Use wholemeal flour to replace up to half of the plain flour, or add a few tablespoons of wheatgerm or oat bran.
  Substituting 2 egg whites for each whole egg increases the moisture when baking. Decrease baking temperature and increase baking time, or use an oven thermometer to check your oven. You can also stir an extra tablespoon of flour or cornflour into the batter to absorb excess moisture.

Reducing the Fat in Salad Dressings

- If you are replacing oil with a liquid that is thinner than oil, whisk 1 to 2 teaspoons of arrowroot into the dressing. Bring to a gentle boil, and cook and stir for 2 minutes. You can also replace the oil with a fat-free or reduced-fat substance that has body, such as buttermilk, yogurt or sour cream.

Low-Fat Eating Out

- Ask your waiter to suggest lower-fat starters, main courses and desserts.
- Start with soups such as onion (without the cheese and buttery toast), clam chowder or

broth with rice or noodles. It's a low-fat way to help your stomach fill up.

- Always order your salad dressing on the side. Light is best, but if all you can get is ordinary, mix it half and half with vinegar or lemon juice.
- If you do order a creamy dressing, dip your fork in the dressing, then spear some salad. You'll get the taste with far less fat.
- Order a baked potato instead of chips or French fries. Limit sour cream to 1 tablespoon, butter to 1 pat.
- In Chinese, Thai, Indian, Mexican or Japanese restaurants, order extra steamed rice. Take it home with half the main course, or share it with a friend.
- Eat plenty of unbuttered bread before and during your meal. Eat plain Italian bread instead of oil-soaked garlic bread.
- In general, order vegetarian, seafood or poultry main courses instead of beef or pork.
- In Italian restaurants, order main courses largely made of pasta. Keep to tomato sauce rather than cream sauces.
- If main dishes are notoriously large, order two starters and ask for one to be served as the main course.
- Ask for lower-fat substitutes such as fresh fruit or vegetables instead of high-fat chips or French fries.
- For dessert, have sorbet, sherbet or fat-free or low-fat frozen yogurt.
- Many fast-food chains now display nutritional information about their food. Focus on those items lower in fat.

- Watch out for sauces and condiments. Scrape off the tartar sauce on a fish sandwich and eliminate two-thirds of the fat. Eliminate the syrup and butter on breakfast pancakes and get rid of two-thirds of the fat. Order a Burger King burger without mayonnaise and eliminate 15 grams of fat.
- Use low-fat dressings on your salads. At the salad bar, avoid pasta salads and potato salad. The mayonnaise can add as much fat as a hamburger.
- French fries or chips usually carry the highest fat of any item on the menu. Think about having a salad with low-fat dressing as a side dish instead.
- Watch out for desserts. A Danish pastry or biscuit can have as much fat and as many calories as a single hamburger.

Low-Fat Eating at Home
- Make extensive use of your microwave. Just about everything can be cooked without fats or oils while retaining all the important vitamins and minerals.
- A modern pressure cooker is great for reducing cooking time without adding any fat.
- Avoid frying or sautéing anything. Instead, grill, bake, poach, griddle or steam.
- Replace your pots and pans with nonstick cooking ware, which makes cooking with little or no oil much easier.
- Use nonstick cooking spray instead of greasing pans and tins for cooking and baking.

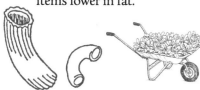

- Season your sauté pans by heating them on high until they smoke, then rub the inside with salt. This helps keep oil from being absorbed by the metal, so you use less when cooking.
- Use butter sprinkles to top vegetables, pasta, rice or potatoes to get a buttery taste without the fat.
- Switch from whole milk to low-fat or nonfat. Note that low-fat milk still contains 5 grams of fat in an 250ml (8fl oz) glass.
- Use margarine instead of butter; it contains no cholesterol, and you can find plenty of varieties of lower-fat margarines and spreads.
- Try using no butter or margarine. Good bread tastes good without it; or think about using a pure-fruit spread.
- For sauces and gravies that call for sour cream or double cream, substitute plain low-fat yogurt. Add a little cornflour to keep it from separating.
- Use nonfat milk or low-fat milk when making cream sauces and gravies. Add a little flour to give thickness.
- Break up flavoured fat-free rice cakes for salads to take the place of fat-filled croutons.
- Chopped chestnuts and water chestnuts are great low-fat replacements for the more standard nuts in salads.
- Substitute wine, lemon juice or vegetable stock for cooking instead of oils or butter. There's no fat, and they add flavour to your recipe.
- When cooking stews, soups and chilli, let the pot cool down. The fat will float to the top and you can skim it off. Then reheat the pot just before serving.
- Keep your meat portions limited to 90g (3oz). This will provide plenty of protein and nutrition, and will cut down considerably the high-fat content of a larger serving.
- Avoid croissants, which are high in butter and fat, in favour of bagels or muffins.
- If meat is essential, consider ham, which usually has less saturated fat than most cuts of beef.
- Don't miss breakfast! It can be a great low-fat meal packed with nutrition and will help keep you from eating fatty foods in the middle of the day.
- Light or dark corn syrup can fill in for some fat in desserts. Substitute 1 tablespoon syrup per 2 tablespoons of fat removed. You'll save 28 grams of fat and 200 calories.
- Read your food labels! Keep a majority of your food choices to those containing 20 per cent of calories or less from fat.
- Be careful in the snacks section of the supermarket. Pretzels are great because they have little or no fat. Watch out for potato crisps and microwave popcorn. Watch the labels on 'new wave' snacks such as vegetable crisps, pitta and bagel crisps. These can have up to 9 grams of fat in a 30g (1oz) serving.
- If you're buying meat, choose chicken and turkey over beef or pork.
- Avoid processed meats such as salami, sausages and hot dogs, all generally very high in fat. Look for healthier vegetarian versions.

- Buy small or medium rather than large eggs. They have less fat and cholesterol.
- If a recipe calls for nuts, try walnuts. They're among the lowest in saturated fat.
- Substitute capers for olives. Using 1 tablespoon of capers in place of 60g (2oz) olives saves 4 grams of fat and 30 calories.
- Exercise! Anything is better than nothing for burning the fat out of your diet. Walk, cycle, stretch, lift weights – it's all great for your heart, mind and body!

Secrets to Healthy Food Shopping

- Never shop on an empty stomach.
- Select tinned fruits and tuna packed in water, not in syrup or oil.
- Check labels for the words *hydrogenated* or *partially hydrogenated*. The earlier they appear in the ingredient list, the higher the amount of unhealthy trans fatty acids a food contains.
- Buy skinless turkey or chicken breasts.
- If selecting frozen dinners, choose those that are not only low in fat, but also low in sodium and cholesterol.
- Try calcium-fortified orange juice if you're not consuming enough dairy products.
- Go for wholemeal breads, rolls and cereals.
- Stock up in the bread, pasta, rice and bean aisles of the supermarket. They all have lots of protein, fibre and nutrition with low fat levels.
- Stock up on fruits and vegetables. Except for a few, they contain little fat and have plenty of nutrition.

- Consider the cantaloupe. For just 95 calories, half a melon provides more than a day's supply of vitamin C and beta carotene.
- Don't be fooled by yogurt-covered raisins or nuts. The coating is usually made of sugar and partially hydrogenated oil.
- Go for these low-fat goodies: pretzels, ginger snaps, crackers and angel food cake.
- Plan your meals before going shopping. Make a shopping list to reduce impulse purchases and to save money and time.
- Consider using own-brand goods; they're usually less expensive than proprietary brands, and the quality is generally comparable.
- Choose a variety of fish, chicken, turkey and veal. And when selecting beef, pork or lamb, look for lean cuts.
- Buy fresh fruits and vegetables and lean meats whenever possible. Tinned soups, frozen dinners and processed meats may be difficult to fit into a healthy diet.

Replacing Fat in the Diet

Replacing fat in the diet is not as easy as it may sound. Contrary to public perception, natural fats actually have many useful roles in the diet. They are one of the nutrient categories essential for proper growth and development and maintenance of good health. They carry the fat-soluble vitamins A, D, E and K, and aid in their absorption in the intestine. They are the only source of linoleic acid, an essential fatty acid. And they are an especially important source of calories for people who are

underweight and for infants and toddlers, who have the highest energy needs per kilogram of body weight of any age group.

Fat also plays important roles in food preparation and consumption. It gives taste, consistency, stability and palatability to foods.

On the other hand, too much fat in the diet can be harmful. Fat is calorie-dense: it contains 9 calories per gram, compared to 4 calories per gram for protein and carbohydrates. So eating a lot of fat can result in excess calorie intake, which in turn can perhaps lead to undesirable weight gain.

Fat intake also is linked to several chronic diseases. There is some evidence of a link between high intakes of fat and a possible increased risk of certain cancers, such as breast, colon and prostate cancers. There also is a link between high intakes of saturated fat and cholesterol and an increased risk of coronary heart disease.

Experts recommend that fat intake be limited to 30 per cent or less of calories and saturated fat to less than 10 per cent. Manufacturers are responding by adding more and more reduced-fat foods to their product lines.

Lifestyle Tips for Low-Fat Eating

- Drink at least 2l (4pts) of water each day. Don't eat dinner until you've finished drinking your daily water requirement.
- Pick one place at home and one at work where you will do all your eating. Make sure you are seated. Don't eat anywhere but in that spot. No worktop eating, sofa eating, car eating or the like.
- Keep healthy foods like fruit or vegetables handy. Eat only if you are hungry.
- Keep a diary of what you eat and your feelings, far away from the kitchen. Write down everything that you eat before you eat it. Describe how you feel in terms of health as you progress. Describe how you feel when you cheat yourself.
- Soups are a great meal. They are filling, tasty and healthy.
- If you are going to a restaurant, decide before you set off what you will be eating. Then stick to it.
- Set up a schedule for when you will eat your food and snacks.
- Keep all food in the kitchen or pantry, not in any other places.
- Never starve yourself, especially before going out to eat (or you will binge). Never miss meals. You must have some kind of regular nourishment or your body's starvation defences will kick in, lower your metabolism and store fat.
- Don't think that just because you are eating low-fat, low-calorie foods that you can eat all that you want. The calories still add up and must be burned off, regardless of what kind of food you eat. Balance is the key.
- Give away or throw away leftover food.
- Get the rest of your family to make their own snacks.

xxi

- Don't put extra food in bowls on the kitchen table. Keep it in the refrigerator or put it away in a cupboard.
- If you get the urge to eat when not truly hungry, go and do something else (go for a walk or do a small chore). Try to accomplish some small thing instead of going backwards in your diet. Try jogging in place for a few minutes when you think you might go off and sneak a snack. This will give you time to think about what you're doing.
- If a certain food shop or restaurant drives you crazy with desire when you drive past it, change your route.
- Try to do at least 30 minutes of low-impact, moderate exercise (walking) at least three times per week. Start off easily and gradually increase in time.
- The best exercise is walking. Plain and simple walking. You should walk briskly but not to the point where you are short of breath. You should be able to carry on a conversation while you are walking.
- Whatever exercise you do to lose weight, make sure it is aerobic. This means that you do not run short of breath. When you run short of breath and have to breathe deeply (anaerobic exercise), your body will burn sugar and not as much fat.
- You should keep track of your measurements (in cm/in) as well as in kg/lb. Write them down every week. Centimetres will come off even though weight is not coming off, or is coming off slowly. This is due to muscle build-up in your body. Muscle is heavier than fat.
- Wherever you work, walk along the longest route possible to get from wherever you are to wherever you're going. (But don't be late!)
- Keep your exercise bike or equipment in full view. This acts as a constant reminder of the effort you have invested, so you don't eat the wrong foods and waste those efforts.
- Always warm up with some stretching before exercising. This will make your body burn more fat when you actually do start exercising, and will help prevent accidental muscle damage.
- Play with your children! It is hard enough for us to find time to be with them with all the pressures of life. Play some kind of game requiring physical movement. They will love you for it, and your overall health will benefit.
- Take the stairs instead of the lift.
- When parking your car at a supermarket, park it as far away from the building as possible. (This will also reduce dents in your car doors from careless people.)
- If you sit a lot at your job or at home, you probably have a flabby stomach. In order to tighten your abdominal muscles, stand or sit with a tall posture, and hold your stomach in as much as possible. Here is the best exercise you can do during the day to tighten those muscles: when you exhale, pull your stomach in, pushing the air out. Pull your stomach in tightly and a little quickly, then let it out naturally while you breathe air back into the lungs.

Pulling the stomach in tightly acts to push the air out of your lungs as you build those abdominal muscles.

- Eat less, and you won't have to exercise as much!
- Eat very slowly and enjoy the tastes.
- Vary your caloric intake so that your body doesn't go into a starvation-prevention mode. If you keep calories low every day, your body will adjust to that amount as if this were all it needed to maintain your weight, and you'll stop losing weight.
- Don't go more than about five hours during the day without eating. This causes you to eat more at mealtime. Eat healthy, low-fat snacks in between meals if you are going to go more than five hours without a meal.
- Don't deprive yourself! If you really enjoy eating a certain food, plan for it. Make it a reward for doing extra sit-ups or for spending more time on cardiovascular exercise. This helps to avoid bingeing.
- Imagine yourself as thin and healthy, and keep that image in mind and recall it once a day, probably in the morning.
- Straight after eating a meal, especially dinner, go straight to the bathroom to brush, floss and gargle with mouthwash so that your mouth is feeling nice and clean. This makes it less appealing to eat more, especially before bedtime.
- If you eat your meals away from the TV and other distracting places, you will enjoy your meal more and you will take a little longer to eat it. In addition, drink at least two glasses of water or one glass of milk during your meal; you'll feel fuller and less likely to go back for seconds.
- Try to work out as much as possible, but at your own pace, and reward yourself, but not with a snack. Instead, put a certain amount of money into a jar every time you work out. The more you work out, the more money you save. Then go on a shopping spree, and buy yourself a new wardrobe for your new thin, trim body.
- Eat to live. Don't live to eat!
- The most important thing to consider before going on a diet is the reason for doing so. Never diet because you think it will make people like you. Diet because you want to look and feel good for yourself. Otherwise you may be disappointed.

Your Low-Fat Choices

Choose a diet low in saturated fat

Fats contain both saturated and unsaturated (monounsaturated and polyunsaturated) fatty acids. Saturated fat raises blood cholesterol more than other forms of fat. Reducing saturated fat to less than 10 per cent of calories will help you lower your blood cholesterol level. The fats from meat, milk and milk products are the main sources of saturated fats in most diets. Many bakery products are also sources of saturated fats.

Vegetable oils supply smaller amounts of saturated fat.

Choose a diet low in monounsaturated and polyunsaturated fat

Olive and sunflower oils are particularly high in monounsaturated fats; most other vegetable oils, nuts and high-fat fish are good sources of polyunsaturated fats. Both kinds of unsaturated fats reduce blood cholesterol when they replace saturated fats in the diet. The fats in most fish are low in saturated fatty acids and contain a certain type of polyunsaturated fatty acid (omega-3) that is being studied because of a possible association with a decreased risk for heart disease in certain people. Remember that fat in the diet should be consumed at a moderate level – that is, no more than 30 per cent of calories. Mono- and polyunsaturated fat sources should replace saturated fats within this limit.

Partially hydrogenated vegetable oils, such as those used in many margarines and fats, contain a particular form of unsaturated fat known as trans-fatty acids that may raise blood cholesterol levels, although not as much as saturated fat.

Choose a diet low in cholesterol

The body makes the cholesterol it requires. In addition, cholesterol is obtained from food. Dietary cholesterol comes from animal sources such as egg yolks, meat (especially organ meats such as liver), poultry, fish and higher-fat milk products. Many of these foods are also high in saturated fats. Choosing foods with less cholesterol and saturated fat will help lower your blood cholesterol levels. You can keep your cholesterol

intake at this level or lower by eating more grain products, vegetables and fruits, and by limiting intake of high cholesterol foods.

Choosing for children

The advice in the previous sections does not apply to infants and toddlers below the age of two years. After that age, children should gradually adopt a diet that, by about five years of age, contains no more than 30 per cent of calories from fat. As they begin to consume fewer calories from fat, children should replace these calories by eating more grain products, fruits, vegetables and low-fat milk products or other calcium-rich foods, and beans, lean meat, poultry, fish or other protein-rich foods.

Facts About Fat

- All oils are 100 per cent fat. This includes olive oil, sesame oil, chilli oil, fish oil, avocado oil, walnut oil, sunflower oil, safflower oil and every other oil. Oils and fats have 9 calories per gram. Of course, oils vary widely in the proportion of saturated, polyunsaturated and monounsaturated fats they contain.
- Vegetables that are high in fat include olives (96 per cent of the calories come from fat), avocados (86 per cent), sunflower seeds (75 per cent), coconut (61 per cent), coconut milk (93 per cent) and, surprisingly, tofu (50 per cent).
- We need some fat in our diet for our bodies to function properly. It would be unhealthy to eliminate all fat. Even with a non-junk-food diet composed of a healthy variety of foods, it

is virtually impossible to eliminate all fat. Almost all foods have fat. A diet consisting only of beans, fruits, vegetables and grains with no added oils or high-fat ingredients will derive up to 10 per cent of its calories from fat.

- We need fat for two main reasons: to help absorb fat-soluble vitamins (such as vitamin A), and to supply two types of essential fatty acids (EFAs) that our bodies need but cannot produce. A diet with at least 10 grams of fat per day will result in normal vitamin absorption (some recommend at least 5 grams per meal, or 15 grams per day). Experts disagree on how much EFA we need, but it is generally a very small amount.

- No Recommended Dietary Allowances (RDA) for either essential fatty acid have been established, primarily because essential fatty acid deficiency has been observed exclusively in patients with medical problems affecting fat intake or absorption. However, the human requirement for linoleic acid has been estimated to be approximately 1 to 2 per cent of the total energy intake (2.7 per cent for infants). This level is generally more than met in varied diets since fats from vegetables are particularly rich sources of linoleic acid. It has been proposed that omega-3 fatty acids should be equal to 10 per cent to 25 per cent of the linoleic acid intake (or 0.1 to 0.5 per cent of total energy intake), particularly during pregnancy, lactation and infancy.

- As long as you eat a varied non-junk-food diet, you are likely to get all the EFAs you need. But if you would like to consume more, the number-one best vegetarian source of both EFAs is flax seeds. However, whole flax seeds are not usually digested well by the body and linoleic acid is very unstable and goes rancid quickly. You should either use cold-pressed flaxseed oil that is no more than three months old, or freshly ground flax seeds. You can eat them raw or use them as an egg replacement in baking. Some people like to add ground flax seed to their breakfast cereal or to make a vinaigrette with flaxseed oil and add it to salad.

Starters

CHAPTER ONE

Amount Per Chapter
16 Recipes

	% Daily Value
Easy to Prepare	**100%**
Low Fat/High Flavour	**100%**
Simple to Understand	**100%**

DELICIOUS, EASY, LOW-FAT RECIPES

We may have become accustomed to going straight into the main course or having only some soup first, but offering a starter before the main dish is too often reserved only for special occasions.

It doesn't have to be this way. In fact, most of the starters that follow can be prepared in just 10 or 15 minutes – something you can do while the rest of the meal is cooking.

Starters are a great way to put the unexpected into a meal, whether it's on a grey day in winter or in the middle of a too-hectic work week. And if you find cooking to be relaxing, making a tasty starter is the perfect antidote to a busy day.

Chillied Bean Dip

Serves: 4

> 500g (1lb) tin kidney beans, drained
>   and rinsed
> 2 jalapeño peppers, finely chopped
> 1 tbsp red wine vinegar
> 1 tsp chilli powder
> 1/4 tsp ground cumin
> 1 tsp finely chopped onion
> 1 tbsp minced fresh parsley

Place the beans, jalapeño peppers, vinegar, chilli powder and cumin in a food processor. Process until smooth. Transfer the mixture to a bowl. Stir in the onion and parsley and serve.

Nutritional Analysis

Calories	43.59	Kcal	Protein	3.05	gm
Fat	0.37	gm	Carbohydrate	7.09	gm
Sodium	74.19	mg	Cholesterol	0.00	mg
Saturated fat	0.02	gm			

Stuffed Celery Stalks

Serves: 12

> 12 long celery stalks with leaves attached
> 185g (6oz) nonfat cream cheese, at room temperature
> 125g (4oz) nonfat cottage cheese
> 1/4 chopped onion (optional)
> 2 tbsp skimmed milk (if needed)
> 12 large pimiento-stuffed green olives, cut into 6mm
>   (1/4 in)-thick slices
> several shakes of paprika

Set the celery stalks on a cutting board, hollow side up. In a small blender or food processor, combine the cream cheese, cottage cheese and onion, if using. Process at high speed for 4 minutes until smooth. If the mixture is very thick, add the milk, a few drops at a time, to thin to spreading consistency.

Using a knife, spread the mixture in the hollows of the celery stalks, dividing it evenly among the stalks. Push olive slices into the spread along the entire length of each stalk. Wrap in cling

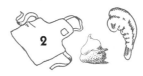

film and chill well. Just before serving, unwrap and sprinkle with paprika.

Nutritional Analysis

Calories	31.02 Kcal	Protein	3.60 gm
Fat	0.54 gm	Carbohydrate	3.03 gm
Sodium	234.03 mg	Cholesterol	2.37 mg
Saturated fat	0.06 gm		

Fruit Smoothie

Serves: 4

250g (8oz) tinned fruit cocktail, chilled
250ml (8fl oz) skimmed milk
60g (2oz) nonfat milk powder
1/2 tsp vanilla extract
2 dashes of ground cinnamon, plus extra for garnish
  (optional)
125g (4oz) ice cubes

In a blender container, combine the undrained fruit cocktail, milk, milk powder, vanilla and cinnamon. Blend until smooth. Add the ice cubes and blend again until smooth. Pour into glasses and sprinkle with additional cinnamon, if desired. Serve immediately.

Nutritional Analysis

Calories	68.64 Kcal	Protein	3.75 gm
Fat	0.67 gm	Carbohydrate	11.95 gm
Sodium	56.14 mg	Cholesterol	3.20 mg
Saturated fat	0.41 gm		

Baked Mushrooms with Spinach and Cheese

Serves: 6

1 tbsp butter
24 medium-sized white mushrooms, quartered
375g (12oz) drained lightly cooked spinach
125ml (4fl oz) Basic Low-Fat White Sauce
  (Chapter 2)
30g (1oz) grated low-fat cheddar cheese
30g (1oz) grated low-fat mozzarella cheese
salt and pepper to taste

Preheat oven to 180°F (350°F), gas mark 4.

In a frying pan over medium-high heat, melt the butter until it foams. Add the mushrooms and sauté until tender and lightly browned, 4 to 6 minutes. Set aside.

Line the bottom of a small baking dish with the spinach. Arrange the mushrooms evenly on top. Pour the white sauce evenly over the mushrooms, then sprinkle with the cheddar and mozzarella cheeses, salt and pepper.

Bake until the cheeses are hot and bubbling, 20 to 25 minutes.

Nutritional Analysis

Calories	73.87 Kcal	Protein	6.84 gm
Fat	2.37 gm	Carbohydrate	8.10 gm
Sodium	169.68 mg	Cholesterol	6.58 mg
Saturated fat	1.26 gm		

Yogurt Dip

Serves: 4

250ml (8fl oz) nonfat plain yogurt
125g (4oz) grated cucumber
1/3 tsp dried dill, crumbled

Combine all the ingredients in a bowl and mix well. Serve with vegetables for dipping.

Nutritional Analysis

Calories	6.72	Kcal	Protein	0.65	gm
Fat	0.02	gm	Carbohydrate	0.94	gm
Sodium	8.69	mg	Cholesterol	0.22	mg
Saturated fat	0.01	gm			

Cheese Coins

Makes: 24 coins

*60g (2oz) buttery light, reduced-fat margarine, at
    room temperature*
250g (8oz) grated low-fat cheddar cheese
1/2 tsp dry mustard
1/2 tsp seasoned salt
2 tsp chopped tinned green chilli peppers
2 tsp minced pimiento
1/2 tsp Worcestershire sauce
185g (6oz) plain flour

Preheat oven to 180°C (350°F), gas mark 4.

In a bowl, using a mixer, beat together the margarine, cheese, mustard, seasoned salt, green chillies, pimiento and Worcestershire sauce until blended. Add the flour, beating it in until a stiff

dough forms. Shape into small balls (about 12mm/1/2in in diameter), and place well-spaced on ungreased baking sheets. Press each ball lightly with the tines of a fork.

Bake until lightly browned, about 15 minutes. Remove from the oven and serve piping hot, or let cool and serve warm or at room temperature. Store in an airtight container at room temperature for up to 2 weeks.

Nutritional Analysis

Calories	47.43	Kcal	Protein	4.00	gm
Fat	1.07	gm	Carbohydrate	5.66	gm
Sodium	108.10	mg	Cholesterol	1.00	mg
Saturated fat	0.25	gm			

Stuffed Mushrooms Parmesan

Serves: 12

12 large mushrooms
1 tbsp buttery light, reduced-fat margarine
1 medium onion, finely chopped
60g (2oz) finely chopped green pepper
1 clove garlic, crushed
125g (4oz) cracker crumbs
11/2 tbsp grated Parmesan cheese
1 tbsp finely chopped fresh parsley
1/4 tsp dried oregano, crumbled
seasoned salt and pepper to taste
80ml (21/2fl oz) reduced-sodium, fat-free chicken stock

Preheat oven to 170°C (325°F), gas mark 3.

Rinse the mushrooms briefly or wipe clean with damp paper towels. Trim off the stem ends, then remove the stems and finely chop; reserve.

Melt the margarine in a frying pan over medium heat. Add the onion, green pepper, garlic and chopped mushroom stems. Cook for about 10 minutes, or until all the vegetables are tender but not browned. Add the crumbs, cheese, parsley and oregano and season with seasoned salt and pepper. Mix well. Stir in the chicken stock until well mixed. Remove from the heat.

Spoon the filling into the mushroom caps, rounding the tops. Place the caps in a shallow baking dish and add water to the dish to a depth of about 6mm (1/4in). Bake uncovered, until the mushrooms are tender and the filling is heated through, about 25 minutes. Serve hot.

Nutritional Analysis

Calories	34.32 Kcal	Protein	1.41 gm
Fat	1.17 gm	Carbohydrate	5.00 gm
Sodium	71.47 mg	Cholesterol	0.49 mg
Saturated fat	0.30 gm		

Buttermilk Quickbread

Serves: 20

300g (10oz) wholemeal flour
185g (6oz) plain flour
1/2 tsp baking soda
1/2 tsp salt
1 tbsp corn oil
250ml (8fl oz) buttermilk

Preheat oven to 220°C (425°F), gas mark 7. Lightly grease a nonstick baking tray.

In a bowl, stir together the flours, baking soda and salt. In another, smaller bowl, stir together the oil and buttermilk. Add the buttermilk mixture to the flour mixture. Mix well to form a stiff dough. Turn out onto a floured board and knead until smooth. Shape into a flat, round loaf on the prepared baking sheet.

Bake 40 to 45 minutes. Cool on a rack for 15 minutes before slicing.

Nutritional Analysis

Calories	55.23 Kcal	Protein	1.94 gm
Fat	1.01 gm	Carbohydrate	9.91 gm
Sodium	83.35 mg	Cholesterol	0.49 mg
Saturated fat	0.16 gm		

Tomato Bruschetta

Serves: 4

8 slices French bread
2 garlic cloves, halved
1 tsp olive oil
2 tbsp finely chopped onion
1 tomato, diced
pinch of dried oregano, crumbled
pinch of pepper
2 tsp grated Parmesan cheese (optional)

Toast the bread on both sides. Rub one side of each piece of toast with the cut side of the cloves of garlic. Keep hot.

(continued)

Heat the oil in a nonstick frying pan over medium-high heat. Add the onion and cook, stirring, until tender. Remove from the heat and stir in the tomato, oregano and pepper.

Spoon the tomato mixture over the garlic-rubbed side of the toast, dividing evenly. Serve immediately. Alternatively, sprinkle with the Parmesan and slip under a preheated grill for 1 minute to brown slightly, then serve.

Nutritional Analysis

Calories	157.68	Kcal	Protein	4.80	gm
Fat	2.72	gm	Carbohydrate	28.32	gm
Sodium	307.67	mg	Cholesterol	0.00	mg
Saturated fat	0.48	gm			

Cold Sesame Noodles

Serves: 6

10 cloves garlic, crushed
50mm (2in) piece fresh ginger, peeled and crushed
3 tbsp water
80ml (2¹/₂ fl oz) tahini (sesame-seed paste)
3 tbsp soy sauce
80ml (2¹/₂ fl oz) cold strong brewed tea
2 tbsp sesame oil
1 tbsp white wine vinegar
1 tbsp sugar
¹/₂ tbsp five-spice powder
chilli oil to taste
6 spring onions, finely chopped
500g (1lb) thin wheat noodles

With Starters, Presentation Is the Key

Because it is served first, a starter will set the tone of a meal. For example, to create a festive atmosphere, serve a dip in the centre of a colourful plate and surround it with lots of different crunchy vegetables. Or to help party guests break the ice and forget their nervousness, set out starters buffet-style so they can help themselves. Starters also make for a casual beginning at the dinner table with children, and make it easier for everyone to talk about their day at school or work.

Purée the garlic, ginger and water together in a food processor. In a medium bowl, stir together the tahini, soy sauce, tea, sesame oil, vinegar, sugar, five-spice powder and chilli oil. Add the garlic-ginger mixture and the spring onions, and stir well.

Cook the noodles in boiling water until al dente. Drain, rinse under cold water and drain again. Transfer to a large bowl.

Add the noodles to the sauce mixture, toss well to coat, and serve.

Nutritional Analysis

Calories	427.12	Kcal	Protein	13.00	gm
Fat	12.89	gm	Carbohydrate	65.47	gm
Sodium	539.10	mg	Cholesterol	0.00	mg
Saturated fat	1.80	gm			

Creamy Garlic–Red Pepper Dip

Serves: 4

220g (7oz) jar or tin roasted red peppers, drained
1 tbsp balsamic vinegar
80ml (2¹/₂fl oz) low-fat cottage cheese
2 cloves garlic, crushed
salt and pepper to taste

Combine the roasted peppers and vinegar in a food processor. Purée until smooth. Add the cottage cheese, garlic, salt and pepper and process until smooth. Serve with vegetable crudité and/or pitta bread triangles.

Nutritional Analysis

Calories	5.75	Kcal	Protein	0.03	gm
Fat	0.00	gm	Carbohydrate	1.63	gm
Sodium	25.96	mg	Cholesterol	0.00	mg
Saturated fat	0.00	gm			

Black Bean Dip

Serves: 8

925g (1lb 14oz) tinned black beans, drained
2 jalapeño peppers, seeded, if desired, and chopped
2 cloves garlic, chopped
1 large tomato, chopped
2 tbsp finely chopped fresh coriander
¹/₂ tsp salt
¹/₂ tsp freshly ground pepper

Combine the beans, jalapeños and garlic in a food processor. Purée until smooth.

Transfer to a bowl and add the tomato and coriander. Mix well and serve with vegetable crudité and/or pitta bread triangles.

Nutritional Analysis

Calories	22.65	Kcal	Protein	1.50	gm
Fat	0.22	gm	Carbohydrate	3.95	gm
Sodium	118.70	mg	Cholesterol	0.00	mg
Saturated fat	0.00	gm			

Herbed Clam Dip

Serves: 4

250ml (8fl oz) low-fat cottage cheese
300g (10oz) tinned clams, finely chopped
80ml (2¹/₂ fl oz) chopped fresh parsley
3 tbsp plain low-fat yogurt
1 tbsp dried basil
l tbsp minced onion
1 tbsp lemon juice
dash of Tabasco sauce

Process the cottage cheese in a food processor until smooth, then transfer to a bowl. Drain the clams, reserving 1 tablespoon of the liquid, and add the clams and reserved liquid to the cottage cheese. Then add the parsley, yogurt, basil, onion, lemon juice and Tabasco. Mix well. Cover and chill for at least 1 hour before serving.

Nutritional Analysis

Calories	27.00 Kcal	Protein	4.29 gm
Fat	0.36 gm	Carbohydrate	1.39 gm
Sodium	72.40 mg	Cholesterol	6.88 mg
Saturated fat	0.12 gm		

Cajun Chicken Fingers

Serves: 8

2 cloves garlic, crushed
60g (2oz) dried breadcrumbs
1 tbsp grated Parmesan cheese
1 tbsp fresh parsley, finely chopped
¹/₂ tsp paprika
¹/₂ tsp dried oregano, crumbled

black pepper to taste
250g (8oz) boneless, skinless chicken breasts, cut into long, narrow strips
60ml (2fl oz) skimmed milk

Preheat oven to 220°C (425°F), gas mark 7. Lightly grease a baking tray.

In a shallow dish, mix together the garlic, breadcrumbs, Parmesan cheese, parsley, paprika, oregano and pepper. Dip the chicken strips in the milk, then roll in the crumb mixture and arrange on the prepared baking tray.

Bake for 5 minutes; turn and bake for 5 more minutes, or until the chicken is done. Serve hot.

Nutritional Analysis

Calories	53.41 Kcal	Protein	7.55 gm
Fat	0.92 gm	Carbohydrate	3.22 gm
Sodium	63.32 mg	Cholesterol	17.24 mg
Saturated fat	0.29 gm		

Candy Corn

Makes: 500g (1lb)

2 tbsp soft brown sugar
1 tbsp butter
1 tbsp golden syrup
500g (1lb) popped corn

Preheat oven to 140°C (275°F), gas mark 1.

Mix together the sugar, butter and golden syrup in a small saucepan. Place over low heat and stir until the butter melts. Remove from the heat. Place the popcorn in a large plastic bag. Pour the sugar-butter mixture over the popcorn and shake

to mix well. Spread on a baking tray and bake, stirring every 5 minutes, or until piping hot and the coating is set, about 20 minutes. Serve cooled to room temperature.

Nutritional Analysis

Calories	96.26 Kcal	Protein	0.99 gm
Fat	3.20 gm	Carbohydrate	16.83 gm
Sodium	38.47 mg	Cholesterol	7.76 mg
Saturated fat	1.82 gm		

Low-Fat Tortilla Crisps

Makes: 500g (1lb) crisps

6 flour tortillas, each 200mm (8in) in diameter
1 tsp ground cumin
2 tsp garlic powder
1/2 tsp salt

Preheat oven to 180°C (350°F), gas mark 4.

Lightly grease one side of each tortilla. Mix the cumin, garlic powder and salt together in a small bowl. Sprinkle over the greased side of the tortillas. Cut each tortilla into six wedges and arrange on a baking sheet. Bake until crisp, about 10 minutes.

Nutritional Analysis

Calories	187.64 Kcal	Protein	4.87 gm
Fat	5.34 gm	Carbohydrate	30.42 gm
Sodium	541.67 mg	Cholesterol	0.00 mg
Saturated fat	0.57 gm		

Popcorn

The advent of air-popped popcorn machines in the 1970s and 1980s made it possible for us to enjoy one of our favourite snacks – popcorn – without all the fat. In the 1990s, of course, microwaveable popcorn packets became all the rage, but even the low-fat versions contain lots more fat than the air-popped variety.

Do your family a favour and use an air-popped machine. Sprinkle Parmesan cheese, a bit of garlic salt, even a bit of honey on your finished popcorn for a flavour that any microwaved popcorn can't match.

Sauces and Relishes

CHAPTER TWO

Amount Per Chapter
27 Recipes

	% Daily Value
Easy to Prepare	100%
Low Fat/High Flavour	100%
Simple to Understand	100%

DELICIOUS, EASY, LOW-FAT RECIPES

Sauces and relishes are the true spice of low-fat cooking. These low-fat, often low-calorie sauces and relishes offer a burst of flavour that can enhance any meal, whether you serve the Special Occasion Tomato Sauce on a bed of fresh pasta topped with freshly grated Parmesan cheese, or a snack such as the zesty Tropical Salsa.

Most of these sauces and relishes can be prepared in advance, which leaves you free to prepare the rest of the meal. Even more inspiring is the fact that, like people, the tastes usually get better with age.

Basic Low-Fat White Sauce

Makes: 250ml (8fl oz) sauce

2 tbsp plain flour
1 tbsp cornflour
1 tsp lemon pepper
250ml (8fl oz) skimmed milk

Place the flour in a small saucepan over medium-low heat and cook until lightly toasted but not browned, stirring constantly. Add the cornflour, lemon pepper and milk, stirring constantly. Continue cooking and stirring until thickened, about 10 minutes. Serve over vegetables or use as a base for cheese sauce or gravy.

Nutritional Analysis

Calories	43.28	Kcal	Protein	2.48	gm
Fat	0.14	gm	Carbohydrate	7.77	gm
Sodium	137.31	mg	Cholesterol	1.22	mg
Saturated fat	0.07	gm			

Special Occasion Tomato Sauce

Makes: 500ml (1pt) sauce

250ml (8fl oz) plain low-fat yogurt
250ml (8fl oz) tomato sauce
60g (2oz) grated Parmesan cheese
handful of fresh basil leaves, torn

Combine all the ingredients in a saucepan, stir well and place over low heat. Heat until hot and well blended; do not allow to boil. Toss with hot pasta to serve.

Nutritional Analysis

Calories	39.84	Kcal	Protein	3.04	gm
Fat	1.26	gm	Carbohydrate	4.49	gm
Sodium	251.12	mg	Cholesterol	3.67	mg
Saturated fat	0.75	gm			

Chunky Pasta Sauce

Makes: 1l (2pt) sauce

1 onion, coarsely chopped
3 cloves garlic, crushed
250g (8oz) mushrooms, sliced
1 green pepper, cut into 25mm (1in) chunks, seeds reserved
1 celery stalk, cut into12mm (1/2-in)-thick slices
850g (1lb 12oz) tinned tomatoes, undrained
180ml (6fl oz) tomato paste
250ml (8fl oz) tomato passata
125ml (4fl oz) red wine or water
1 tsp brown sugar
1 tsp dried oregano, crumbled
2 tbsp dried basil, crumbled, or
*   4 tbsp chopped fresh basil*
2 tsp chopped fresh parsley
1/8 tsp red pepper flakes (optional)
salt to taste

In a nonstick frying pan over low heat, combine the onion and garlic with several tablespoons of water and cook until tender, about 4 minutes.

Add the mushrooms and continue cooking over low heat for about 3 minutes. Add the pepper, pepper seeds and celery and cook until barely tender, about 4 minutes. Add the tomatoes and their juice. In a small bowl, whisk together the tomato paste and passata and the wine or water, and add to the pan along with the sugar, oregano, basil, parsley, red pepper flakes and salt and cook, stirring occasionally, for an additional 15 minutes to blend the flavours. Toss with hot pasta to serve.

Nutritional Analysis

Calories	41.26 Kcal	Protein	1.63 gm
Fat	0.30 gm	Carbohydrate	8.05 gm
Sodium	254.54 mg	Cholesterol	0.00 mg
Saturated fat	0.02 gm		

Low-Fat Gravy

Makes: 375ml (12fl oz) sauce

1 tbsp Worcestershire sauce
2 tbsp dried onion soup mix
1/4 tsp dried thyme, crumbled
1/4 tsp garlic powder
250ml (8fl oz) Low-Fat White Sauce (see page 12)
skimmed milk, if needed

In a saucepan, combine the Worcestershire sauce, soup mix, thyme, garlic powder and white sauce. Place over low heat and heat until the soup mix is well dissolved and the onions are limp, just a few minutes. If sauce becomes too thick, add a little skimmed milk to thin to desired consistency. Serve hot.

Nutritional Analysis

Calories	43.65 Kcal	Protein	2.24 gm
Fat	0.32 gm	Carbohydrate	7.93 gm
Sodium	477.37 mg	Cholesterol	1.01 mg
Saturated fat	0.10 gm		

Low-Fat Cheese Sauce

Makes: 300ml (10fl oz) sauce

250ml (8fl oz) Low-Fat White Sauce (see page 12)
60g (2oz) grated low-fat cheese of choice

Pour the white sauce into a saucepan and heat to serving temperature. Add the cheese and continue heating until the cheese is melted and the sauce is smooth. Serve hot.

Nutritional Analysis

Calories	43.62	Kcal	Protein	3.98	gm
Fat	0.11	gm	Carbohydrate	6.61	gm
Sodium	151.86	mg	Cholesterol	1.58	mg
Saturated fat	0.06	gm			

Cranberry Chutney

Makes: 2l (4pt)

375g (12oz) walnut pieces, toasted
500g (1lb) cranberries
250g (4oz) golden raisins
1 small red onion, sliced
250g (4oz) orange marmalade
125ml (4fl oz) orange juice
2 tbsp orange zest
80ml (2¹/₂ fl oz) white wine vinegar
250g (8oz) granulated sugar
250g (4oz) firmly packed brown sugar
¹/₂ tsp salt
¹/₄ tsp cayenne pepper
¹/₂ tsp ground ginger
1 cinnamon stick
1 bay leaf

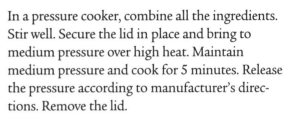

In a pressure cooker, combine all the ingredients. Stir well. Secure the lid in place and bring to medium pressure over high heat. Maintain medium pressure and cook for 5 minutes. Release the pressure according to manufacturer's directions. Remove the lid.

Remove the cinnamon stick and bay leaf and discard. Stir the chutney well, then ladle into sterilized jars. Cover tightly, cool and store in the refrigerator for up to 4 weeks.

Nutritional Analysis

Calories	27.54	Kcal	Protein	0.25	gm
Fat	0.87	gm	Carbohydrate	5.02	gm
Sodium	10.47	mg	Cholesterol	0.00	mg
Saturated fat	0.07	gm			

California Salsa

Makes: About 500ml (1pt)

500g (1lb) peeled and chopped tomatoes
1 celery stalk, cut
1 onion, cut
1 green pepper, cut up
1¹/₂ tsp salt
1 tbsp cider vinegar
1 tbsp sugar
1 green chilli pepper, seeded, if desired,
*   and chopped*

In a food processor, combine all the ingredients and process until well blended. If a finer texture is desired, pass the ingredients through a food mill using a fine blade. Transfer to a bowl, cover tightly and chill overnight before serving.

Nutritional Analysis

Calories	6.94	Kcal	Protein	0.17	gm
Fat	0.03	gm	Carbohydrate	1.60	gm
Sodium	111.31	mg	Cholesterol	0.00	mg
Saturated fat	0.00	gm			

Nectarine Chutney

Makes: About 500ml (1pt)

3 nectarines, peeled, stoned and cut into
  12mm ($1/2$in) chunks
1 onion, roughly chopped
250g (4oz) firmly packed brown sugar
250g (4oz) golden raisins
60ml (2fl oz) cider vinegar
$1/2$ tsp chilli powder
$1/2$ tsp ground allspice
90g (3oz) almonds, toasted and chopped

In a microwave-safe container, combine all the
ingredients except the almonds. Microwave on
high for 25 to 30 minutes, stirring every 5
minutes, or until the mixture is very thick and the
fruit and onion are tender. Let cool, cover and
refrigerate until well chilled. Stir in the almonds
before serving. Serve on sandwiches or as a relish
with poultry, lamb or pork.

Nutritional Analysis

Calories	40.43	Kcal	Protein	0.64	gm
Fat	1.12	gm	Carbohydrate	7.65	gm
Sodium	2.40	mg	Cholesterol	0.00	mg
Saturated fat	0.10	gm			

Chilli Pepper Primer

**Do you know your poblano from
your jalapeño? Here's how to tell
the difference:**

Jalapeño: **The jalapeño is short, fat
and dark green. It's the most popular
fresh chilli pepper sold in supermarkets
and can be eaten raw or cooked. It is
very hot.**

Poblano: **Like the jalapeño, the
poblano is dark green, but is shaped
like a cone and is milder in flavour.
The strength intensifies when the
pepper is roasted.**

Anaheim: **Also known as a New
Mexico chilli, the Anaheim ranges
from 75 to 150mm (3 to 6in) in length.
It is a lighter green than either the
jalapeño or poblano, and it is also the
chilli with the least bite.**

Fig Jam

Makes: 750ml (1¹/₂pt)

8 large ripe figs
60ml (2fl oz) lemon juice
60g (2oz) powdered pectin
1.4kg (3lb) sugar

Cut off the ends from the figs, then force the fruits through a food mill or coarse strainer. Measure 1l (2 pints) pulp into a deep saucepan. Add the lemon juice and pectin and mix well.

Place over high heat and heat to boiling, stirring constantly. Add the sugar and mix well. Bring to a full rolling boil, stirring constantly. Boil without stirring for 4 minutes. Remove from the heat and alternately stir and skim for 5 minutes to cool slightly.

Spoon into hot, sterilized jars and seal with sterilized lids. Let cool and check for seal. If the seal is good, store in a cool, dark place for up to one year. If the seal is not good, store in the refrigerator for up to one month.

Nutritional Analysis

Calories	105.65 Kcal	Protein	0.03 gm
Fat	0.01 gm	Carbohydrate	27.37 gm
Sodium	2.61 mg	Cholesterol	0.00 mg
Saturated fat	0.00 gm		

Raspberry and Plum Butter

Makes: 1l (2pt)

1kg (2lb) plums, stoned and quartered
300g (10oz) frozen raspberries, thawed and liquid reserved
250ml (8fl oz) water
750g (1lb 8oz) sugar
2 tbsp lemon juice

Combine the plums, thawed raspberries and their liquid and the water in a heavy saucepan. Place over high heat and bring to the boil. Reduce the heat to low and cook, stirring occasionally, for 5 minutes, or until the fruit is very tender. Remove from the heat and purée in a blender. Return the purée to the saucepan and add the sugar and lemon juice. Cook over low heat, stirring occasionally, until the sugar is dissolved. Raise the heat to medium and cook, stirring constantly, for 5 minutes, or until the butter is thick and glossy. The butter is ready when it drips from a spoon. Alternatively, drop a spoonful on a plate; if no rim of liquid forms around the edge of the butter, it's ready. Ladle into hot, sterilized jars and seal with sterilized lids. Let cool and check for seal. If the seal is good, store in a cool, dark place for up to 6 months. If the seal is not good, store in the refrigerator for up to 2 weeks. Serve with bread or fruit, or over ice cream.

Nutritional Analysis

Calories	40.08 Kcal	Protein	0.14 gm
Fat	0.12 gm	Carbohydrate	10.18 gm
Sodium	0.16 mg	Cholesterol	0.00 mg
Saturated fat	0.00 gm		

Apricot Salsa

Makes: About 500 ml (1pt)

500g (1lb) tinned apricots in light syrup, drained,
  rinsed and cut into chunks
2 tbsp chopped red onion
1½ tsp olive oil
1 tbsp chopped fresh coriander
1½ tsp lime juice
½ tsp white vinegar
½ tsp finely chopped jalapeño pepper
¼ tsp grated lime zest
¼ tsp ground cumin
salt and white pepper to taste

Combine all the ingredients in a bowl and stir gently. Cover and refrigerate until ready to serve.

Nutritional Analysis

Calories	44.77	Kcal	Protein	0.35	gm
Fat	0.87	gm	Carbohydrate	9.67	gm
Sodium	2.81	mg	Cholesterol	0.00	mg
Saturated fat	0.11	gm			

Tangy Peach Salsa

Makes: 500 ml (1pt)

4 fresh peaches, stoned and chopped
125g (4oz) orange marmalade
125g (4oz) thinly sliced spring onions
2 tbsp cider vinegar
1 tsp peeled and grated fresh ginger

In a bowl, combine all the ingredients. Cover and refrigerate until ready to serve. Serve as a sauce for lamb, pork or fish.

Nutritional Analysis

Calories	20.01	Kcal	Protein	0.14	gm
Fat	0.01	gm	Carbohydrate	5.28	gm
Sodium	3.05	mg	Cholesterol	0.00	mg
Saturated fat	0.00	gm			

Fresh Peach Salsa

Makes: 500 ml (1pt)

2 fresh peaches, stoned and diced
2 fresh plums, stoned and diced
90g (3oz) raisins
60g (2oz) diced red onion
1 tbsp lemon juice
1 tbsp chopped fresh mint

In a bowl, combine all the ingredients and stir gently to mix. Cover and refrigerate until ready to serve, preferably 1 day in advance. Serve spooned onto warm flour tortilla quarters.

Nutritional Analysis

Calories	43.82	Kcal	Protein	0.64	gm
Fat	0.14	gm	Carbohydrate	11.13	gm
Sodium	1.84	mg	Cholesterol	0.00	mg
Saturated fat	0.00	gm			

Chinese (Snow) Pear, Quince and Apple Sauce

Makes: About 1.2l (2½pt)

250g (8oz) sugar
500ml (1pt) water
1 cinnamon stick

(continued)

*2 quinces, peeled, cored and cut into
    50mm (2in) chunks
2 Chinese (snow) pears, peeled, cored and cut into
    50mm (2in) chunks
2 pippin apples, peeled, cored and cut into
    50mm (2in) chunks*

In a large, heavy saucepan over medium heat, combine the sugar, water and cinnamon stick and cook, stirring often, until the sugar is dissolved. Add the quinces and bring to a low simmer. Cover and cook, stirring occasionally, until fruit is tender, about 40 minutes.

Add the pears and apples and continue cooking for about 30 minutes, stirring occasionally, or until the apples have softened. Remove and discard the cinnamon stick. If you prefer a puréed, sauce-like consistency, purée the sauce in the pot with a hand blender to achieve the desired consistency. Serve warm, at room temperature or chilled. If storing, spoon into containers, cover and refrigerate for up to 1 week.

Nutritional Analysis

Calories	56.49 Kcal	Protein	0.10 gm
Fat	0.05 gm	Carbohydrate	14.61 gm
Sodium	0.47 mg	Cholesterol	0.00 mg
Saturated fat	0.00 gm		

Smoky Salsa

Makes: 500ml (1pt)

*5 plum tomatoes, halved
1 small red onion, thickly sliced*

*3 spring onions
1/3 bunch fresh coriander, tough stem ends removed
1 clove garlic
1 tsp chopped tinned red pepper
1 tsp cider vinegar
1 tsp salt
60ml (2fl oz) reduced-sodium, fat-free chicken stock, or
    more as needed*

Prepare a fire in a charcoal grill. In a grill basket, grill the tomatoes, red onion slices and spring onions over medium-hot coals until partially charred, turning occasionally. The red onions will take the longest. Transfer to a plate. Grill the coriander for about 30 seconds, just until it wilts and gives off a slight smoky scent.

With the motor running, add the garlic to a food processor and purée. Add the grilled vegetables and all the remaining ingredients, and process until all the vegetables are puréed. Taste and adjust for seasonings. For a thinner consistency, add more stock. Cover and refrigerate until ready to serve or for up to 1 week.

Serve with crisps or as a condiment for grilled chicken or meat.

Nutritional Analysis

Calories	14.07 Kcal	Protein	0.66 gm
Fat	0.10 gm	Carbohydrate	3.05 gm
Sodium	318.83 mg	Cholesterol	0.00 mg
Saturated fat	0.01 gm		

Mock Sour Cream

Makes: 500ml (1pt)

250ml (8fl oz) nonfat milk, or more as needed
185g (6oz) low-fat cottage cheese, or more as needed
2 to 4tsp white wine vinegar

Pour the milk and cottage cheese into a blender. Blend on medium speed until smooth. Add more cottage cheese or milk to bring the mixture to the consistency of sour cream. Stir in the vinegar to taste to give the mix a 'tang'.

Nutritional Analysis

Calories	26.22 Kcal	Protein	3.66 gm
Fat	0.26 gm	Carbohydrate	2.11 gm
Sodium	101.94 mg	Cholesterol	1.45 mg
Saturated fat	0.16 gm		

Marinara Sauce

Makes: About 1l (2pt)

850g (1lb 12oz) tinned plum tomatoes, drained
4 large cloves garlic, c rushed
185g (6oz) tomato paste
2 tsp oregano, dried
black pepper to taste
60g (2oz) finely chopped fresh basil

Place the tomatoes in a food processor and blend until smooth. Lightly oil a large frying pan and place over low heat, add the garlic and sauté briefly. Add the puréed tomatoes, tomato paste, oregano and pepper. Bring to the boil, then reduce the heat to low and simmer, uncovered, to blend

the flavours and thicken slightly, about 10 minutes. Remove from the heat and stir in basil. Toss with pasta to serve.

Nutritional Analysis

Calories	21.69 Kcal	Protein	0.97 gm
Fat	0.27 gm	Carbohydrate	4.62 gm
Sodium	165.08 mg	Cholesterol	0.00 mg
Saturated fat	0.02 gm		

Barbecue Sauce

Makes: 250ml (8fl oz) sauce

80ml (2½fl oz) cider vinegar
125ml (4fl oz) water
1 tbsp Dijon mustard
2 tbsp firmly packed brown sugar
½ tsp black pepper
60ml (2fl oz) lemon juice
1 large onion, finely chopped
60ml (2fl oz) Worcestershire sauce
80ml (2½fl oz) tomato ketchup

In a saucepan, mix together all ingredients except the ketchup. Bring to the boil, then reduce the heat to low and simmer for 20 minutes. Remove from the heat and stir in the ketchup.

For barbecued chicken, place a layer of skinless chicken breasts in a baking pan. Spoon the sauce over the chicken, cover the pan with a piece of foil and bake in a 170°F (325°F), gas mark 3 oven for 1 hour, or until done.

(continued)

Nutritional Analysis

Calories	93.36 Kcal	Protein	1.78 gm
Fat	0.20 gm	Carbohydrate	22.28 gm
Sodium	497.69 mg	Cholesterol	0.00 mg
Saturated fat	0.01 gm		

Dijon Mustard Sauce

Makes: 80ml (2¹/₂fl oz)

2 tbsp plain nonfat yogurt
2 tbsp low-fat cottage cheese
2 tbsp low-fat mayonnaise
¹/₂ tsp Dijon mustard
¹/₄ tsp soy sauce

For a smooth sauce, combine all the ingredients in a blender and process until smooth. Otherwise, for a chunkier texture, stir the ingredients together thoroughly and serve.

Nutritional Analysis

Calories	44.73 Kcal	Protein	2.59 gm
Fat	1.15 gm	Carbohydrate	5.52 gm
Sodium	280.16 mg	Cholesterol	0.84 mg
Saturated fat	0.11 gm		

Tomato-Lime Salsa

Makes: 500ml (1pt)

2 large tomatoes, finely chopped
1 clove garlic, crushed
2 tsp finely chopped fresh coriander
1 red onion, finely chopped

1 jalapeño pepper, seeded, if desired, and finely chopped
juice of 1 lime
salt and pepper to taste

In a bowl, stir together the tomatoes, garlic, coriander, onion and jalapeño pepper. Add the lime juice, salt and pepper. Mix well, cover and chill before serving. Serve with low-fat tortilla crisps or as a topping on cold chicken or salad.

Nutritional Analysis

Calories	22.62 Kcal	Protein	0.88 gm
Fat	0.20 gm	Carbohydrate	5.13 gm
Sodium	7.59 mg	Cholesterol	0.00 mg
Saturated fat	0.02 gm		

Easy Apple Sauce

Makes: 375ml (12fl oz)

4 apples, peeled, cored and diced
80ml (2¹/₂fl oz) unsweetened apple juice

Put the apples and apple juice in a food processor and purée thoroughly.

Nutritional Analysis

Calories	55.05 Kcal	Protein	0.12 gm
Fat	0.27 gm	Carbohydrate	14.25 gm
Sodium	0.40 mg	Cholesterol	0.00 mg
Saturated fat	0.04 gm		

Cooked Apple Sauce

Makes: 1l (2pt)

10 large apples, cored and thinly sliced
l tsp ground cinnamon
80ml (2½fl oz) apple juice
3 tbsp lemon juice

Put all the ingredients except the lemon juice into a slow cooker or a heavy saucepan. Cover. If you are using a slow cooker, turn it to the slow setting and leave overnight or longer, until the apples are cooked. If you are cooking on top of the stove, cook over medium-high heat, checking that it is done after 45 minutes. Stir in the lemon juice. Serve hot or at room temperature.

Nutritional Analysis

Calories	67.15	Kcal	Protein	0.21	gm
Fat	0.38	gm	Carbohydrate	17.36	gm
Sodium	0.77	mg	Cholesterol	0.00	mg
Saturated fat	0.06	gm			

Tuna Tomato Sauce

Makes: 625ml (1¼pt)

1 tbsp olive oil
2 large cloves garlic, crushed
1 tsp anchovy paste
1 tsp red pepper flakes
500ml (1pt) tomato passata
1 tsp black pepper
220g (7oz) water-packed tuna, drained and flaked
90g (3oz) finely chopped fresh parsley

Heat the oil and garlic in a saucepan over medium-high heat for 1 minute. Remove from the heat and add the anchovy paste and pepper flakes. Stir in the passata and black pepper, and bring to the boil over high heat. Reduce the heat to low and cook for 20 minutes, stirring occasionally. Stir in the tuna and half of the parsley and cook for another 10 minutes. Toss with pasta to serve. Sprinkle on the remaining parsley.

Nutritional Analysis

Calories	59.55	Kcal	Protein	6.32	gm
Fat	1.56	gm	Carbohydrate	5.63	gm
Sodium	281.75	mg	Cholesterol	7.68	mg
Saturated fat	0.22	gm			

Herbed Yogurt Dressing

Makes: 625ml (1¼pt)

500ml (1pt) plain low-fat yogurt
125g (4oz) chopped fresh parsley
125g (4oz) chopped fresh dill
2 cloves garlic, crushed
2 tbsp lemon juice
1 tbsp Dijon mustard
salt and pepper to taste

In a small bowl, stir together all the ingredients. Cover and chill before serving. Serve over grilled chicken or beef or on a bed of lettuce.

(continued)

Nutritional Analysis

Calories	8.16	Kcal	Protein	0.60	gm
Fat	0.17	gm	Carbohydrate	0.92	gm
Sodium	17.45	mg	Cholesterol	0.68	mg
Saturated fat	0.11	gm			

Tropical Salsa

Makes: About 680ml (1³/₄pt)

250g (8oz) diced cantaloupe melon
250g (8oz) diced honeydew melon
150g (5oz) chopped mild green chillies
6 spring onions, finely chopped
60g (2oz) chopped fresh coriander
2 tbsp lime juice
¹/₄ tsp cayenne pepper

In a bowl, stir together all the ingredients. Chill for at least 1 hour before serving.

Nutritional Analysis

Calories	46.19	Kcal	Protein	1.27	gm
Fat	0.24	gm	Carbohydrate	11.42	gm
Sodium	207.73	mg	Cholesterol	0.00	mg
Saturated fat	0.00	gm			

Black Bean and Corn Salsa

Makes: 560ml (1¹/₈pt)

kernels from 2 large ears corn, lightly cooked
2 jalapeño peppers, seeded, if desired, and chopped
425g (14oz) tinned black beans, drained and rinsed

2 large tomatoes, chopped
2 tbsp lemon juice
salt and pepper to taste

In a bowl, stir together all the ingredients. Chill for at least 1 hour before serving. Serve with crisps or use as a condiment for grilled chicken.

Nutritional Analysis

Calories	77.54	Kcal	Protein	4.26	gm
Fat	0.88	gm	Carbohydrate	15.08	gm
Sodium	175.02	mg	Cholesterol	0.00	mg
Saturated fat	0.07	gm			

Fannie Flagg Salsa

Makes: 375ml (12fl oz)

2 jalapeño peppers, seeded, if desired, and finely
    chopped
6 small green tomatoes, chopped
2 tbsp chopped fresh coriander
1 tsp ground cumin
2 tbsp red wine vinegar
60g (2oz) diced red onion

In a bowl, stir together all the ingredients. Chill for at least 1 hour before serving. Serve as a side dish with grilled chicken or fish.

Nutritional Analysis

Calories	15.67	Kcal	Protein	0.70	gm
Fat	0.15	gm	Carbohydrate	3.29	gm
Sodium	6.57	mg	Cholesterol	0.00	mg
Saturated fat	0.01	gm			

Soups

CHAPTER THREE

Amount Per Chapter

40 Recipes

% Daily Value

Easy to Prepare	**100%**
Low Fat/High Flavour	**100%**
Simple to Understand	**100%**

DELICIOUS, EASY, LOW-FAT RECIPES

I love soups because you can usually throw all the ingredients together into one pot, they don't require a lot of attention while cooking, and they provide sustenance for a full meal, supplemented only by a salad and a loaf of crusty bread.

The soups here range from traditional stick-to-the-ribs dishes suitable for winter fare to no-cooking gems light enough for the hottest summer days. Many of the recipes are as easy to prepare as opening a few tins of soup. In addition, because you're making it yourself, the soup will be lower in fat and sodium, a claim that supermarkets and major soup manufacturers can't make.

Onion Soup

Serves: 8

2 tbsp olive oil
6 large onions, thinly sliced
1 clove garlic, crushed
250ml (8fl oz) dry red wine
125ml (4fl oz) dry sherry
125ml (4fl oz) Marsala wine
1 tbsp dried thyme, crumbled
1 tbsp black pepper
1 tbsp dried rosemary
1l (2pt) reduced-sodium, fat-free chicken stock
1l (2pt) reduced-sodium, fat-free beef stock
8 slices French bread, each 12mm (1/2in) thick
60g (2oz) grated Parmesan cheese

Heat the oil in a soup pot over low heat, add the onions and garlic, and sauté until tender and lightly caramelized, about 30 minutes. Add all three wines, bring to the boil, and boil for about 15 minutes. Add the thyme, pepper, rosemary and the stocks, reduce the heat to medium, and simmer for 1 hour.

Preheat the oven to 190°C (375°F), gas mark 5. Sprinkle 1 teaspoon of cheese on each bread slice. Place the slices on a baking sheet, cheese side up, and bake for 8 minutes.

Preheat the grill. Ladle the soup into individual ovenproof crocks, and top each serving with a slice of prepared bread. Broil for a minute or two until the bread is lightly browned. Serve at once.

Nutritional Analysis

Calories	219.33 Kcal	Protein	9.55 gm
Fat	6.00 gm	Carbohydrate	32.52 gm
Sodium	850.43 mg	Cholesterol	3.95 mg
Saturated fat	1.66 gm		

Summertime Strawberry Soup

Serves: 6

> *750g (1lb 8oz) strawberries, destemmed*
> *1/2 tsp ground cinnamon*
> *125g (4oz) frozen orange juice concentrate*
> *125ml (4fl oz) water*
> *60ml (2fl oz) dry red wine*
> *dash of ground cloves*
> *2 tbsp cornflour*
> *2 tbsp water*
> *500ml (1pt) vanilla low-fat frozen yogurt*
> *500ml (1pt) low-fat plain yogurt*

Mix the strawberries, cinnamon, orange juice concentrate, water, wine and cloves in a saucepan. Bring to the boil, reduce the heat to medium-low, and simmer for 10 minutes.

Mix together the cornflour and water in a small bowl. Stir 80ml (2 1/2fl oz) of the strawberry mixture into the cornflour mixture until smooth and then add to the saucepan. Bring to the boil and cook, stirring, until thick, about 5 minutes. Remove from the heat, let cool for at least 1 hour, then add both yogurts. Stir until the frozen yogurt melts. Cover and refrigerate for 1 hour before serving.

Nutritional Analysis

Calories	278.76 Kcal	Protein	10.51 gm
Fat	3.74 gm	Carbohydrate	50.67 gm
Sodium	142.82 mg	Cholesterol	11.79 mg
Saturated fat	2.14 gm		

Cioppino

Serves: 6

> *1 1/2 tbsp olive oil*
> *1 large onion, chopped*
> *1 large green pepper, chopped*
> *2 cloves garlic, crushed*
> *500ml (1pt) bottled clam juice*
> *500g (1lb) coarsely chopped tomatoes*
> *125ml (4fl oz) dry white wine*
> *2 tbsp minced fresh parsley*
> *1 bay leaf*
> *salt and pepper to taste*
> *4 soft-shelled crabs*
> *12 mussels, well scrubbed and debearded*
> *12 clams, well scrubbed*
> *12 large prawns, peeled and deveined*
> *500g (1lb) cod fillet, cubed*

In a nonstick frying pan, add the olive oil, onion, pepper and garlic and sauté for 3 minutes, or until the onion is translucent. Stir in the clam juice, tomatoes, wine, parsley and bay leaf. Bring to the boil, reduce the heat to medium-low, cover and simmer for 30 minutes. Add the salt and pepper and remove and discard the bay leaf.

Discard any open mussels and clams, and add them, the crabs, prawns and fish and stir gently. Bring to the boil, reduce the heat to low, and cook for 5 to 10 minutes, or until the shellfish and fish are cooked. Discard any mussels or clams that remain closed. Serve at once.

(continued)

Nutritional Analysis

Calories	211.18	Kcal	Protein	30.14	gm
Fat	6.26	gm	Carbohydrate	8.02	gm
Sodium	528.69	mg	Cholesterol	130.05	mg
Saturated fat	1.10	gm			

Cream of Mushroom Soup

Serves: 4

500g (1lb) button or other mushrooms, sliced or
chopped
1 large onion or 6 spring onions, coarsely chopped
1 clove garlic, crushed (optional)
1 celery stalk, sliced or chopped
60ml (2fl oz) water
1l (2pt) skimmed milk
1/4 tsp ground nutmeg
3 tbsp Madeira, Marsala, dry white wine, dry
vermouth or dry sherry
2 tbsp plain flour
2 tbsp cornflour
salt and pepper to taste
125g (4oz) chopped fresh parsley or enoki mushrooms
for garnish

Combine the mushrooms, onion (or spring
onions), garlic, celery and water in a saucepan over
medium heat. Bring to a simmer and cook until
soft, about 5 minutes. Add three-quarters of the
milk, the nutmeg and the wine. Reduce the heat to
very low, cover and simmer for 20 minutes.

In a small bowl, combine the remaining milk,
the flour and cornflour and whisk well until

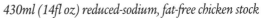

smooth. Add to the soup and stir continuously
for at least 4 minutes (to cook the flour), until
thick. Add more milk (or stock) to adjust the
thickness, if needed. Season with salt and pepper.
Ladle into bowls and garnish with the parsley (or
enoki mushrooms).

Nutritional Analysis

Calories	175.35	Kcal	Protein	12.03	gm
Fat	1.11	gm	Carbohydrate	30.93	gm
Sodium	146.74	mg	Cholesterol	4.90	mg
Saturated fat	0.39	gm			

Light and Lean Chowder

Serves: 8

430ml (14fl oz) reduced-sodium, fat-free chicken stock
250g (8oz) small broccoli florets
250g (8oz) sliced mushrooms
125g (4oz) chopped onion
1 tbsp buttery light, reduced-fat margarine
2 tbsp plain flour
1/4 tsp salt
1/8 tsp pepper
425g (14oz) evaporated skimmed milk
250g (8oz) corn kernels, drained
1 tbsp chopped pimiento

In a small saucepan, combine the stock and broccoli and bring to the boil. Reduce the heat to low,
cover and simmer for 5 minutes. Do not drain.
Set aside.

In a large saucepan over medium heat, cook
the mushrooms and onions in the margarine until

tender. Stir in the flour, salt and pepper. Add the milk all at once. Cook, stirring until bubbling, then 1 minute more. Stir in broccoli and stock, corn and pimiento. Heat through and serve.

Nutritional Analysis

Calories	92.10	Kcal	Protein	6.26	gm
Fat	1.84	gm	Carbohydrate	13.34	gm
Sodium	321.95	mg	Cholesterol	2.15	mg
Saturated fat	0.32	gm			

Curried Mushroom Soup

Serves: 4

250g (8oz) mixed dried morel and porcini mushrooms (30g/1oz dried mushrooms)
500ml (1pt) boiling water
2 or 3 chopped leeks, white part only
2 tbsp plain flour
1 tbsp curry powder
1l (2pts) skimmed milk
1 chicken bouillon cube
500g (1lb) chopped fresh portobello mushrooms (3 large mushrooms)
1 tbsp dry sherry (optional)
1 tbsp chopped fresh chervil

Combine the dried mushrooms and boiling water in a bowl and set aside to soak for 15 to 30 minutes.

Preheat a saucepan over medium heat for about 1 minute, then oil it lightly. Add the leeks and sauté, stirring constantly until translucent, about 3 minutes. Add the flour and curry powder and stir until the leeks are well coated. Add the milk and bouillon cube. Raise the heat to high and cook just until bubbles begin to form around the edges. Reduce the heat to low and whisk until all ingredients are thoroughly combined. Stir in the fresh mushrooms and cook for 5 minutes.

Meanwhile, drain the reconstituted mushrooms and squeeze out moisture. Chop roughly. Add to the saucepan and cook for 1 minute more. Stir in the sherry, if using. Ladle into bowls and garnish with the chervil. Serve at once.

Nutritional Analysis

Calories	163.02	Kcal	Protein	11.13	gm
Fat	1.57	gm	Carbohydrate	27.81	gm
Sodium	380.28	mg	Cholesterol	4.90	mg
Saturated fat	0.32	gm			

Apple-Squash Soup

Serves: 8 to 10

1 tbsp safflower or sunflower oil
375g (12oz) thinly sliced leeks, white and light green parts, or coarsely chopped onions
1l (2pt) boiling water
1.5kg (3lb) butternut squash, seeded and cut into 38mm (1 1/2 in) chunks
3 Granny Smith apples, peeled, cored and quartered
90g (3oz) porridge oats

(continued)

2 tbsp peeled and finely minced fresh ginger
1½ tbsp mild curry powder
1 tbsp salt, or to taste

Heat the oil in the pressure cooker over medium-high heat. Add the leeks and cook, stirring frequently, for 1 minute. Add the water (stand back to avoid splashing oil), squash, apples, oats, ginger, curry powder and salt.

Secure the lid in place. Bring to high pressure over high heat. Adjust the heat to maintain high pressure and cook for 5 minutes. Turn off the heat and allow the pressure to come down naturally, or use a quick-release method. Remove the lid, tilting it away from you to allow any excess steam to escape. If the squash is not fork-tender, replace (but do not lock) the lid, and cook for a few more minutes in the residual heat.

Purée the soup in two or three batches in a blender (preferred) or food processor. Return to the cooker and reheat to serving temperature.

Nutritional Analysis

Calories	121.21	Kcal	Protein	2.21	gm
Fat	2.13	gm	Carbohydrate	26.44	gm
Sodium	268.26	mg	Cholesterol	0.00	mg
Saturated fat	0.20	gm			

Luscious Corn Chowder

Serves: 8

3 slices bacon
125g (4oz) finely chopped onions
½ tsp crushed garlic
125g (4oz) finely chopped green pepper
500g (1lb) corn kernels
500ml (1pt) water
500ml (1pt) skimmed milk
1 medium potato, cut into 25mm (1in) cubes
125g (4oz) chopped fresh parsley
pepper to taste
2 dashes of Tabasco sauce

In a frying pan, fry the bacon until crisp. Using tongs, transfer to paper towels to drain. Pour off all but 1 tablespoon of the dripping from the pan and add the onions, garlic and green pepper to the bacon dripping and sauté over medium heat until wilted.

Transfer the sautéed onion mixture to a saucepan and add all the remaining ingredients except the bacon. Bring to the boil, reduce the heat to low, cover and simmer until the potato is tender, about 20 minutes. Ladle into bowls and sprinkle with the bacon.

Nutritional Analysis

Calories	107.74	Kcal	Protein	4.64	gm
Fat	3.57	gm	Carbohydrate	15.63	gm
Sodium	85.96	mg	Cholesterol	5.60	mg
Saturated Fat	1.27	gm			

Italian Bean Soup

Serves: 8

1 tbsp olive oil
125g (4oz) chopped onions
1 clove garlic, crushed
750g (1lb 8oz) mixed dried beans picked over and
  soaked overnight in water to cover
1l (2 pints) salt- and fat-free beef broth
1 tsp dried oregano, crumbled
375g (12oz) crushed tomatoes
185g (6oz) carrots cut into strips
125g (4oz) celery cut into strips
650g (1lb 5oz) loosely packed torn spinach
125g (4oz) cooked small pasta shells
salt to taste
125g (4oz) grated romano cheese

In a saucepan, heat the oil over medium heat. Add the onion and garlic and sauté for about 5 minutes, or until translucent. Drain the beans and add to the saucepan along with the stock and oregano. Bring to a simmer, cover and cook until the beans are tender, about 40 minutes.

Add the tomatoes, carrots and celery. Simmer for 15 minutes. Stir in the spinach and pasta; adjust the seasoning with salt. Simmer for 5 minutes, or until heated through, then sprinkle with cheese and serve.

Nutritional Analysis

Calories	332.69 Kcal	Protein	23.69 gm
Fat	3.89 gm	Carbohydrate	53.03 gm
Sodium	727.21 mg	Cholesterol	5.20 mg
Saturated fat	1.25 gm		

Cooking Beans

Place dried beans in a vessel with two to three times as much water as beans. Remove and discard any beans or any debris that float. Soak overnight and bring to boil. Reduce heat and simmer until beans are tender.

If you have failed to soak the beans overnight, cover them with cold water, bring to a boil and simmer for 2 minutes. Remove from the heat and let stand tightly covered for 1 hour before continuing with the recipe. Do not overcook the beans to the point of mushiness. One test is to scoop up a few cooked beans in a spoon and blow on them. If the skins burst, the beans are cooked.

Black Bean Soup

Serves: 8

*625g (1lb 4oz) dried black beans, picked over and
    soaked overnight in water to cover*
60ml (2fl oz) olive oil
1 large onion, chopped
1 large bunch fresh coriander, destemmed and chopped
8 cloves garlic, crushed
2 1/2 tsp ground cumin
2 tsp ground coriander
1/2 tsp dried oregano, crumbled
1 1/2 tbsp chilli powder
1 1/2 tbsp crushed dried red chillies
830g (1lb 12oz) tomato purée
1 tsp black pepper
750ml (1 1/2pt) reduced-sodium, fat-free chicken stock
60ml (2fl oz) brandy or dry sherry
30g (1oz) grated Parmesan cheese for garnish
chopped fresh coriander for garnish

Drain the beans and place in a large pot. Add water to cover, bring to the boil, reduce the heat to low, cover and simmer up to 1 hour, or until the beans are very tender.

In a large frying pan, heat the oil over medium-high heat. Add the onion, fresh coriander, garlic, cumin, ground coriander, oregano, chilli powder and crushed chillies until the onion is tender. Stir in the tomatoes, black pepper and chicken stock. Cook for 5 minutes over medium heat, then set aside.

Drain the beans and let cool for 10 minutes. Purée in a blender or food processor. Return to the pot, add the contents of the frying pan and stir well. Place over medium heat and cook until heated through. Add additional stock if the soup is too thick. Stir in the brandy or sherry. Ladle the soup into bowls. Garnish with the Parmesan cheese and fresh coriander, and serve.

Nutritional Analysis

Calories	285.29	Kcal	Protein	12.67	gm
Fat	8.62	gm	Carbohydrate	37.80	gm
Sodium	673.72	mg	Cholesterol	1.97	mg
Saturated fat	1.53	gm			

Broccoli-Leek Soup

Serves: 8

2 tbsp olive oil
2 medium leeks, white parts only, finely chopped
500g (1lb) red potatoes, peeled and finely chopped
*750g (1lb 8oz) broccoli florets and stalks, cut into
    25mm (1in) pieces*
1.25l (2 1/2pt) reduced-sodium, fat-free chicken stock
salt and white pepper to taste

Parmesan Topping:
125ml (4fl oz) plain nonfat yogurt
60g (2oz) grated Parmesan cheese
pinch of white pepper
2tbsp snipped fresh chives for garnish

In a large soup pot, heat the olive oil over medium heat. Add the leeks and sauté, until softened, 3 to 5 minutes. Add the potatoes and broccoli and sauté, stirring frequently, for 2 minutes. Add the stock and bring to a simmer. Cover partially and simmer until the vegetables are tender when pierced with a knife, 15 to 20 minutes.

Purée the soup in the pot with a hand blender or in a food processor. Add salt and pepper and taste for seasoning. Reheat, if necessary, to serving temperature.

To make the Parmesan topping, combine the yogurt, cheese and pepper in a small bowl and whisk until combined.

Ladle the soup into bowls and spoon the Parmesan topping on top, dividing it between the bowls. Garnish with the chives. Serve immediately.

Nutritional Analysis

Calories	141.37 Kcal	Protein	7.66 gm
Fat	4.60 gm	Carbohydrate	18.88 gm
Sodium	585.49 mg	Cholesterol	2.25 mg
Saturated fat	0.99 gm		

Cauliflower Soup

Serves: 8

2 tbsp olive oil
2 small white onions, thinly sliced
3 small leeks, white parts only, chopped
2 shallots, chopped
2l (4pt) plus 250ml (8fl oz) reduced-sodium, fat-free chicken stock
2 large cauliflowers, cut into florets

about 250ml (8fl oz) plain low-fat yogurt
salt and white pepper to taste
16 asparagus tips

In a medium sauté pan, heat the olive oil over medium heat. Add the onions, leeks and shallots and sauté, stirring often, until tender, 3 to 4 minutes; do not let them brown.

In a large saucepan, combine the sautéed vegetables, the 2 litres chicken stock and the cauliflower florets. Bring to the boil over high heat, reduce the heat to low and simmer, uncovered, until the cauliflower florets are tender, about 30 minutes.

Working in batches, purée the cauliflower mixture until smooth. Strain through a sieve into a clean saucepan and add the yogurt in small amounts, stirring it in until the desired consistency is achieved.

Season the soup with salt and white pepper.

In a small saucepan, heat the 250ml chicken stock until it simmers. Add the asparagus tips and cook until just tender, 3 to 5 minutes; do not overcook. Drain the asparagus.

Ladle the soup into bowls, and float 2 asparagus tips on each serving.

Nutritional Analysis

Calories	119.98 Kcal	Protein	7.88 gm
Fat	4.08 gm	Carbohydrate	14.07 gm
Sodium	674.21 mg	Cholesterol	1.70 mg
Saturated fat	0.76 gm		

Chilli Bean Soup

Serves: 6

> 500g (1lb) dried pinto or kidney beans, picked over
>   and soaked overnight in cold water to cover
> 1.5 to 2l (3 to 4pt) water
> 1/4 tsp dried thyme
> 1/4 tsp dried marjoram
> 375g (12fl oz) reduced-sodium, fat-free beef or chicken
>   stock
> 500g (1lb) tinned chopped tomatoes
> 1 packet chilli seasoning mix
> 250ml (8fl oz) hot water

Drain the beans and place in a large pot. Add the water, thyme and marjoram. Bring to the boil, reduce the heat to low, cover, and simmer until tender, up to about 1 hour. Don't let the beans boil dry; add hot water as needed.

Spoon out 250g (8oz) of the cooked beans to use another day in another way. Using a potato masher, mash the remaining beans with their liquid. Add the stock, tomatoes, chilli mix and hot water. Stir well and heat for at least 10 minutes to blend the flavours. Ladle into soup bowls and serve.

Nutritional Analysis

Calories	298.11	Kcal	Protein	17.84	gm
Fat	1.35	gm	Carbohydrate	55.36	gm
Sodium	904.57	mg	Cholesterol	0.00	mg
Saturated fat	0.24	gm			

Pumpkin Cheese Soup

Serves: 8

> 1 large pumpkin
> 2 tsp butter, melted
> 1 large onion, chopped
> 2 large carrots, grated
> 2 celery stalks, chopped
> 1.2l (2 1/4pt) reduced-sodium vegetable stock
> 1 clove garlic, crushed
> 1/2 tsp salt
> 1/2 tsp pepper
> 1/2 tsp nutmeg
> 180ml (6fl oz) plus 2 tsp skimmed milk
> 125g (4oz) low-fat cheddar cheese, grated
> 6 tbsp dry white wine
> 90g (3oz) finely chopped fresh parsley

Preheat oven to 180°C (350°F), gas mark 4. Grease a baking tray.

To prepare the pumpkin, cut off the top and scoop out the seeds. Brush the inside with the melted butter. Replace the top and place the pumpkin on the baking tray. Bake until tender when pierced with a fork, about 45 minutes. The pumpkin should be a bit droopy but still hold its shape well.

Meanwhile, melt the butter in a large saucepan. Add the onion, carrots and celery and sauté until soft, about 10 minutes. Add the stock, garlic, salt, pepper and nutmeg. Cover and simmer for 20 minutes. Remove from the heat and let cool slightly.

Working in two or batches batches, purée the vegetable mixture in a blender or food processor.

Pour back into the saucepan and stir in the milk. Reheat gently. Add the cheese and wine and heat until the cheese melts, stirring frequently to avoid scorching.

Place the hot pumpkin on a serving platter and ladle in the soup. Sprinkle with the parsley.

To serve, ladle out soup at the table, scooping a little bit of pumpkin into each serving. The pumpkin then makes a great centrepiece for your table, while allowing people to have second helpings. After the soup is finished, the pumpkin can be peeled, cut up, rinsed and used in pumpkin pie. It may need more baking to become soft enough to purée for the pie filling.

Nutritional Analysis

Calories	122.45 Kcal	Protein	8.31 gm
Fat	3.80 gm	Carbohydrate	13.48 gm
Sodium	458.45 mg	Cholesterol	11.62 mg
Saturated fat	2.29 gm		

Hearty Bean Soup

Serves: 4

2 tbsp buttery light, reduced-fat margarine
125g (4oz) chopped celery
60g (2oz) diced onions
2 tbsp plain flour
250ml (8fl oz) water
180ml (6fl oz) skimmed milk
500g (1lb) tinned white beans, drained
500g (1lb) tinned whole kernel corn with liquid
250g (8oz) crushed tomatoes

185g (6oz) low-fat grated cheddar or gruyere cheese
1/4 tsp salt
1/8 tsp pepper
dash of Tabasco sauce
sourdough or soda bread for serving

In a saucepan, melt the margarine over medium heat. Add the celery and onion and sauté until onion is translucent, about 10 minutes. Stir in the flour until well blended. Slowly pour in the water and milk while stirring constantly, then cook, stirring, for 5 minutes, or until thickened and smooth. Add the beans, corn (with liquid), tomatoes and cheese. Heat through, stirring often, but do not boil. Season to taste with salt, pepper and Tabasco sauce. Serve with wedges of sourdough or soda bread.

Nutritional Analysis

Calories	328.79 Kcal	Protein	18.27 gm
Fat	9.64 gm	Carbohydrate	46.36 gm
Sodium	1130.38 mg	Cholesterol	16.63 mg
Saturated fat	4.18 gm		

Cuban Black Bean Soup

Serves: 6

250g (8oz) dried black beans, picked over and soaked
*   overnight in water to cover*
1 tbsp butter
250g (8oz) chopped onion
1l (2pt) water
1 beef bouillon cube
2 bay leaves

(continued)

Blanching Vegetables

One way to make sure that vegetables are well cooked before you add them to a soup and to ensure that they don't turn soggy during cooking is to blanch them beforehand. In a saucepan, bring about 1 litre (2 pints) of water to a boil. Add the vegetables, cook for 3 minutes, then remove and immediately rinse under cold water. This last step prevents the vegetables from absorbing excess liquid, in essence forming a seal on the skin, and rinsing stops the vegetables losing their bright colour.

$^1/_2$ *tsp dried thyme, crumbled*
$^1/_2$ *tsp dried oregano, crumbled*
$^1/_2$ *tsp salt*
1 red pepper, chopped
1 green pepper, chopped
500g (1lb) hot cooked white rice

Drain the beans. In a large pot, melt the butter over medium heat. Add the onion and sauté for 5 minutes, or until onion is translucent. Add the drained beans, water, bouillon cube, bay leaves, thyme, oregano, salt and red pepper. Bring to the boil, reduce the heat to low, cover and simmer until the beans are tender, 1 to 1$^1/_2$ hours.

Remove 125g (4oz) of the beans and mash in a bowl with a potato masher or fork. Return the mashed beans to the pot and mix well to thicken. Remove and discard the bay leaves. Add the green pepper to the beans. Cover and simmer for 15 minutes to blend the flavours. To serve, ladle the beans over the rice in shallow bowls.

Nutritional Analysis

Calories	431.43	Kcal	Protein	19.83	gm
Fat	3.40	gm	Carbohydrate	81.22	gm
Sodium	362.77	mg	Cholesterol	5.19	mg
Saturated gat	1.55	gm			

Tortilla Soup

Serves: 6

1 tbsp vegetable or olive oil
1 small onion, chopped
4 or 5 green chilli peppers, roasted, peeled, seeded and chopped
2 cloves garlic, crushed
185g (6oz) peeled and chopped tomatoes
430ml (14fl oz) reduced-sodium, fat-free beef stock
430ml (14fl oz) reduced-sodium, fat-free chicken stock
375ml (12fl oz) water
375ml (12fl oz) tomato juice
1 tsp ground cumin
1 tsp chilli powder
1 tsp salt
1/8 tsp pepper
2 tsp Worcestershire sauce
1 tbsp barbecue sauce
3 corn tortillas, cut in 12mm (1/2in)-wide strips
60g (2oz) grated fat-free or low-fat cheddar cheese

In a large saucepan, heat the oil over medium heat. Add the onion, chillies and garlic and cook until soft, about 5 minutes. Add the tomatoes, both stocks, water, tomato juice, cumin, chilli powder, salt, pepper and Worcestershire and barbecue sauces. Bring to the boil, reduce the heat to low, cover and simmer for 1 hour.

Add the tortillas and cheese, stir well and simmer for 10 minutes longer. Ladle into soup bowls and serve.

Nutritional Analysis

Calories	110.38 Kcal	Protein	5.97 gm
Fat	2.92 gm	Carbohydrate	16.81 gm
Sodium	1082.45 mg	Cholesterol	0.49 mg
Saturated fat	0.33 gm		

Split Pea Soup

Serves: 6

2 tbsp olive oil
1 medium onion, finely chopped
2 carrots, diced
2 celery stalks, diced
2 cloves garlic, crushed
1/2 tsp dried thyme, crumbled
1 tsp pepper
1 tsp Worcestershire sauce
1/2 tsp Tabasco sauce
500g (1lb) dried green split peas, picked over and soaked overnight in 2l (4pt) cold water
2 bay leaves
2 whole cloves
2 pounds ham hocks
500g (1lb) white potatoes, peeled and diced
salt and pepper

In a soup pot, heat the oil over medium heat. Add the onion, carrots, celery, garlic, thyme, pepper and Worcestershire and Tabasco sauces and sauté for 5 minutes, or until the vegetables soften. Add the split peas along with their soaking liquid, the bay leaves, cloves, ham hocks and potatoes and

(continued)

bring to the boil. Skim off any foam that appears on the surface. Reduce the heat to low and simmer gently for 2 hours, or until the peas are tender.

Remove the ham hocks and, when cool enough to handle, remove the meat and cut into small cubes. Add to the pot and heat through, then ladle soup into bowls and serve.

Nutritional Analysis

Calories	456.77 Kcal	Protein	27.56 gm
Fat	10.04 gm	Carbohydrate	66.04 gm
Sodium	992.01 mg	Cholesterol	21.56 mg
Saturated fat	2.00 gm		

Autumn Soup

Serves: 6

1l (2pt) reduced-sodium, fat-free chicken stock
250g (8oz) chopped onion
2 slices bread, cut into cubes
2 tart apples, cored and coarsely chopped
500g (1lb) butternut squash, peeled, washed, seeded and cubed
1 tsp salt
1 tsp diced marjoram
1 tsp diced rosemary
1 tsp pepper
2 eggs
125g (4fl oz) buttermilk

Combine the stock, onion, bread cubes, apples, squash, salt, marjoram, rosemary and pepper in a large, heavy saucepan. Bring to the boil, reduce the

heat to low, and simmer, covered, for 45 minutes. Remove from the heat.

Working in batches, purée the soup in a blender. Return the purée to the pan. In a small bowl, beat together the eggs and buttermilk. Stir a little of the hot soup into the egg mixture, and then add it to the soup. Reheat gently for 5 minutes to blend the flavours; do not boil. Ladle into bowls and serve.

Nutritional Analysis

Calories	132.86 Kcal	Protein	6.48 gm
Fat	2.43 gm	Carbohydrate	22.42 gm
Sodium	853.44 mg	Cholesterol	71.72 mg
Saturated fat	0.72 gm		

Corn Chowder

Serves: 8

1kg (2lb) baking potatoes, peeled and cut into large chunks
1 large onion, coarsely chopped
1 green pepper, chopped
500g (1lb) corn kernels
250ml (8fl oz) low-fat evaporated milk

In a large soup pot, combine the potatoes, onion and pepper. Add just enough water to cover the vegetables, bring to the boil, reduce the heat to low and simmer for 10 minutes.

Add the corn and simmer for another 10 minutes, or until the potatoes are tender. Stir in the evaporated milk, bring back to the boil and ladle into bowls to serve.

Tuna Chowder

Nutritional Analysis

Calories	130.61 Kcal	Protein	5.18 gm
Fat	1.06 gm	Carbohydrate	26.83 gm
Sodium	46.38 mg	Cholesterol	5.00 mg
Saturated fat	0.08 gm		

Tuna Chowder

Serves: 8

> 2 tbsp buttery light, reduced-fat margarine
> 3 celery stalks, chopped
> 1 large onion, chopped
> 1 large baking potato, cut into 12mm (1/2in) dice
> 3 tbsp plain flour
> 750ml (1 1/2pt) low-fat milk
> 425g (14oz) tinned water-packed tuna, drained
>   and flaked
> 250g (8oz) grated non-fat cheddar cheese
> 1 tsp dried thyme, crumbled
> 1 tsp dried dill, crumbled
> salt and pepper to taste
> 60g (2oz) chopped fresh parsley

In a large, heavy pot, melt the margarine over medium-high heat. Add the celery, onion and potato and sauté until the potato is tender. Add the flour and milk and blend thoroughly. Cook, stirring, until the mixture thickens, about 5 minutes. Add the tuna, cheese, thyme and dill. Mix well and season with salt and pepper. Heat over medium-low heat for 5 to 10 minutes. Ladle into bowls and garnish with parsley, then serve.

Nutritional Analysis

Calories	173.28 Kcal	Protein	21.55 gm
Fat	2.78 gm	Carbohydrate	15.57 gm
Sodium	327.50 mg	Cholesterol	22.38 mg
Saturated fat	1.03 gm		

Grandma's Cabbage Soup

Serves: 8

> 1 tbsp butter
> 1 tbsp vegetable oil
> 500g (1lb) chopped celery
> 500g (1lb) chopped carrots
> 2 onions, coarsely chopped
> 500g (1lb) chopped green cabbage
> 2l (4pt) reduced-sodium, fat-free chicken stock
> 500g (1lb) desirée or red potatoes, diced
> 1/2 tsp dried marjoram, crumbled
> 1 tsp dried dill, crumbled
> salt and pepper to taste

In a large pot, melt the butter with the oil over medium heat. Add the celery, carrots and onions and sauté until tender, about 15 minutes. When the vegetables are tender, add the cabbage and cook for 5 more minutes. Add the stock, bring to the boil, reduce the heat to low and simmer, uncovered, for 15 minutes. Add the potatoes and herbs and cook for another 15 minutes.

Working in three batches, purée the soup in a food processor or blender and return to the pot. Cook for another 10 minutes to blend the

(continued)

flavours. Season with salt and pepper, then ladle into bowls to serve.

Nutritional Analysis

Calories	125.98 Kcal	Protein	5.31 gm
Fat	3.41 gm	Carbohydrate	18.74 gm
Sodium	620.67 mg	Cholesterol	3.88 mg
Saturated fat	1.12 gm		

Cream of Carrot Soup

Serves: 6

1 tbsp olive oil
500g (1lb) carrots
1 large onion, chopped
125g (4oz) chopped celery
500g (1lb) peeled and diced potato
1 clove garlic, crushed
1 tsp sugar
4 whole cloves
pepper to taste
1l (2pt) reduced-sodium, fat-free chicken stock

In a saucepan, heat the oil over medium heat. Add the carrots, onion, celery, potato, garlic and sugar and sauté until onion is translucent, about 3 minutes. Reduce the heat to low, cover and cook for 10 minutes. Uncover, add the cloves, pepper and stock, and bring to the boil. Reduce the heat to low and cook, covered, until vegetables are tender, 15 to 30 minutes.

Remove and discard the cloves, then allow the soup to cool slightly. Working in batches, purée the soup in a food processor or blender until

smooth. Return to a clean saucepan, reheat to serving temperature, and ladle into bowls to serve.

Nutritional Analysis

Calories	121.45 Kcal	Protein	4.33 gm
Fat	2.51 gm	Carbohydrate	21.15 gm
Sodium	413.67 mg	Cholesterol	0.00 mg
Saturated fat	0.34 gm		

Winter Potato and Vegetable Soup

Serves: 8

1 tbsp butter
1 clove garlic, crushed
1 large onion, chopped
1.5l (3pt) reduced-sodium, fat-free chicken stock
3 medium pink fir or anya potatoes, peeled and diced
2 medium carrots, sliced
2 medium celery stalks, finely chopped
1 courgette, sliced
1 tsp dried dill
1 bunch fresh parsley, finely chopped
salt and pepper to taste
2 tbsp cornflour mixed with 2 tbsp cold water

In a sauté pan, melt the butter over medium heat. Add the garlic and onion and sauté for 4 minutes, or until the onion is soft. Add the stock, potatoes, carrots, celery and courgette and bring to the boil. Reduce the heat to low and cook, covered, until the potatoes are tender, about 20 minutes.

Add the dill, parsley, salt, pepper and corn-flour-water mixture, stir well and continue to

cook for about 15 minutes, or until the soup is slightly thickened. Ladle into bowls to serve.

Nutritional Analysis

Calories	103.07 Kcal	Protein	4.28 gm
Fat	1.64 gm	Carbohydrate	17.79 gm
Sodium	458.36 mg	Cholesterol	3.88 mg
Saturated fat	0.89 gm		

Zesty Gazpacho

Serves: 4

1 large cucumber, peeled and cut in half
2 large tomatoes, peeled and chopped
1 green pepper, chopped
1 medium onion, halved
750g (1½pt) tomato juice
60ml (2fl oz) red wine vinegar
1 tbsp olive oil
1 tsp Tabasco sauce
½ tsp salt
1 tsp pepper
4 cloves garlic, crushed

Place half the cucumber, 1 tomato, half the pepper, half the onion and 250ml (8fl oz) of the tomato juice in a food processor and process until blended. Chop the remaining cucumber, tomato, pepper and onion, and place in a large bowl. Stir in the purée and add the remaining tomato juice along with the vinegar, oil, Tabasco, salt, pepper and garlic. Cover and chill for at least 2 hours before serving.

(continued)

Reduced-Sodium Soy Sauce

It's always a good idea to choose the reduced-sodium soy sauce at the supermarket. But did you know it's easy to make your own soy sauce with less salt than the bottled variety – and cheaper, too?

Pour a bottle of regular soy sauce into a measuring cup. Add an equal amount of water, stir well, and you've made low-salt (relatively speaking) soy sauce. Pour into bottles and store in a cool cupboard.

Rich Potato Soup

Nutritional Analysis

Calories	121.39 Kcal	Protein	3.57 gm
Fat	3.99 gm	Carbohydrate	21.44 gm
Sodium	973.53 mg	Cholesterol	0.00 mg
Saturated fat	0.52 gm		

Serves: 8

1 tbsp butter
250g (8oz) sliced leeks
750g (1lb 8oz) red potatoes, peeled and sliced
750ml (1½pt) reduced-sodium, fat-free chicken stock
Dash of ground nutmeg
750ml (1½pt) low-fat milk
salt and pepper to taste

In a saucepan, melt the butter over medium heat. Add the leeks and sauté for 5 to 10 minutes, or until tender. Add the potatoes, stock and nutmeg, and bring to the boil. Reduce the heat to low and simmer, covered, for 30 minutes, or until the potatoes are very tender.

Let cool slightly. Working in batches, purée in a food processor or blender until smooth. Pour into a bowl and stir in the milk, salt and pepper. Cover and chill well before serving.

Lentil Soup

Nutritional Analysis

Calories	120.27 Kcal	Protein	5.29 gm
Fat	2.40 gm	Carbohydrate	19.22 gm
Sodium	271.71 mg	Cholesterol	6.93 mg
Saturated Fat	1.39 gm		

Serves: 10

2 tbsp olive oil
3 large onions, chopped
3 carrots, grated
1 tsp dried marjoram, crumbled
1 tsp dried thyme, crumbled
875g (1lb 12oz) tinned tomatoes with their juice, coarsely chopped
2l (4pt) reduced-sodium, fat-free chicken stock
375g (12oz) dried brown lentils
salt and pepper to taste
125ml (4fl oz) dry white wine
60g (2oz) chopped fresh parsley
60g (2oz) grated Parmesan cheese

In a large saucepan, heat the oil over medium heat. Add the onions, carrots, marjoram and thyme, and sauté until onion is translucent, about 5 minutes. Add the tomatoes, stock and lentils, and bring to the boil. Reduce the heat to low, cover and cook until the lentils are tender, about 1 hour. Add the salt, pepper, wine and parsley, and mix well. Ladle into bowls and sprinkle with the cheese.

Nutritional Analysis

Calories	202.39 Kcal	Protein	13.09 gm
Fat	3.91 gm	Carbohydrate	28.28 gm
Sodium	629.39 mg	Cholesterol	1.58 mg
Saturated fat	0.83 gm		

Turkey Chowder

Serves: 10

2 tbsp butter
1 large onion, thinly sliced
1 green pepper, chopped
500ml (1pt) reduced-sodium, fat-free chicken stock
3 medium carrots, sliced
3 medium baking potatoes, peeled and diced
2 celery stalks, thinly sliced
1 tsp salt
750g (1lb 8oz) cooked, diced turkey
500g (1lb) corn kernels, drained
1/2 tsp dried thyme, crumbled
pepper to taste
750ml (1 1/2pt) low-fat milk
60g (2oz) finely chopped fresh parsley

In a large frying pan, melt the butter over medium heat. Add the onion and pepper, and sauté for 10 minutes, or until the onion is translucent. Stir in the stock and carrots, and bring to the boil. Reduce the heat to low, cover and cook for 5 minutes. Add the potatoes, celery and salt. Cover and simmer until the potatoes and carrots are tender, about 10 minutes.

Add the turkey, corn, thyme, pepper and milk. Heat through. Ladle into bowls, sprinkle with the parsley and serve.

Nutritional Analysis

Calories	203.23 Kcal	Protein	17.62 gm
Fat	5.46 gm	Carbohydrate	21.50 gm
Sodium	524.72 mg	Cholesterol	41.46 mg
Saturated fat	2.60 gm		

Hearty Corn Chowder

Serves: 8

1kg (2lb) potatoes cut into large chunks
1 large onion, chopped
1 green pepper, chopped
500g (1lb) frozen sweetcorn kernels
250ml (8fl oz) low-fat evaporated milk

In a saucepan, combine the potatoes, onion and pepper with water to cover. Bring to the boil, reduce the heat to low and simmer for 10 minutes. Add the corn and cook until vegetables are tender, about 10 more minutes. Stir in the milk and bring to serving temperature, stirring well. Ladle into bowls and serve.

Nutritional Analysis

Calories	133.58 Kcal	Protein	5.18 gm
Fat	0.92 gm	Carbohydrate	28.03 gm
Sodium	41.76 mg	Cholesterol	5.00 mg
Saturated fat	0.06 gm		

Using Lamb in Soup

Lamb has a stronger taste than either beef or chicken, so it is a good choice to use in soups, as a little goes a long way. Nearly any cut of lamb will work well; shank or shoulder, for example, is less costly than most other cuts and provides plenty of good flavour. Just make sure to add the lamb early in the cooking, as it tastes best when tender, and this comes from long, slow simmering.

Chilled Cucumber-Mint Soup

Serves: 4

1 cucumber, halved, peeled and seeded
60g (2oz) chopped spring onions
30g (1oz) chopped fresh mint
500ml (1pt) low-fat milk
250ml (8fl oz) plain low-fat yogurt
salt and pepper to taste

Purée the cucumber, spring onions and mint in a food processor or blender. Add the milk and yogurt and process until smooth. Transfer to a large bowl and stir in the yogurt. Season with salt and pepper. Cover and chill for 1 to 2 hours before serving.

Nutritional Analysis

Calories	99.12 Kcal	Protein	7.59 gm
Fat	2.26 gm	Carbohydrate	12.49 gm
Sodium	106.68 mg	Cholesterol	8.28 mg
Saturated fat	1.37 gm		

Red Bean and Rice Soup

Serves: 6

1 tbsp olive oil
1 onion, finely chopped
4 celery stalks, chopped
2 cloves garlic, crushed
2 tbsp plain flour
500ml (1pt) water
500ml (1pt) reduced-sodium, fat-free chicken stock
500g (8oz) chopped tomatoes

125g (4oz) washed white rice
1 tbsp chilli powder
1/2 tsp salt
425g (14oz) tinned kidney beans, drained
1 tbsp lemon juice

In a large frying pan, heat the oil over medium heat. Add the onion, celery and garlic, and cook for 5 minutes. Stir in the flour and cook for 1 minute. Add the water, stock, tomatoes, rice, chilli powder and salt. Bring to the boil, reduce the heat to low, cover, and cook until rice is tender, about 20 minutes.

Add the beans and lemon juice and heat through. Ladle into bowls to serve.

Nutritional Analysis

Calories	181.27 Kcal	Protein	7.97 gm
Fat	3.23 gm	Carbohydrate	30.34 gm
Sodium	532.55 mg	Cholesterol	0.00 mg
Saturated fat	0.37 gm		

Hearty Scotch Broth

Serves: 8

500g (1lb) chopped cooked or raw lamb, all visible fat removed
2l (4pt) water
1 bay leaf
2 medium onions, chopped
2 celery stalks, diced
4 medium potatoes, peeled and diced
90g (3oz) pearl barley
500g (1lb) chopped cabbage

3 carrots, grated
90g (3oz) chopped fresh parsley
salt and pepper to taste

Put the lamb, water, bay leaf and onions in a large pot. Bring to the boil, reduce the heat to low, cover and simmer until the onions are translucent and the lamb is tender, about 45 minutes. Stir in the celery, potatoes and barley and cook, covered, for 15 minutes. Add the cabbage and carrots and continue to cook until the vegetables are tender, about 15 minutes.

Discard the bay leaf and add the parsley, salt and pepper. Ladle into bowls to serve.

Nutritional Analysis

Calories	182.23 Kcal	Protein	12.24 gm
Fat	3.59 gm	Carbohydrate	25.81 gm
Sodium	51.85 mg	Cholesterol	30.47 mg
Saturated fat	1.30 gm		

Summertime Potato Soup

Serves: 6

310ml (10fl oz) tinned condensed cream of potato soup
310ml (10fl oz) reduced-sodium, fat-free chicken stock
low-fat milk, as needed to fill the soup tin
1 small onion, cut into chunks
2 spring onions, finely chopped

Place the cream of potato soup, chicken stock and 1 soup tin of milk into a blender or food processor and purée for 10 seconds until blended. Add the

(continued)

onion and purée until smooth. Transfer to a serving bowl, cover and chill overnight. Ladle into chilled bowls and sprinkle with the spring onions.

Nutritional Analysis

Calories	64.81 Kcal	Protein	3.41 gm
Fat	1.55 gm	Carbohydrate	9.24 gm
Sodium	550.43 mg	Cholesterol	4.71 mg
Saturated fat	0.85 gm		

Quick Borscht

Serves: 6

500g (1lb) bottled pickled beetroot, drained
500ml (1pt) buttermilk
1 tbsp sugar
2 tbsp lemon juice
60g (2oz) snipped fresh chives

Place the beetroot, buttermilk, sugar and lemon juice in a blender or food processor. Purée until smooth. Ladle into bowls and top with the chives.

Nutritional Analysis

Calories	91.43 Kcal	Protein	3.37 gm
Fat	0.79 gm	Carbohydrate	18.68 gm
Sodium	286.54 mg	Cholesterol	3.26 mg
Saturated Fat	0.44 gm		

Sweet Potato–Ginger Soup

Serves: 6

1 tbsp olive oil
1 onion, chopped
2 tbsp peeled and crushed fresh ginger
750g (1lb 8oz) butternut squash, peeled, seeded and diced
750g (1lb 8oz) sweet potatoes, peeled and diced
1 large maris piper potato, peeled and diced
2l (4 pints) reduced-sodium, fat-free chicken stock
1/4 tsp salt
125g (4fl oz) plain low-fat yogurt

Heat the oil over medium heat in a soup pot for 30 seconds. Add the onion and sauté until translucent, about 5 minutes. Add the ginger and cook for about 1 minute. Add the squash, sweet potatoes, maris piper potato and stock. Bring to the boil, reduce the heat to low, cover and cook until the vegetables are tender, about 30 minutes.

Let cool slightly, then, working in 250ml (8fl oz) batches, purée in a food processor or blender until smooth. Pour into a clean saucepan, stir in the yogurt, season to taste and reheat gently. Ladle into bowls and serve.

Nutritional Analysis

Calories	220.14 Kcal	Protein	8.28 gm
Fat	2.98 gm	Carbohydrate	41.15 gm
Sodium	779.73 mg	Cholesterol	1.13 mg
Saturated fat	0.53 gm		

Creamy Vegetable Soup

Serves: 6

> 500ml (1½pt) water
> 750g (1lb 8oz) broccoli florets
> 1 large carrot, diced
> 1 onion, chopped
> 250g (8oz) coarsely chopped cauliflower
> salt and pepper to taste
> ¼ tsp dry mustard
> 250ml (8fl oz) low-fat milk
> 185g (6oz) grated low-fat cheddar cheese
> 125g (4oz) diced yellow courgette

Bring the water to the boil in a saucepan. Add 500g (1lb) of the broccoli, half the carrot and the onion, and return to the boil. Reduce the heat to low, cover and cook until the vegetables are tender, about 15 minutes.

Let cool slightly, then transfer to a food processor and purée until smooth. Return the broccoli purée to the saucepan. Add the remaining broccoli and carrot, cauliflower, salt, pepper, mustard and milk. Bring to the boil, reduce the heat to low and cook, covered, until the vegetables are tender, about 10 minutes. Add the cheese and courgette, stir well and cook, stirring, until the cheese melts and the courgette is tender, about 5 minutes more. Ladle into bowls to serve.

Nutritional Analysis

Calories	83.87 Kcal	Protein	9.45 gm
Fat	0.92 gm	Carbohydrate	11.58 gm
Sodium	162.39 mg	Cholesterol	3.12 mg
Saturated fat	0.30 gm		

Potato and Corn Chowder

Serves: 6

> 4 King Edward potatoes, peeled and diced
> 625ml (1¼pt) water
> 1 onion, chopped
> 3 cloves garlic, crushed
> 1 red pepper, diced
> 1 tsp ground cumin
> 1 tsp dried basil, crumbled
> 1 tsp salt
> ½ tsp black pepper
> 125g (4oz) tinned diced green chilli peppers
> 300g (10z) frozen sweetcorn, thawed
> 500ml (1 pint) low-fat milk

Place the potatoes and 500ml (1 pint) of the water in a large saucepan. Bring to the boil, reduce the heat to low, cover and cook for 20 minutes, or until potatoes are tender. Heat 250ml (8fl oz) water in a saucepan, add the onion, garlic and pepper, and cook for 5 minutes. Add the cumin, basil, salt and black pepper, and cook until the vegetables are tender, about 5 minutes longer. Meanwhile, mash the potatoes in their cooking water and add the onion mixture with the chillies, sweetcorn and milk. Stir to blend. Heat gently for 5 more minutes, or until heated through. Ladle into bowls to serve.

Nutritional Analysis

Calories	181.58 Kcal	Protein	6.81 gm
Fat	1.55 gm	Carbohydrate	37.29 gm
Sodium	555.72 mg	Cholesterol	3.25 mg
Saturated fat	0.58 gm		

Lime-Chicken Soup

Serves: 6

250g (8oz) boneless, skinless chicken breasts
1l (2pt) reduced-sodium, fat-free chicken stock
juice of 2 limes
1 tsp dried oregano, crumbled
1 tsp dried basil, crumbled
1 jalapeño pepper, finely chopped
1 bay leaf
salt and black pepper to taste
1 tomato, peeled and chopped
1 red onion, chopped
1 tbsp finely chopped fresh coriander
125g (4oz) low-fat gruyere or cheddar cheese, cubed
2 corn tortillas, cut into strips
4 lime slices
4 fresh coriander sprigs

Place the chicken breasts in a saucepan, add water to cover, bring to a simmer and poach for about 10 minutes or until cooked through. Drain and let cool, then shred the meat. Set aside.

Combine the stock, lime juice, oregano, basil, jalapeño, bay leaf, salt and pepper in a saucepan. Bring to the boil, reduce the heat to low and simmer for 15 minutes. Add the chicken, tomato, red onion and chopped coriander. Return to simmer and cook for 5 minutes. Ladle the soup into a large bowl. Add the cheese cubes. Garnish with the tortillas, lime slices and coriander sprigs.

Nutritional Analysis

Calories	146.10 Kcal	Protein	16.68 gm
Fat	4.79 gm	Carbohydrate	9.39 gm
Sodium	577.87 mg	Cholesterol	35.28 mg
Saturated fat	2.81 gm		

Savoury Tomato Soup

Serves: 4

1 tsp butter
2 tbsp finely chopped shallots
5 large tomatoes, diced
250ml (8fl oz) reduced-sodium, fat-free chicken stock
250ml (8fl oz) low-fat milk
1 tsp dried oregano
1 tsp dried basil

In a large pan, melt the butter over medium heat. Add the shallots and sauté for 5 minutes, or until shallots are tender. Add the tomatoes and chicken stock, and simmer for 15 minutes.

Let cool slightly. Transfer to a food processor and purée until smooth. Return to the saucepan and add the milk. Reheat gently for 10 minutes to blend the flavours. Add the oregano and basil, and ladle into bowls to serve.

Nutritional Analysis

Calories	103.11 Kcal	Protein	5.38 gm
Fat	2.56 gm	Carbohydrate	17.37 gm
Sodium	206.88 mg	Cholesterol	5.03 mg
Saturated fat	1.13 gm		

Onion and Garlic Soup

Serves: 6

> 3 onions, sliced
> 3 large shallots, finely chopped
> 1 head garlic, cloves separated and peeled
> 1 tbsp olive oil
> 1l (2pt) reduced-sodium, fat-free chicken stock
> 1 tsp thyme, dried, crumbled
> salt and pepper to taste

Combine the onions, shallots, garlic and oil in a large pan. Place over very low heat and sauté for 15 minutes, or until the onions are golden. Pour in 250ml (8fl oz) of the chicken stock. Stir, loosening the caramelized bits stuck to the pan bottom. Transfer to a saucepan and add the thyme and the remaining stock. Bring to the boil, reduce the heat to low, cover and simmer until onion is tender, about 30 minutes. Season with salt and pepper.

Nutritional Analysis

Calories	78.10	Kcal	Protein	3.61	gm
Fat	2.42	gm	Carbohydrate	10.90	gm
Sodium	378.81	mg	Cholesterol	0.00	mg
Saturated fat	0.32	gm			

Reduced-Fat Stock

Although meat and chicken stocks are relatively low fat already, you may want to go a step further and make them virtually fat-free. First, place a lamb shank, beef bone or chicken carcass in a large soup pot with enough water to cover. Add 1 bay leaf and 1 onion, chopped. Bring to the boil, lower the heat to low and simmer, uncovered, for 1 hour. Remove the bone or carcass and strain the stock through a sieve into a clean container. Cover and place in the refrigerator overnight. The next day, skim off the fat that has solidified on top. You can store in the refrigerator for up to two weeks, taking it out and bringing it to the boil and letting it cool again regularly.

Salads

CHAPTER FOUR

Amount Per Chapter
47 Recipes

	% Daily Value
Easy to Prepare	**100%**
Low Fat/High Flavour	**100%**
Simple to Understand	**100%**

DELICIOUS, EASY, LOW-FAT RECIPES

I love salads, not only in hot weather but at any time of year. They're easy to make, usually requiring little preparation besides chopping and stirring for a couple of minutes, and they satisfy my urge for crunchy foods, a craving that commonly comes over me at least once a day.

In addition, most of the following recipes call for only a single bowl for the making, which reduces stress by producing a minimum of dirty dishes to wash. This is an admirable goal to strive for, no matter what the season.

Summertime Potato Salad
Serves: 8

Dressing:
250ml (8fl oz) plain low-fat yogurt
1 tsp ground cumin
1 tsp ground coriander
1 tsp pepper

1kg (2lb) medium potatoes, peeled, boiled until tender and cut into chunks
1 large onion, thinly sliced into rings
2 tbsp finely chopped fresh basil
dash of paprika

Whisk together all the dressing ingredients in a serving bowl. Add the potatoes and toss them gently to coat thoroughly. Place the onion rings on top and sprinkle the salad with basil and paprika. Cover and refrigerate for at least 30 minutes.

Nutritional Analysis

Calories	97.98 Kcal	Protein	3.65 gm
Fat	0.60 gm	Carbohydrate	20.08 gm
Sodium	26.45 mg	Cholesterol	1.70 mg
Saturated fat	0.30 gm		

Seafood Pasta Salad
Serves: 4

250g (8oz) dry tricolore spiral pasta, cooked and chilled
250g (8oz) cooked and peeled prawns
1 green pepper, diced
60g (2oz) sliced carrots
125g (4oz) sliced courgette
80ml (2¹/₂fl oz) Worcestershire sauce
80ml (2¹/₂fl oz) low-fat mayonnaise
salt and pepper to taste

In a bowl, combine the pasta, prawns, pepper, carrots and courgette, mixing gently. Add the Worcestershire sauce, mayonnaise, salt and pepper, and toss lightly to combine. Cover and refrigerate for at least 30 minutes before serving.

Nutritional Analysis

Calories	306.36 Kcal	Protein	16.25 gm
Fat	2.34 gm	Carbohydrate	54.07 gm
Sodium	509.63 mg	Cholesterol	69.10 mg
Saturated fat	0.18 gm		

Chinese Coleslaw

Serves: 6

1kg (2lb) shredded Chinese cabbage
250g (8oz) tinned crushed pineapple, drained
250g (8oz) tinned water chestnuts, drained and sliced
250g (8oz) chopped fresh parsley
60g (2oz) sliced spring onions
60ml (2fl oz) low-fat mayonnaise
1 tbsp mustard
1 tsp peeled and grated fresh ginger

In a bowl, combine the cabbage, pineapple, water chestnuts, parsley and spring onions. Toss to mix. Cover and chill. In a small bowl, whisk together the mayonnaise, mustard and ginger. Cover and chill. To serve, spoon the mayonnaise dressing over the cabbage mixture and toss to coat all the ingredients thoroughly.

Nutritional Analysis

Calories	66.43	Kcal	Protein	1.42	gm
Fat	0.93	gm	Carbohydrate	14.41	gm
Sodium	138.02	mg	Cholesterol	0.00	mg
Saturated fat	0.04	gm			

Crispy Caesar Salad

Serves: 4

1 large head romaine lettuce, chilled
nonstick olive oil-flavoured cooking spray
2 large cloves garlic, crushed
1/2 tsp anchovy paste
1 tsp Worcestershire sauce

60ml (2fl oz) lemon juice
grated Parmesan cheese (optional)
coarsely ground pepper

Place the romaine leaves in a serving bowl and spray lightly with the olive oil spray. In a small bowl, whisk together the garlic, anchovy paste, Worcestershire sauce and lemon juice until blended. Pour the dressing on the romaine and toss well. Sprinkle with pepper (or cheese) and serve.

Nutritional Analysis

Calories	26.02	Kcal	Protein	2.21	gm
Fat	0.45	gm	Carbohydrate	4.04	gm
Sodium	39.30	mg	Cholesterol	0.27	mg
Saturated fat	0.04	gm			

Apricot-Coriander Salad

Serves: 6

500g (1lb) beansprouts
boiling water as needed
500ml (1lb) tinned apricot halves in syrup
3 tbsp white wine vinegar
1 tsp peanut oil
2 tbsp soy sauce
1 1/2 tsp grated fresh ginger
1kg (2lb) shredded lettuce
60g (2oz) finely chopped fresh coriander
2 spring onions, sliced on the diagonal
250g (8oz) tinned water chestnuts, drained and sliced

(continued)

Place the beansprouts in a colander or large sieve. Pour boiling water over them; drain and cool. Drain the apricots, reserving 2 tablespoons syrup. Cut the apricots into strips and set aside.

In a jar with screw-top lid, combine the syrup, vinegar, oil, soy sauce and ginger. Cover and shake well. Place the lettuce into a bowl or onto a platter. Top with the coriander, spring onions, beansprouts and water chestnuts. Place the apricot strips over the salad. Shake the dressing again and pour over the salad. Toss well and serve.

Nutritional Analysis

Calories	139.97 Kcal	Protein	3.98gm
Fat	1.48 gm	Carbohydrate	31.28 gm
Sodium	532.83 mg	Cholesterol	0.00 mg
Saturated fat	0.24 gm		

Artichoke Hearts Salad

Serves: 4

Salad:
4 artichoke hearts, quartered
4 endives, cut on the diagonal into 12mm (1/2in) pieces
2 bunches watercress, chopped
4 large tomatoes, sliced
1 tbsp snipped fresh chives

Chutney Vinaigrette:
juice of 1 lemon
1/4 tsp curry powder
1 tsp red wine vinegar
1/2 tsp dry mustard
1/2 tsp salt
1/4 tsp white pepper
1 tbsp virgin olive oil
125g (4oz) mango chutney

On a large serving platter, arrange the artichoke hearts, endives, watercress and tomato slices in an attractive way. Cover and chill.

To make the chutney vinaigrette, combine the lemon juice, curry powder, vinegar, mustard, salt and white pepper in a small bowl. Mix well. Add the olive oil and whisk until fully incorporated. Stir in the chutney. Chill the dressing in the refrigerator for at least an hour.

Spoon the vinaigrette over the salad. Sprinkle on the chives and serve.

Nutritional Analysis

Calories	232.33 Kcal	Protein	5.83 gm
Fat	4.45 gm	Carbohydrate	44.18 gm
Sodium	987.50 mg	Cholesterol	0.00 mg
Saturated fat	0.64 gm		

Black and White Bean Salad

Serves: 6

250g (8oz) dry small white beans, cooked and drained
250g (8oz) dry black beans, cooked and drained
185g (6oz) frozen corn kernels, thawed
1 tomato, diced
250g (8oz) diced red onions
2 tbsp minced fresh coriander
1 tbsp finely chopped fresh mint
1/2 tsp salt
1/8 tsp cayenne pepper

3 tbsp lime juice
1 tbsp vegetable oil
2 tbsp reduced-sodium, fat-free
  chicken stock

In a medium bowl, mix together all ingredients. Serve chilled or at room temperature. The salad may be made and refrigerated for up to 2 days before serving.

Nutritional Analysis

Calories	210.74 Kcal	Protein	11.51 gm
Fat	3.18 gm	Carbohydrate	36.03 gm
Sodium	211.93 mg	Cholesterol	0.00 mg
Saturated fat	0.49 gm		

Black Bean and Rice Salad

Serves: 8

310ml (10fl oz) reduced-sodium, fat-free
  chicken stock
60ml (2fl oz) water
250g (8oz) long-grain white rice
500g (1lb) tinned black beans, drained and rinsed
1 red pepper, chopped
1/2 green pepper, chopped
1/2 medium red onion, chopped

Dressing:
1 tbsp olive oil
3 tbsp orange juice
1 tbsp red wine vinegar
2 tsp fresh coriander leaves
1 1/2 tsp ground cumin

1 tsp garlic salt
1/2 tsp chilli powder

In a large saucepan, bring the chicken broth and water to the boil. Add the rice, cover, reduce the heat to low and simmer for 20 minutes, or until all the liquid has been absorbed. Uncover, fluff with a fork and turn into a large salad bowl.

Add the beans, red and green peppers and onion, and stir gently to combine.

In a small bowl, combine all the dressing ingredients and beat with a fork until well combined.

Pour the dressing over the rice mixture and stir gently. Cover and refrigerate for at least 4 hours before serving.

Nutritional Analysis

Calories	155.35 Kcal	Protein	5.34 gm
Fat	2.35 gm	Carbohydrate	28.22 gm
Sodium	436.42 mg	Cholesterol	0.00 mg
Saturated fat	0.26 gm		

California Black Bean Salad

Serves: 8

500g (1lb) tinned black beans, drained and rinsed
375g (12oz) tinned sweetcorn kernels, drained
1 tomato, chopped
125g (4oz) chopped red onion
125g (4oz) chopped green pepper
2 cloves garlic, crushed
180ml (6fl oz) low-fat Italian dressing
2 tsp finely chopped fresh parsley
3/4 tsp tabasco sauce

(continued)

Fruit Salad Days

Fruit salads can easily be enhanced or even turned into a main meal with a few judicious additions. Choose your favourites: a little shredded coconut, a handful of walnuts, a drizzle of honey, a scattering of raisins. Just a sprinkle or handful will do, so as not to overpower the delicate fruit and also to keep the fat content low.

¹/₂ tsp pepper
¹/₂ tsp garlic powder
¹/₂ tsp chilli powder

In a bowl, mix together all the ingredients. Cover and chill for 30 minutes before serving.

Nutritional Analysis

Calories	135.85	Kcal	Protein	4.02	gm
Fat	0.77	gm	Carbohydrate	16.39	gm
Sodium	415.70	mg	Cholesterol	0.00	mg
Saturated fat	0.04	gm			

Fruity Brown Rice Salad

Serves: 6

500g (1lb) tinned fruit cocktail
250g (8oz) warm cooked brown rice
1 tomato, diced
250g (8oz) sliced celery
125g (4oz) sliced spring onions
2 tbsp red wine vinegar
1 tbsp vegetable oil
1 tbsp Dijon mustard
¹/₂ tsp dried tarragon, crumbled
¹/₈ tsp garlic powder

Drain the fruit cocktail, reserving 60ml (2fl oz) of the liquid; save the remaining juice for another use. In a bowl, toss together the rice, fruit cocktail, tomato, celery and spring onions. Combine the reserved liquid, the vinegar, oil, mustard, tarragon and garlic powder. Stir into the rice mixture. Cover and chill for at least an hour before serving.

Nutritional Analysis

Calories	104.82 Kcal	Protein	1.67 gm
Fat	2.65 gm	Carbohydrate	18.97 gm
Sodium	85.30 mg	Cholesterol	0.00 mg
Saturated fat	0.34 gm		

Chilli Pepper Potato Salad

Serves: 10

6 medium potatoes, peeled and chopped
250ml (8fl oz) low-fat mayonnaise
1 tbsp vinegar
1 tbsp mustard
1 tsp salt
1/4 tsp pepper
2 celery stalks, chopped
1 medium onion, chopped
125g (4oz) tinned chopped green chilli peppers,
  drained
1 avocado
2 tomatoes, chopped

Place the potatoes in a saucepan with water to
cover, bring to the boil and cook for about 20
minutes, or until tender. Drain and let the potatoes cool slightly.

In a large glass or plastic bowl, mix together
the mayonnaise, vinegar, mustard, salt and
pepper. Add the potatoes, celery and onion; toss
well. Stir in the chillies. Cover and refrigerate for
at least 4 hours. Just before serving, peel, stone
and chop the avocado, then stir it and the tomatoes into the salad.

Nutritional Analysis

Calories	143.36 Kcal	Protein	2.41 gm
Fat	4.90 gm	Carbohydrate	23.90 gm
Sodium	561.61 mg	Cholesterol	0.00 mg
Saturated fat	0.53 gm		

Sunshine Bean Salad with Golden Gate Dressing

Serves: 8

Golden Gate Dressing:
90g (3oz) sugar
1/2 tsp dry mustard
1 tsp salt
2 tbsp plain flour
1 egg
125ml (4fl oz) white wine vinegar
125ml (4fl oz) water
1 tbsp butter

500g (1lb) tinned chick peas, drained
250g (8oz) tinned sweetcorn kernels,
  drained
250g (8oz) diced celery
125g (4oz) chopped onion
2 tbsp diced pimiento
60g (2oz) diced green peppers

To make the dressing, in a small bowl stir
together the sugar, mustard, salt and flour. In
another small bowl, beat the egg with a fork.
Beat the dry mixture into the egg. In a small
saucepan, heat together the vinegar, water and
butter over low heat until the mixture simmers.

(continued)

Remove from the heat and gradually add to the egg mixture, stirring vigorously. Return to the heat and cook, stirring constantly, until smooth and thick, 2 or 3 minutes. Chill. You should have about 310ml (15fl oz). Leftover dressing is fine for potato, cabbage, tuna or other salads, and will keep in a refrigerator for up to a week.

In a large glass bowl, combine the chick peas, sweetcorn, celery, onion, pimiento and green pepper. Moisten to taste with the dressing. Chill before serving.

Nutritional Analysis

Calories	125.46	Kcal	Protein	3.79	gm
Fat	3.19	gm	Carbohydrate	21.27	gm
Sodium	431.56	mg	Cholesterol	30.44	mg
Saturated fat	1.14	gm			

Fruity Chicken Salad

Serves: 8

600g (1lb 4oz) shredded cooked chicken
600g (1lb 4oz) peeled melon chunks
600g (1lb 4oz) peeled cucumber chunks
600g (1lb 4oz) seedless green grapes
125ml (4fl oz) low-fat mayonnaise
2 tbsp plain nonfat yogurt
1¹/₂ tsp cider vinegar
¹/₈ tsp salt
¹/₈ tsp pepper

80ml (2¹/₂fl oz) chopped fresh coriander
2 tbsp lime juice

In a medium bowl, combine the chicken, melon, cucumber and grapes. In a larger bowl, whisk together the remaining ingredients to make a dressing. Add the chicken-fruit mixture to the dressing and toss to mix. Cover and chill for at least an hour before serving.

Nutritional Analysis

Calories	146.71	Kcal	Protein	13.46	gm
Fat	4.50	gm	Carbohydrate	13.27	gm
Sodium	222.60	mg	Cholesterol	39.00	mg
Saturated fat	0.94	gm			

Chicken Pasta Salad

Serves: 6

1 head broccoli, chopped
¹/₄ tsp salt
750g (1lb 8oz) diced cooked chicken
250g (8oz) pasta shells, cooked and drained
2 large tomatoes, cubed
125g (4oz) coarsely chopped red onion
¹/₂ tsp pepper
250ml (8fl oz) low-calorie Italian dressing

Steam the broccoli over boiling water for about 5 minutes. Chill by rinsing in cold water, drain, place in a large bowl and sprinkle with the salt. Add the chicken, pasta, tomatoes and onion, and

sprinkle with the pepper. Pour the dressing over the salad and mix gently but thoroughly. Cover and chill before serving.

Nutritional Analysis

Calories	374.67 Kcal	Protein	28.01 gm
Fat	11.60 gm	Carbohydrate	39.41 gm
Sodium	612.48 mg	Cholesterol	62.30 mg
Saturated fat	2.22 gm		

Avocado-Citrus Salad

Serves: 6

> *3 corn tortillas, each 150mm (6in) in diameter*
> *4 oranges*
> *4 grapefruit*
> *2 tbsp honey*
> *2 tbsp raspberry vinegar*
> *1 avocado*
> *6 fresh mint sprigs*

Preheat oven to 140°C (275°F), gas mark 1. Slice the corn tortillas into very narrow strips. Spread out on a baking tray and bake until lightly brown, about 15 minutes. Set aside to cool.

Grate enough zest from the oranges to give about 4 tablespoons. Set aside. Using a sharp knife, peel the oranges and grapefruit, removing all the bitter white membrane, then free the sections from the membranes by cutting along either side of each section. Remove any seeds and set the sections to one side.

In a large bowl, mix together the honey, vinegar and orange and grapefruit sections, tossing to coat evenly. Add the orange zest and tortilla strips, and toss gently to distribute evenly. Transfer to individual plates. Peel, stone and cut the avocados into slices and arrange each serving with the slices and a mint sprig.

Nutritional Analysis

Calories	205.76 Kcal	Protein	3.16 gm
Fat	5.81 gm	Carbohydrate	39.82 gm
Sodium	23.97 mg	Cholesterol	0.00 mg
Saturated fat	0.89 gm		

Curried Bean and Rice Salad

Serves: 6

> *1 tbsp butter or buttery light, reduced-fat margarine*
> *1 tsp curry powder*
> *180ml (6fl oz) reduced-sodium, fat-free chicken stock*
> *90g (3oz) long-grain rice*
> *60g (2oz) chopped celery*
> *2 tbsp chopped spring onions*
> *2 tbsp chopped green peppers*
> *1 tbsp lime juice*
> *500g (1lb) tinned kidney beans, drained and rinsed*
> *60ml (2fl oz) plain nonfat yogurt*
> *2 tbsp toasted slivered blanched almonds*
> *1/4 tsp salt*
> *dash of pepper*
> *1 large tomato, cut into wedges*
> *1 fresh parsley sprig*

In a small saucepan, melt the butter or margarine over medium-high heat. Add the curry powder and sauté for several seconds. Stir in the chicken stock and bring to the boil. Add the rice, cover, reduce to low and cook for 20 minutes, or until all the liquid is absorbed and the rice is tender.

Stir in the celery, spring onions, pepper and lime juice. Transfer to a bowl, let cool, cover and chill thoroughly. Stir in the beans, yogurt, almonds and salt and pepper. Garnish with the tomato and parsley, and serve.

Nutritional Analysis

Calories	142.76	Kcal	Protein	6.55	gm
Fat	4.03	gm	Carbohydrate	20.45	gm
Sodium	295.68	mg	Cholesterol	5.35	mg
Saturated fat	1.38	gm			

Mixed Greens with Honey and Oranges

Serves: 6

> 60ml (2fl oz) water
> 60ml (2fl oz) honey
> 60ml (2fl oz) white vinegar
> 2 heads lettuce
> 2 heads radicchio
> 3 oranges

In a small saucepan, bring the water, honey and vinegar to the boil; reduce the heat and simmer for 2 minutes. Remove from the heat; let cool.

Arrange the lettuce and radicchio on 6 salad plates. Using a sharp knife, peel the oranges, removing all the bitter white membrane, then free the sections from the membranes by cutting along either side of each section. Remove any seeds and divide the orange sections among the salad plates. Drizzle each salad with the cooled dressing and serve.

Nutritional Analysis

Calories	94.63	Kcal	Protein	1.80	gm
Fat	0.35	gm	Carbohydrate	23.80	gm
Sodium	11.69	mg	Cholesterol	0.00	mg
Saturated fat	0.05	gm			

Mai Fun Chicken Salad with Hoisin Dressing

Serves: 6

Hoisin Dressing:
> 3 tbsp rice vinegar or white wine vinegar
> 2 tbsp peanut oil
> 1 tbsp hoisin sauce
> 2 tsp toasted sesame seeds
> 2 tsp peeled and minced fresh ginger
>
> savoy cabbage leaves
> 250g (8oz) mai fun (rice sticks), cooked and chilled,
>   or white rice, cooked and chilled
> 250g (8oz) finely grated carrots
> 2 whole chicken breasts, cooked, skinned, boned
>   and sliced

*125g (4oz) sugar snap peas, blanched briefly, drained
and chilled*
1 cucumber, peeled and chopped

To make the dressing, combine the vinegar, oil,
hoisin sauce, sesame seeds and ginger in a jar with
a screw-top lid. Cover and shake well. Chill.

For each serving, line a salad plate with
cabbage leaves and arrange a layer of the rice
sticks or cooked rice on top. Arrange the carrots,
chicken slices and sugar snap peas on top.
Garnish with cucumber and carrot, as desired.
Shake dressing again, and pass around the table.

Nutritional Analysis

Calories	293.36 Kcal	Protein	18.58 gm
Fat	7.09 gm	Carbohydrate	37.41 gm
Sodium	170.15 mg	Cholesterol	48.73 mg
Saturated fat	1.39 gm		

Manhattan Deli-Style Salad

Serves: 6

300g (10oz) pitted black olives, sliced
250g (8oz) chopped red or green pepper or pimiento
1 small red onion, thinly sliced into rings
60g (2oz) grated Parmesan cheese
60g (2oz) finely chopped fresh parsley
1 tbsp capers
180ml (6fl oz) low-fat Italian dressing
*375g (12oz) fusilli, cooked, drained
and cooled*

(continued)

Parsley Hints

Lots of fruit and vegetable salads
benefit from a couple of sprigs of
parsley. The problem is that you
need to buy a whole bunch to get
those few sprigs. Parsley, however,
will stay crisp and fresh for up to
a week if you store it standing in a
glass of iced water in the refrigerator.
Change the water every couple of
days – and give some parsley to the
dog to freshen his breath.

In a large bowl, combine the olives, pepper (or pimiento), onion, cheese, parsley, capers and dressing. Mix well. Add the cooled pasta and toss to coat evenly. Serve at room temperature or chilled.

Nutritional Analysis

Calories	351.72 Kcal	Protein	9.34 gm
Fat	4.94 gm	Carbohydrate	49.36 gm
Sodium	621.94 mg	Cholesterol	2.63 mg
Saturated fat	1.15 gm		

Mariner Bean Salad Plate

Serves: 8

600g (1lb 4oz) well-drained cooked small white beans
600g (1lb 4oz) well-drained cooked pink beans
600g (1lb 4oz) diced, skinned cooked chicken
250g (8oz) low-fat cheddar cheese, cut into 12mm (1/2 in) cubes
1/4 tsp dried basil, crumbled
1 tbsp sugar
125ml (4fl oz) low-fat Italian dressing
1 head iceberg lettuce, separated into leaves
185g (6oz) tinned marinated artichoke hearts, drained and halved
1 lemon, cut into wedges

In a bowl, combine the beans, chicken and cheese. In a small bowl, stir the basil and sugar into the dressing. Pour over the bean mixture and toss well. Cover and chill for about 1 hour.

Line 8 individual salad plates with the lettuce. Make a mound of about 250g (8oz) of the bean mixture in the centre of each plate. Garnish each plate with artichoke hearts and a lemon wedge.

Nutritional Analysis

Calories	394.44 Kcal	Protein	35.62 gm
Fat	5.79 gm	Carbohydrate	44.25 gm
Sodium	488.30 mg	Cholesterol	41.93 mg
Saturated fat	1.30 gm		

Peach-Spinach Salad

Serves: 6

600g (1lb 4oz) spinach, stems removed and leaves torn
250g (8oz) cucumbers, scored and sliced
1 fresh peach, stoned, peeled and sliced
2 fresh plums, stoned and sliced
60g (2oz) spring onions, sliced
250ml (8fl oz) plain low-fat yogurt
1 tbsp lemon juice
1 tbsp water
1/4 tsp dried dill, crumbled

In a large bowl or on 6 salad plates, combine the spinach, cucumber, peach, plums and spring onions. In a small bowl, whisk together the yogurt, lemon juice, water and dill until smooth. Toss with salad, or pour over salad plates and serve.

Calories	52.58 Kcal	Protein	2.86 gm
Fat	0.78 gm	Carbohydrate	9.44 gm
Sodium	38.54 mg	Cholesterol	2.26 mg
Saturated fat	0.38 gm		

Summer Peach Pasta Salad

Serves: 3

1 tbsp olive oil
2 spinach leaves, torn
1/2 courgette, cut into strips
185g (6oz) penne or rigatoni, cooked and drained, chilled
4 peaches, pitted, stoned and sliced
90g (3oz) grated Parmesan cheese
60g (2oz) chopped fresh basil leaves
2 tbsp white wine vinegar
1/2 tsp pepper

In a medium pan, heat the oil over medium heat. Add the spinach and courgette, and sauté until the spinach is limp, about 5 minutes. In a salad bowl, toss together the pasta, peaches, cheese, basil, vinegar, spinach mixture and pepper, mixing well. Serve chilled.

Nutritional Analysis

Calories	373.02 Kcal	Protein	12.62 gm
Fat	8.26 gm	Carbohydrate	63.59 gm
Sodium	170.75 mg	Cholesterol	6.95 mg
Saturated fat	2.41 gm		

Warm Chinese Chicken Salad

Serves: 4

250ml (8fl oz) low-fat Italian dressing
2 tsp low-sodium soy sauce
1 tsp peeled and finely chopped fresh ginger
2 skinless, boneless whole chicken breasts, split
500g (1lb) torn salad greens
60g (2oz) chopped fresh coriander (optional)
60g (2oz) diagonally sliced spring onions
5 peaches, peeled
60g (2oz) sliced almonds, toasted
2 tbsp sesame seeds, toasted (optional)

In a large resealable plastic bag, combine the dressing, soy sauce and ginger. Add the chicken, seal the bag securely, and turn to coat the chicken well. Refrigerate for 30 minutes.

Prepare a fire in a charcoal grill or preheat a griddle.

Arrange greens on 4 salad plates. Sprinkle with the coriander, if using. Top with the spring onions. Stone and slice 3 of the peaches and arrange on the lettuce. Remove the chicken from the marinade, reserving the marinade. Grill or griddle the chicken, turning once and basting occasionally with the marinade, until browned and cooked through. Set aside; keep warm.

Halve and stone the remaining 2 peaches. Baste with the marinade. Grill or griddle, turning once, until browned and tender, about 5 minutes. Slice the chicken breasts and arrange the chicken and grilled peach halves on the lettuce.

(continued)

In a small saucepan, bring the remaining marinade to the boil (this can be done on the grill, if desired). Add the almonds and sesame seeds (if using). Pour over the salads and serve immediately.

Nutritional Analysis

Calories	417.38	Kcal	Protein	31.28	gm
Fat	4.93	gm	Carbohydrate	27.54	gm
Sodium	679.27	mg	Cholesterol	68.44	mg
Saturated fat	0.71	gm			

White Bean Salad with Pistachios

Serves: 4

475g (15oz) tinned small white beans, drained and rinsed
1 head sliced celery
125g (4oz) diced red onions
90g (3oz) shelled pistachio nuts, coarsely chopped
1 tsp pepper
2 tbsp fresh thyme leaves
1 tsp dried tarragon, crumbled
80ml (2½fl oz) distilled white vinegar
2 tbsp sugar
500g (1lb) mixed greens

In a bowl, combine all the ingredients except the salad greens and toss well. Cover and chill for 1 to 2 hours, to allow the flavours to blend.

Divide the greens among 6 salad plates and spoon the bean mixture on top, dividing it evenly.

Nutritional Analysis

Calories	118.96	Kcal	Protein	6.11	gm
Fat	3.78	gm	Carbohydrate	20.70	gm
Sodium	284.32	mg	Cholesterol	0.00	mg
Saturated fat	0.44	gm			

Curried Coleslaw

Serves: 6

1kg (2lb) shredded cabbage
250g (8oz) shredded carrot
1 medium green pepper, cut into slivers
60ml (2fl oz) cider vinegar
1 tbsp low-fat mayonnaise
60g (2oz) finely chopped onion
2 tsp lemon juice
1 tbsp sugar
1 tsp curry powder
pepper to taste

Combine the cabbage, carrot and green pepper in a large bowl. In a small bowl, combine all the remaining ingredients, mixing well. Pour over the cabbage mixture, toss well, and chill for at least 2 hours. Stir again briefly before serving.

Nutritional Analysis

Calories	36.10	Kcal	Protein	0.86	gm
Fat	0.32	gm	Carbohydrate	8.41	gm
Sodium	36.02	mg	Cholesterol	0.00	mg
Saturated fat	0.00	gm			

Fruity Coleslaw

Serves: 6

> 3 firm pears, peeled, cored and diced
> 1 firm tart apple, peeled, cored and diced
> 3 tbsp lemon juice
> 750g (1lb 8oz) shredded cabbage
> 90g (3oz) raisins or dried currants
> 250ml (8fl oz) plain low-fat yogurt
> 1 tsp grated lemon zest
> 1 tbsp honey

Toss the diced pears and apples with 2 table-spoons of the lemon juice. Add the cabbage and raisins (or currants), mixing well. In a small bowl, combine all the remaining ingredients, including the remaining lemon juice, and mix well. Add to the cabbage mixture. Toss well and chill for 1 hour before serving.

Nutritional Analysis

Calories	129.82	Kcal	Protein	3.04	gm
Fat	1.08	gm	Carbohydrate	29.99	gm
Sodium	35.46	mg	Cholesterol	2.26	mg
Saturated fat	0.40	gm			

Apple Salad

Serves: 4

> 2 large Red Delicious apples, peeled, cored and cut
>   into chunks
> 185g (6oz) tinned crushed pineapple, drained, juice
>   reserved
> 90g (3oz) diced celery

> 2 tbsp raisins
> 60ml (2fl oz) plain low-fat yogurt
> 1 tbsp low-fat mayonnaise
> 1/4 tsp ground cinnamon

In a large bowl, combine the apples, pineapple, celery and raisins. In a small bowl, combine all the remaining ingredients, including 2 tablespoons of the reserved juice, and mix well. Add to the fruit mixture and mix gently to coat, then serve.

Nutritional Analysis

Calories	98.11	Kcal	Protein	1.23	gm
Fat	0.73	gm	Carbohydrate	23.61	gm
Sodium	54.52	mg	Cholesterol	0.85	mg
Saturated fat	0.17	gm			

Four-Bean Salad

Serves: 8

> 425g (14oz) tinned chick peas, drained and
>   rinsed
> 425g (14oz) red kidney beans, drained and
>   rinsed
> 425g (14oz) black beans, drained and
>   rinsed
> 425g (14oz) pinto or butter beans, drained and
>   rinsed
> 1 large onion, diced
> 125g (4oz) diced celery
> 250ml (8fl oz) low-fat Italian dressing
> salt and pepper to taste
> 1 tbsp chopped fresh parsley

(continued)

In a large bowl, combine all the beans. Add the onion and celery. Toss gently with the dressing until the ingredients are thoroughly coated. Season with salt and pepper, and sprinkle with parsley. Cover and refrigerate for 2 hours before serving.

Nutritional Analysis

Calories	284.70 Kcal	Protein	13.33 gm
Fat	2.34 gm	Carbohydrate	35.33 gm
Sodium	700.41 mg	Cholesterol	0.00 mg
Saturated fat	0.09 gm		

Waldorf Salad

Serves: 6

2 Red Delicious apples, unpeeled, cored and cubed
24 red grapes
24 green grapes
2 oranges, peeled and sectioned
250ml (8fl oz) plain nonfat yogurt
1 tbsp honey
4 large lettuce leaves
2 bananas
60g (3oz) walnuts, chopped

In a bowl, toss together the apples, grapes and oranges. In a small bowl, stir together the yogurt and honey. Mix into the fruit, tossing to coat evenly.

Place a lettuce leaf on each salad plate and top with the fruit salad, dividing it evenly. Just before serving, peel and slice the bananas and place them

around the circumference of the plates, and sprinkle the walnuts over everything.

Nutritional Analysis

Calories	190.48 Kcal	Protein	4.30 gm
Fat	3.90 gm	Carbohydrate	38.61 gm
Sodium	54.59 mg	Cholesterol	0.75mg
Saturated fat	0.50 gm		

Busy Day Salad

Serves: 2

1 head lettuce, torn into bite-sized pieces
60g (2oz) grated carrot
60g (2oz) chick peas
1 small tomato, sliced
1/2 small red onion, sliced
4 pitted black olives
125ml (4fl oz) low-fat dressing of choice

In a large salad bowl, combine the lettuce, carrots, chick peas, tomato, onion and olives. Toss well. Drizzle with the dressing, toss again, and serve.

Nutritional Analysis

Calories	240.37 Kcal	Protein	3.61 gm
Fat	1.71 gm	Carbohydrate	18.37 gm
Sodium	573.06 mg	Cholesterol	0.00 mg
Saturated fat	0.19 gm		

Herbed Pasta Salad

Serves: 4

1kg (2lb) cooked rotelle pasta
250g (8oz) cooked broccoli florets
250g (8oz) cooked cauliflower florets
125g (4oz) thinly sliced carrots
1 red pepper, chopped
125g (4oz) bottled marinated artichoke hearts,
*   drained*
125g (4oz) pitted black olives
1 tomato, chopped
4 spring onions, thinly sliced
125ml (4fl oz) low-calorie bottled Italian dressing

In a large bowl, combine the pasta, broccoli, cauliflower, carrots, pepper, artichoke hearts, black olives, tomato and spring onions. Toss well. Pour the dressing over the pasta and vegetables and toss to coat thoroughly. Refrigerate for several hours before serving.

Nutritional Analysis

Calories	353.48 Kcal	Protein	9.62 gm
Fat	5.23 gm	Carbohydrate	51.18 gm
Sodium	566.43 mg	Cholesterol	0.00 mg
Saturated fat	0.68 gm		

Citrus Rice Salad

Serves: 4

1 celery stalk, thinly sliced
4 spring onions, sliced
125g (4oz) tinned mandarin oranges, drained

(continued)

Cooking Pasta for Salad

When preparing a cold pasta salad, you can save time by cooking a batch of pasta in advance. Once cooked, rinse it immediately under cold water and drain thoroughly, then pat it with paper towels to absorb the excess moisture. Place in a large resealable plastic bag and store in the refrigerator. This way, the pasta will keep for up to 3 days.

Buying Fresh Herbs

It used to be that one could only find fresh herbs in the summertime. Today, suppliers have recognized that people all over the country appreciate fresh basil, dill and other herbs all year round. Some are sold prepackaged, while others are sold loose. Look for them in the fresh produce department of your supermarket.

Before you buy, check for any brown or dry leaves. Sniff the herbs: they should be fully aromatic. If none of the herbs appear fresh, tell the produce manager. A new shipment of herbs may be sitting in the stock room, ready to be put out.

125g (4oz) sliced cucumber
60g (2oz) raisins
500g (1lb) cooked white rice, at room temperature
250ml (8fl oz) plain low-fat yogurt
2 tbsp orange juice
2 tbsp honey
½ tsp ground ginger

In a large bowl, combine the celery, spring onions, oranges, cucumber and raisins. Gently stir in the rice. In a small bowl, stir together the yogurt, orange juice, honey and ginger, mixing well. Pour over the salad and toss gently to coat.

Nutritional Analysis

Calories	269.07 Kcal	Protein	6.93 gm
Fat	5.83 gm	Carbohydrate	49.58 gm
Sodium	56.05 mg	Cholesterol	3.40 mg
Saturated fat	1.03 gm		

Tomato and Red Onion Salad

Serves: 6

4 large tomatoes, sliced
1 tsp dried basil, crumbled
2 tsp olive oil
1 tbsp red wine vinegar
2 cloves garlic, crushed
salt and pepper to taste
1 red onion, sliced

Make a layer with about one-third of the tomato slices in a shallow serving dish. Sprinkle with

about a quarter of the basil, olive oil, vinegar, garlic, salt and pepper. Cover with half the onion slices, and sprinkle with more of the oil, vinegar and seasoning. Cover with another layer of tomato slices and more of the seasoning. Repeat the layers, using the remaining tomatoes, onions and seasoning. Chill before serving.

Nutritional Analysis

Calories	59.01	Kcal	Protein	1.83	gm
Fat	2.02	gm	Carbohydrate	10.20	gm
Sodium	16.88	mg	Cholesterol	0.00	mg
Saturated fat	0.27	gm			

Mediterranean Lentil and Bean Salad

Serves: 6

3 red peppers
425g (14oz) tinned haricot beans, drained and rinsed
500g (1lb) well-drained cooked puy lentils
125g (4oz) diced celery
60g (2oz) chopped fresh basil
60g (2oz) chopped fresh parsley
80ml (2¹/₂fl oz) balsamic vinegar
salt and pepper to taste

Preheat a grill.

Grill the peppers under the grill for 15 minutes, turning once or twice, until the skin is blackened and blistered. Remove from the grill and put in a bowl and cover with cling film. When

cool enough to handle, pull away the blackened skin. Remove the skins and seeds and cut into narrow strips. Combine the peppers, beans, lentils, celery, basil and parsley in a medium bowl. Add vinegar and mix thoroughly. Season with salt and pepper. Chill for at least 1 hour and serve.

Nutritional Analysis

Calories	196.59	Kcal	Protein	12.98	gm
Fat	0.61	gm	Carbohydrate	36.44	gm
Sodium	17.03	mg	Cholesterol	0.00	mg
Saturated fat	0.40	gm			

Light Chinese Chicken Salad

Serves: 6

2 tbsp soy sauce
1 tbsp white wine vinegar
1 tbsp sesame oil
1 tbsp peanut oil
1 tbsp peeled and finely chopped fresh ginger
3 cloves garlic, crushed
¹/₂ tsp pepper
¹/₄ tsp dry mustard
1 whole chicken breast, poached, boned, skinned and diced
750g (1lb 8oz) cooked white rice
1 red pepper, chopped
250g (8oz) sliced celery
250g (8oz) beansprouts
250g (8oz) sliced spring onions
250g (8oz) sugar snap peas

(continued)

In a medium bowl, stir together the soy sauce, vinegar, sesame oil, peanut oil, ginger, garlic, pepper and mustard. Add the chicken, toss well and chill for 1 hour.

Add the rice, red pepper, celery, beansprouts, spring onions and sugar snaps to the chicken mixture. Stir gently and serve.

Nutritional Analysis

Calories	230.14 Kcal	Protein	13.56 gm
Fat	5.95 gm	Carbohydrate	30.22 gm
Sodium	388.20 mg	Cholesterol	24.36 mg
Saturated fat	1.05 gm		

Daikon Salad

Serves: 4

2 tbsp rice vinegar
1 tbsp sake
1 tbsp soy sauce
1 tsp sugar
10 medium radishes, sliced
1 carrot, sliced

In a bowl, stir together the rice vinegar, sake, soy sauce and sugar, mixing well. Add the radishes and carrot, and toss well with the dressing. Cover and chill for 2 hours before serving.

Nutritional Analysis

Calories	29.71 Kcal	Protein	0.79 gm
Fat	0.37 gm	Carbohydrate	5.67 gm
Sodium	279.11 mg	Cholesterol	0.00 mg
Saturated Fat	0.01 gm		

Sugar Snap Salad

Serves: 4

500g (1lb) sugar snap peas
1 small red onion, chopped
60g (2oz) fresh mint leaves, chopped
250g (8oz) cooked, chilled rice
2 tbsp raspberry vinegar
1 tbsp olive oil
salt and pepper to taste
$1/4$ tsp sugar

Steam the sugar snaps for 3 minutes. Rinse under cold water, drain and place in the refrigerator for 30 minutes to chill.

Place the sugar snaps in a serving bowl. Add the rice, onion and mint; toss well. In a small bowl, stir together the vinegar, oil, salt, pepper and sugar. Pour the dressing over the salad and toss again. Chill for 30 minutes before serving.

Nutritional Analysis

Calories	140.62 Kcal	Protein	4.78 gm
Fat	3.76 gm	Carbohydrate	22.38 gm
Sodium	9.62 mg	Cholesterol	0.00 mg
Saturated fat	0.52 gm		

Macaroni and Bean Salad

Serves: 4

> 250g (8oz) macaroni
> 60g (2oz) grated Parmesan cheese
> 500g (1lb) tinned kidney beans, drained, liquid
>   reserved and rinsed
> 1 onion, chopped
> 3 celery stalks, finely chopped
> 1 tsp curry powder
> 1 tbsp honey
> 80ml (2¹/₂fl oz) cider vinegar
> 60g (2oz) raisins

Cook the macaroni for 8 to 10 minutes, until done. Drain, transfer to a serving bowl and toss with the cheese. Add the beans, onion and celery. Pour the liquid from the beans into a measuring cup and add enough water to make 250ml (8fl oz). Put the liquid into a small saucepan. Add the curry powder, honey, vinegar and raisins, and stir well. Bring to the boil, reduce the heat to low and cook for 5 to 10 minutes, or until the raisins are plump. Pour the dressing over the macaroni mixture and toss well. Chill for 1 hour before serving.

Chick Peas

It's simple to pick up a couple of cans of chick peas at the supermarket, but if you really like the taste of these peas, cook your own.

First, soak 500g (1lb) dried chick peas in 1l (2pt) of water overnight. Drain, place in a saucepan and add water to cover. Bring to the boil for 10 minutes, then reduce the heat to low. Cover and cook very gently for at least 2 hours, or until tender.

Nutritional Analysis

Calories	307.98 Kcal	Protein	12.67 gm
Fat	2.51 gm	Carbohydrate	61.57 gm
Sodium	518.63 mg	Cholesterol	3.95 mg
Saturated fat	1.10 gm		

Tricolore Pepper Salad

Serves: 8

> 2 red peppers, chopped
> 2 yellow peppers, chopped
> 2 green peppers, chopped
> 2 celery stalks, minced
> 2 large cucumbers, diced
> 1 red onion, chopped
> 500g (1lb) cherry tomatoes, halved
> 3 tbsp lime juice
> 1 tbsp lemon juice
> 2 tbsp white wine vinegar
> 1 tbsp olive oil
> 4 cloves garlic, crushed
> $1/2$ tsp salt
> cayenne pepper to taste
> 60g (2oz) chopped fresh parsley

In a large salad bowl, combine the peppers, celery, cucumbers, onion and tomatoes. In a small bowl, stir together the lime and lemon juices, vinegar, oil, garlic, salt, cayenne and parsley. Add the dressing to the salad; toss well to combine. Cover and chill for 1 hour, tossing occasionally, before serving.

Nutritional Analysis

Calories	60.08	Kcal	Protein	1.64	gm
Fat	1.98	gm	Carbohydrate	10.43	gm
Sodium	162.87	mg	Cholesterol	0.00	mg
Saturated fat	0.25	gm			

Orzo Salad

Serves: 4

> 250g (8oz) fresh basil leaves, finely chopped
> 60g (2oz) finely chopped fresh parsley
> 4 cloves garlic, crushed
> $1/2$ tsp salt
> 60ml (2fl oz) olive oil
> 500g (1lb) orzo pasta, cooked, drained and cooled
> 1 red pepper, chopped

In a serving bowl, stir together the basil, parsley, garlic, salt and oil. Add the orzo and red pepper, and mix well. Chill for 1 hour. Toss the salad before serving.

Nutritional Analysis

Calories	563.79	Kcal	Protein	16.08	gm
Fat	15.60	gm	Carbohydrate	89.29	gm
Sodium	302.95	mg	Cholesterol	0.00	mg
Saturated fat	2.09	gm			

Carrot, Apple and Raisin Salad

Serves: 8

> 180ml (6fl oz) frozen orange juice concentrate, thawed
> 1kg (2lb) carrots, grated
> 3 large Granny Smith apples, peeled, cored and grated
> 125g (4oz) black raisins
> 125g (4oz) golden raisins

Place the orange juice concentrate in a medium serving bowl. Fill the concentrate can with water and add to the bowl, stirring to combine. Add the carrots, apples and raisins. Toss well and serve.

Nutritional Analysis

Calories	177.11	Kcal	Protein	2.46	gm
Fat	0.51	gm	Carbohydrate	44.21	gm
Sodium	42.67	mg	Cholesterol	0.00	mg
Saturated fat	0.07	gm			

Cool Beans Salad

Serves: 4

475g (15oz) tinned butter beans, drained and rinsed
60g (2oz) cubed cooked lean pork
1 red pepper, chopped
2 cloves garlic, chopped
1/2 tsp dried sage, crumbled
1/2 tbsp olive oil
1 tbsp red wine vinegar

In a medium bowl, combine the beans, pork, pepper, garlic and sage. Add the oil and vinegar and toss well. Chill for 30 minutes before serving.

Nutritional Analysis

Calories	111.33	Kcal	Protein	8.66	gm
Fat	3.29	gm	Carbohydrate	17.79	gm
Sodium	375.29	mg	Cholesterol	7.26	mg
Saturated fat	0.64	gm			

Salmon Tortellini Salad

Serves: 4

250g (8oz) frozen or fresh cheese tortellini
4 carrots, thinly sliced
1 courgette, sliced
1 red pepper, cut into narrow strips
400g (13oz) tinned salmon, drained and flaked
250ml (8fl oz) plain low-fat yogurt
60g (2oz) grated Parmesan cheese
60g (2oz) chopped fresh parsley
1 tbsp low-fat milk
1 tsp dried oregano, crumbled

Cook the tortellini as directed on the packet. Drain, rinse under cold water and drain again. In a medium bowl, gently toss together the pasta, carrots, courgette and pepper. Add the salmon and mix. In a small bowl, stir together the yogurt, cheese, parsley, milk and oregano until well mixed. Add to the pasta mixture and toss gently to coat evenly. Cover and refrigerate for several hours before serving.

Nutritional Analysis

Calories	385.64	Kcal	Protein	30.38	gm
Fat	10.86	gm	Carbohydrate	41.90	gm
Sodium	728.90	mg	Cholesterol	60.66	mg
Saturated fat	4.35	gm			

Potato and Tuna Salad

Serves: 8

1kg (2lb) red potatoes, cubed
250g (8oz) green beans
60ml (2fl oz) cider vinegar
1 tbsp water
1 tbsp Dijon mustard
1 tbsp anchovy paste
2 tbsp olive oil
2 cloves garlic, crushed
pepper to taste
3 celery stalks, finely chopped
1 red pepper, chopped
1 medium onion, chopped
60g (2oz) fresh parsley leaves, coarsely chopped
220g (7oz) tinned water-packed tuna, drained and flaked

In a saucepan, combine the potatoes with water to cover. Bring to the boil, reduce the heat to medium and simmer until nearly tender, about 10 minutes. Add the green beans to the pan and cook until the potatoes and beans are tender, about 5 minutes; drain well and place in a bowl.

In another bowl, mix together the vinegar, water, mustard, anchovy paste, oil, garlic and pepper. Add the dressing to the potatoes and beans, and toss well. Add celery, pepper, onion, parsley and tuna, and toss well.

Nutritional Analysis

Calories	182.27	Kcal	Protein	9.99	gm
Fat	3.99	gm	Carbohydrate	26.77	gm
Sodium	226.13	mg	Cholesterol	9.86	mg
Saturated fat	0.52	gm			

Creamy Dill-Parsley Dressing

Makes: About 250ml (8fl oz)

250ml (8fl oz) plain nonfat yogurt
1 tsp dried dill, crumbled
1/2 tsp lemon juice
1 tsp chopped fresh parsley

In a bowl, mix ingredients well.

Nutritional Analysis

Calories	8.14	Kcal	Protein	0.82	gm
Fat	0.02	gm	Carbohydrate	1.12	gm
Sodium	10.96	mg	Cholesterol	0.28	mg
Saturated fat	0.02	gm			

Buttermilk Salad Dressing

Makes: About 250ml (8fl oz)

125ml (4fl oz) buttermilk
¹125ml (4fl oz) low-fat mayonnaise
3 tbsp minced fresh parsley
3 tbsp snipped fresh chives
1 clove garlic, crushed
1 tbsp finely chopped fresh tarragon

1 tbsp lemon juice
dash of Worcestershire sauce
salt and coarse pepper to taste

In a bowl, gently fold all the ingredients together. Cover and refrigerate until serving time. Serve spooned over torn lettuce or mixed salad greens.

Nutritional Analysis

Calories	16.62 Kcal	Protein	0.29 gm
Fat	0.55 gm	Carbohydrate	2.57 gm
Sodium	78.80 mg	Cholesterol	0.30 mg
Saturated fat	0.04 gm		

Horseradish Salad Dressing

Makes: About 160ml (5fl oz)

1 tbsp lemon juice
2 tbsp rice wine vinegar
2 tbsp fresh, grated horseradish
1 tsp honey
125ml (4fl oz) plain nonfat yogurt

In a bowl, stir together all the ingredients until well mixed.

Nutritional Analysis

Calories	11.20 Kcal	Protein	0.72 gm
Fat	0.02 gm	Carbohydrate	2.08 gm
Sodium	9.16 mg	Cholesterol	0.22 mg
Saturated fat	0.01 gm		

A Salad a Day . . .

Nothing beats a salad for low fat and high nutritional eating. And sometimes the very best salads are very simple recipes. For example, consider how good thick slices of juicy tomatoes sprinkled with fresh basil, coarsely ground black pepper and freshly chopped chives taste.

Salads can also be meals in themselves. Start with fresh greens including dark-green spinach leaves, soft green lettuce, curly red-tipped leaf lettuce and add crisp carrots, thinly sliced cucumbers, tomatoes, fresh mushrooms, green peppers, fresh courgettes, or even broccoli and cauliflower. Add cold pasta or rice and serve with a hearty bread – a crunchy, crispy, delicious low-fat meal!

Sandwiches

CHAPTER FIVE

Amount Per Chapter
21 Recipes

	% Daily Value
Easy to Prepare	100%
Low Fat/High Flavour	100%
Simple to Understand	100%

DELICIOUS, EASY, LOW-FAT RECIPES

With all the delicious bread varieties available today in supermarkets and in bakeries – let alone those you can make yourself – there's no excuse for a boring low-fat sandwich anymore. And having an equally diverse choice of tasty and exotic vegetables available, such as red- and green-leaf lettuces, fresh basil and vine-ripened tomatoes all year round, doesn't hurt either.

You can use the recipes I've provided here as a springboard for countless sandwiches – a different one for every day of the year. For instance, if you're a mustard connoisseur, experiment with some of the recipes here by substituting wholegrain Dijon mustard for the low-fat mayonnaise.

Use your imagination, and you'll look forward to having wonderfully creative sandwiches for lunch – and dinner, too.

French Bread Pizzas

Serves: 4

1 loaf French bread
2 tbsp olive oil
1 large onion, chopped
1 green pepper, chopped
2 garlic cloves, crushed
2 tsp dried basil, crumbled
2 tsp dried oregano, crumbled
500ml (1pt) spaghetti sauce, from a jar
*   or homemade*
2 large tomatoes, sliced
250g (8oz) pitted black olives, sliced
500g (1lb) finely grated carrots
90g (3oz) grated Parmesan cheese

Preheat oven to 230°C (450°F), gas mark 8.
Slice the bread in half lengthways. Drizzle the cut sides of both halves with 1 tablespoon of the

oil and place on a baking tray. In a small pan, heat the remaining tablespoon of oil over medium heat. Add the onion, pepper, garlic, basil and oregano, and cook for 5 minutes, or until softened. Remove from the heat. Spoon 250g (8oz) of the spaghetti sauce on each piece of bread. Top evenly with the onion-pepper mixture, tomatoes and black olives. Then sprinkle evenly with the carrots and Parmesan cheese.

Bake for 12 to 15 minutes, or until bubbling and until the bread is lightly browned. Cut across to serve. Serve hot.

Nutritional Analysis

Calories	655.70 Kcal	Protein	17.86 gm
Fat	22.34 gm	Carbohydrate	99.40 gm
Sodium	1758.23 mg	Cholesterol	5.21 mg
Saturated fat	4.27 gm		

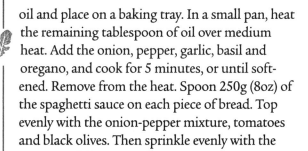

Grilled Chicken Breast Sandwiches with Onions

Serves: 4

>1 tbsp butter
>4 large onions, sliced
>125g (4oz) oil-packed sun-dried tomatoes, drained and
>   chopped
>2 cloves garlic, crushed
>1 tbsp water
>2 boneless, skinless whole chicken breasts, split
>4 burger buns

Prepare a fire in a charcoal grill.

In a large frying pan, melt the butter over medium heat. Add the onions and cook, stirring occasionally, for 10 minutes, or until translucent. Add the tomatoes, garlic and water, and cook for 5 minutes, stirring occasionally.

Meanwhile, place the chicken over medium-hot coals and grill, turning once, until done, about 10 minutes. Spread some of the onion mixture over the bottom half of each bun. Top with a piece of the chicken, the remaining onion mixture and then the tops of the buns. Serve hot.

Nutritional Analysis

Calories	436.66 Kcal	Protein	35.63 gm
Fat	10.87 gm	Carbohydrate	49.69 gm
Sodium	473.81 mg	Cholesterol	76.20 mg
Saturated fat	2.73 gm		

Grilled Vegetable Sandwich

Serves: 6

Dressing:
>250ml (8fl oz) plain nonfat yogurt
>3 tbsp Dijon mustard
>pepper to taste
>2 tbsp nonfat cottage cheese
>1/3 tsp Tabasco sauce
>2 tbsp finely sliced shallot
>1 clove garlic, crushed
>**1** tsp lemon juice

Sandwiches:
>1 small aubergine, cut into 6mm (1/4in) thick rounds
>1 medium-sized yellow courgette, cut into 6mm (1/4in)
>   thick rounds
>1 medium-sized green courgette, cut into 6mm (1/4in)
>   thick rounds
>1 medium onion
>1 tbsp Italian seasoning
>1/4 tsp cayenne pepper
>2 baguettes
>1 large tomato, sliced
>pepper to taste
>2 tbsp chopped jalapeño pepper
>8 fresh basil leaves
>8 rocket leaves
>2 red peppers, roasted and quartered

To make the dressing, combine all the ingredients and blend until smooth. Transfer to a bowl, cover and refrigerate.

Preheat grill.

(continued)

Low-Fat Toasted Sandwiches

The toasted cheese sandwiches I remember from my childhood – a pat of butter on each bread slice, a big hunk of cheddar cheese in the middle, and sometimes a slice of salami, too – have rightly earned the sobriquet of high-fat cooking.

Today, however, you can grill a sandwich on a griddle or in a pan that has been sprayed with nonstick cooking spray, resulting in a wonderful melted cheese sandwich without a heavy, greasy taste. One bite and you will be transported back to a childhood when a rainy day meant sitting down to a mug of tomato soup and a toasted cheese sandwich.

Spray a baking tray with nonstick cooking spray. Arrange the aubergine, yellow and green courgettes and onion in a single layer on the baking tray. Sprinkle the Italian dressing and cayenne pepper over all the rounds. Grill, turning once, for about 5 minutes on each side, or until browned. Remove the baking tray, but leave the grill on.

Cut each of the baguettes in half lengthways and scoop out the soft inner dough. Place in the grill and toast for 2 minutes on each side.

Put a few slices of tomato into the well in each baguette half. Dust with black pepper and sprinkle with the jalapeño pepper.

Place 4 basil leaves, 4 rocket leaves and 4 pieces of roasted pepper onto the bottom half of each baguette. Layer slices of aubergine, yellow and green courgette and onion on top. Coat the inside of the remaining half of each baguette with the dressing and place it on top of the vegetables. Cut each baguette across into 3 equal pieces and serve.

Nutritional Analysis

Calories	286.41 Kcal	Protein	11.35 gm
Fat	2.64 gm	Carbohydrate	53.11 gm
Sodium	706.29 mg	Cholesterol	1.16 mg
Saturated fat	0.56 gm		

California-Style Turkey Burger

Serves: 6

> 500g (1lb) ground turkey breast
> 250g (8oz) rolled oats
> 60ml (2fl oz) ketchup
> 1 egg, beaten
> 60g (2oz) minced onion
> 1½ tsp garlic salt
> ½ tsp pepper
> 1 tsp Worcestershire sauce
> ¼ tsp Tabasco sauce
> 6 burger buns

Prepare a fire in a charcoal grill.

Combine all the ingredients except the buns in a large bowl. Mix well and shape into 6 patties. Place the patties on the grill rack and grill for about 6 minutes on each side, or until done; the timing will depend on the thickness. Serve plain or on buns.

Nutritional Analysis

Calories	285.45 Kcal	Protein	25.73 gm
Fat	4.40 gm	Carbohydrate	34.32 gm
Sodium	778.18 mg	Cholesterol	82.32 mg
Saturated fat	1.05 gm		

Chicken Pocket Sandwich

Serves: 5

> 425g (14oz) diced cooked chicken
> 250ml (8fl oz) plain low-fat yogurt
> 125g (4oz) chopped almonds
> 60g (2oz) chopped nectarine
> 90g (3oz) chopped spring onions
> 1 tbsp lemon juice
> ⅛ tsp pepper
> ⅛ tsp dried dill, crumbled
> 5 large pitta breads
> 10 lettuce leaves

In a bowl, combine all the ingredients except the pitta bread and lettuce. Toss gently to mix well. Using a sharp knife, cut each pitta bread in half, forming 10 pockets. Line each pitta half with 1 lettuce leaf. Spoon in the chicken mixture, dividing it evenly. Serve at once.

Nutritional Analysis

Calories	437.05 Kcal	Protein	26.61 gm
Fat	12.04 gm	Carbohydrate	55.29 gm
Sodium	532.44 mg	Cholesterol	44.33 mg
Saturated fat	2.18 gm		

Corn Dogs

Serves: 8

> 250g (8oz) plain flour
> 2 tbsp sugar
> 1½ tsp baking soda
> 1 tsp salt
> 185g (6oz) cornmeal

(continued)

2 tbsp lard
1 egg
180ml (6fl oz) milk
500g (1lb) frankfurters
ketchup
mustard

Preheat oven to 180°C (350°F), gas mark 4.

In a bowl, sift together the flour, sugar, baking soda and salt. Stir in the cornmeal. Using a pastry blender or 2 knives, cut in the lard until the mixture resembles coarse meal. In a separate bowl, whisk together the egg and milk until blended and stir into the cornmeal mixture, again mixing until blended. Insert a wooden skewer into the end of each hot dog. Working in batches, coat the hot dogs evenly with the batter and arrange on a biscuit tray sprayed with nonstick spray. Bake for 15 minutes or until batter is lightly browned. Serve immediately with ketchup and mustard.

Nutritional Analysis

Calories	233.87 Kcal	Protein	11.08 gm
Fat	6.53 gm	Carbohydrate	30.34 gm
Sodium	930.10 mg	Cholesterol	59.62 mg
Saturated fat	1.99 gm		

Grilled Chicken Sandwich with Tarragon Mayonnaise

Serves: 6

2 tbsp red wine vinegar
2 tbsp dried tarragon, crumbled
2 tbsp butter

4 tsp finely chopped shallots
250ml (8fl oz) low-fat mayonnaise
1/2 tsp white pepper
3 boneless whole chicken breasts, 250g (8oz) each, skin and visible fat removed
salt and pepper to taste
6 buns, split
6 lettuce leaves
6 slices tomato

Prepare a fire in a charcoal grill.

In a small saucepan, combine the vinegar and tarragon, and bring to the boil. Cook until reduced by half, and set aside. In a small frying pan, melt the butter over medium heat. Add the shallots and sauté for 10 minutes, or until tender. Transfer to a small bowl and add the mayonnaise, tarragon reduction and white pepper. Mix well.

Pound the chicken breasts lightly with the fine side of a meat-tenderizing mallet. Cut in half down the natural seam, removing any cartilage at the centre. Season with salt and pepper.

Place the chicken on the grill rack on medium fire and grill, turning once and basting each side with 1 tablespoon of the mayonnaise mixture, for about 7 minutes on each side, or until done. Just before the chicken is ready, place the buns, cut sides down, on the grill rack to warm.

Spread the cut sides of the buns generously with the flavoured mayonnaise. Place one chicken piece on the bottom of each bun. Top with lettuce and tomato and then the bun top. Serve immediately.

Nutritional Analysis

Calories	369.65 Kcal	Protein	29.65 gm
Fat	11.75 gm	Carbohydrate	34.53 gm
Sodium	716.58 mg	Cholesterol	79.80 mg
Saturated fat	3.71 gm		

Curried Chicken Pockets

Serves: 4

> 250ml (8fl oz) plain low-fat yogurt
> 1/2 tsp curry powder
> 1/4 tsp ground mace
> 375g (12oz) deboned, cubed, cooked chicken breasts
> 125ml (4fl oz) low-fat Italian dressing
> 1 green apple, cored and cubed
> 60g (2oz) thinly sliced celery
> 60g (2oz) sliced almonds, toasted
> 4 tbsp raisins
> 1 avocado
> 4 pitta breads
> 8 curly lettuce leaves

In a small bowl, stir the yogurt until smooth and creamy. Add the curry powder and mace, and mix well. Cover and refrigerate for at least 4 hours or up to 24 hours to blend the flavours.

In a medium bowl, combine the chicken and Italian dressing. Cover and marinate in the refrigerator for at least 4 hours, up to 8 hours.

Add the apple, celery, almonds and raisins to the chicken. Stir the curry-yogurt dressing into the chicken mixture. Peel, stone and cut the avocado into cubes and fold in gently. Cut the pitta breads in half, forming 8 pockets. Line each

pocket with 1 lettuce leaf, then spoon in the chicken mixture, dividing it evenly. Serve the pitta breads immediately.

Nutritional Analysis

Calories	507.66 Kcal	Protein	23.49 gm
Fat	13.26 gm	Carbohydrate	57.77 gm
Sodium	654.75 mg	Cholesterol	34.23 mg
Saturated fat	2.38 gm		

Peach Pitta Sandwiches

Serves: 2

> 2 pitta breads
> 4 curly lettuce leaves
> 250g (8oz) low-fat cottage cheese
> 4 tomato slices
> 4 extra-lean smoked ham slices
> 500g (1lb) tinned cling peach slices, drained

Cut the pitta breads in half, forming 4 pockets. Line each pocket with 1 lettuce leaf. Fill the pockets with the cottage cheese, tomato slices, ham slices and peach slices, dividing them evenly. Serve at once.

Nutritional Analysis

Calories	427.92 Kcal	Protein	32.23 gm
Fat	4.85 gm	Carbohydrate	64.85 gm
Sodium	1603.11 mg	Cholesterol	31.16 mg
Saturated fat	1.74 gm		

Roast Beef Pitta Bread Sandwich with Tomato

Serves: 6

125g (4oz) chopped fresh basil
30g (1oz) prepared horseradish
125ml (4fl oz) plain low-fat yogurt
375g (12oz) thin-sliced roast beef
1 head round lettuce, separated into leaves
3 pitta breads
1 large tomato, cored and cut into 12 slices

In a large bowl, stir together the basil, horseradish and yogurt. Spread the horseradish-yogurt mixture on the beef slices and wrap each slice in a lettuce leaf. Cut the pitta breads in half, making 6 pockets. Put the lettuce-wrapped beef and 2 slices of tomato into each half. Serve immediately.

Nutritional Analysis

Calories	174.20	Kcal	Protein	15.76	gm
Fat	2.85	gm	Carbohydrate	21.54	gm
Sodium	761.34	mg	Cholesterol	26.10	mg
Saturated fat	1.03	gm			

Bruschetta with Basil

Serves: 16 to 20

250g (8oz) plum tomatoes, sliced lengthwise
60g (2oz) diced red onion
1 tbsp olive oil
2 tbsp chopped fresh parsley
1 tbsp chopped fresh basil
1 clove garlic, crushed

salt and pepper to taste
1 soft baguette, about 300g (10oz), cut on the diagonal into 25mm (1in) slices and lightly toasted
16 to 20 small fresh basil leaves

In a medium bowl, combine the tomatoes, onion, olive oil, parsley, chopped basil, garlic, salt and pepper. Mix gently. Top each toasted bread slice with about 1 heaped tablespoon of the tomato-avocado mixture. Garnish each with a small basil leaf.

Nutritional Analysis

Calories	53.76	Kcal	Protein	1.52	gm
Fat	1.26	gm	Carbohydrate	9.03	gm
Sodium	97.46	mg	Cholesterol	0.00	mg
Saturated fat	0.20	gm			

Black Bean and Vegetable Dip

Serves: 6

Black Bean Dip:
185g (6oz) dried black beans, picked over and soaked for 2 hours in water to cover
125g (4oz) chopped fresh basil
125ml (4fl oz) plain nonfat yogurt
pepper to taste

Corn Tortilla Crisps:
1 tsp olive oil
6 corn tortillas, each 150mm (6in) in diameter
6 flour tortillas, each 150mm (6in) in diameter
185g (6oz) low-fat mozzarella cheese, grated
125g (4oz) diced green pepper
125g (4oz) diced red pepper

125g (4oz) chopped tomatoes
125g (4oz) chopped fresh basil
1 avocado

To make the black bean dip, drain the beans and place them in a saucepan with water to cover by 50mm (2in). Bring to the boil for 10 minutes, cover, reduce the heat to low and cook until tender, about 45 minutes. Drain and mash with a fork. Cool, then add the basil, yogurt and pepper.

To make the tortilla crisps, preheat the oven to 150°C (300°F), gas mark 2. Brush the corn tortillas on both sides with the olive oil. Place on a baking tray. Cut each tortilla into 6 wedges. Bake until crispy. Leave the oven on.

Place a nonstick frying pan over medium heat. One at a time, heat the flour tortillas, turning once, until crispy. Remove and top each one with equal portions of the grated cheese, green and red peppers, tomato and basil. Place the tortillas on a baking tray and bake until the cheese is melted and bubbling, about 10 minutes. Remove from the oven and cut each tortilla into 6 wedges. Peel, stone and dice the avocado, then top each tortilla with a slice of avocado.

Serve the tortillas, dip and crisps together.

Nutritional Analysis

Calories	325.78 Kcal	Protein	19.73 gm
Fat	8.43 gm	Carbohydrate	45.16 gm
Sodium	366.99 mg	Cholesterol	3.36 mg
Saturated fat	1.31 gm		

Pitta Bread

Although pitta bread has long been a Middle Eastern staple, Westerners have become familiar with this pocket bread only comparatively recently.

It's not surprising that it has caught on so quickly. You can stuff a pitta with everything from vegetables to peanut butter and, unlike a conventional sandwich, the filling won't fall out of the sides. That makes a pitta sandwich a genuinely portable meal. In addition, pitta bread is virtually fat-free. Try some of the new flavours, from onion to coriander and garlic.

Lemon-Sesame Tuna Sandwiches

Serves: 4

> 2 tbsp lemon juice
> 1 tbsp soy sauce
> l tbsp sesame oil
> 4 tuna fillets, about 150g (5oz) each
> 3 spring onions, finely chopped
> pinch of pepper
> 4 burger buns, split and toasted
> 4 green leaf lettuce leaves

In a small bowl, stir together the lemon juice, soy sauce and sesame oil to form a marinade. Place the tuna steaks on a baking tray and drizzle the marinade over the fish. Chill for 1 hour.

Preheat oven to 200°C (400°F), gas mark 6. Bake the fish until it is opaque throughout, about 10 minutes, or until done to your liking. Sprinkle with the spring onions and pepper, and serve on the buns with the lettuce.

Nutritional Analysis

Calories	379.55 Kcal	Protein	39.42 gm
Fat	13.04 gm	Carbohydrate	23.61 gm
Sodium	560.96 mg	Cholesterol	57.36 mg
Saturated fat	2.89 gm		

Greek Lamb Pitta Sandwiches

Serves: 4

> 250g (8oz) lean minced lamb
> 1 onion, finely chopped
> 3 cloves garlic, crushed
> 1 celery stalk, chopped

> 300g (10oz) chopped frozen spinach, thawed and well drained
> 1 tsp dried oregano, crumbled
> salt and pepper to taste
> 125g (4oz) crumbled feta cheese
> 4 pitta breads
> 8 lettuce leaves
> 1 tomato, diced
> 60ml (2fl oz) plain low-fat yogurt

In a large nonstick pan, combine the lamb, onion, garlic and celery over medium heat. Sauté until the vegetables are tender, about 5 minutes. Drain off any liquid. Add the spinach, oregano, salt and pepper, and cook, stirring, for 5 minutes until heated through and the flavours are blended. Remove from the heat and add the feta. Cut each pitta bread in half, making 8 pockets. Slip the lettuce leaves, some tomato and 1 tablespoon yogurt into each pocket. Spoon the lamb mixture into the pitta halves, then serve.

Nutritional Analysis

Calories	385.20 Kcal	Protein	22.14 gm
Fat	12.78 gm	Carbohydrate	45.91 gm
Sodium	628.11 mg	Cholesterol	54.15 mg
Saturated fat	6.08 gm		

Sweet-and-Sour Turkey Burgers

Serves: 6

> 1 tbsp soy sauce
> 1 tbsp honey
> 4 spring onions, minced
> 500g (1lb) lean minced turkey

6 slices tinned pineapple
6 burger buns, split and toasted

Stir the soy sauce and honey together in a bowl until blended. Add the minced turkey and spring onions, and mix well. Shape into 4 patties. In a nonstick frying pan over medium heat, fry the patties, turning once, until done, about 8 minutes. To serve, place a burger on the base of each bun and top with a pineapple ring.

Nutritional Analysis

Calories	299.79 Kcal	Protein	17.71 gm
Fat	9.85 gm	Carbohydrate	34.61 gm
Sodium	460.41 mg	Cholesterol	38.11 mg
Saturated fat	2.58 gm		

Mozzarella Sandwiches with Basil and Tomato

Serves: 4

185g (6oz) chopped dry-packed sun-dried tomatoes
2 cloves garlic, chopped
1/4 tsp salt
1 tbsp olive oil
1 tbsp lemon juice
1/4 tsp red pepper flakes
4 black olives, chopped
8 slices French bread
125g (4oz) low-fat mozzarella cheese, sliced
pepper to taste
3 tomatoes, sliced
salt to taste
2 tsp balsamic vinegar
250g (8oz) fresh basil leaves, torn

Place the sun-dried tomatoes in a bowl and cover with boiling water. Let stand for 10 minutes. Drain.

In a medium bowl, mash together the garlic and salt. Add the oil, lemon juice and red pepper flakes. Mix well. Add the rehydrated tomatoes and the olives, and again mix well. Divide among 4 of the bread slices, spreading evenly. Top with the cheese slices and sprinkle with the pepper. Place the tomato slices on top, and season with salt and vinegar. Top with the basil and then the remaining bread slices. Cut in half to serve.

Nutritional Analysis

Calories	298.54 Kcal	Protein	18.11 gm
Fat	5.91 gm	Carbohydrate	44.75 gm
Sodium	755.36 mg	Cholesterol	3.00 mg
Saturated fat	0.90 gm		

A Year in Provence Sandwich

Serves: 2

1 tsp olive oil
1 onion, chopped
1 tsp dried oregano, crumbled
1 tsp dried basil, crumbled
1 tbsp water
60g (2oz) pitted black olives, sliced
2 tbsp grated Parmesan cheese
8 to 12 spinach leaves
2 French rolls, split
125g (4oz) low-fat mozzarella cheese, sliced
2 plum tomatoes, sliced

(continued)

Heat the oil in a large pan over medium heat. Add the onion, oregano and basil, and cook, stirring, for 2 minutes. Add the water, reduce the heat to low, cover and cook until the onion is tender, about 5 minutes. Remove from the heat and stir in the olives and Parmesan.

Arrange 2 or 3 spinach leaves on the bottom half of each French roll. Spoon half the onion mixture onto each, top with the cheese slices and then the tomato slices. Arrange the remaining spinach leaves on top and then the tops of the rolls. Cut in half to serve.

Nutritional Analysis

Calories	348.10 Kcal	Protein	27.10 gm
Fat	8.39 gm	Carbohydrate	42.44 gm
Sodium	1026.64 mg	Cholesterol	9.94 mg
Saturated fat	2.08 gm		

Portobello, Basil and Tomato Sandwich

Serves: 4

1 tbsp low-fat mayonnaise
1/2 tsp lemon juice
2 large portobello mushrooms
1 tsp olive oil
2 cloves garlic, crushed
4 half baguettes, split
1 tomato, sliced
185g (6oz) fresh basil leaves, finely chopped
4 leaves green leaf lettuce

Preheat grill.

In a small bowl, mix together the mayonnaise and lemon juice. Brush the mushrooms with the oil and place on a griddle. Grill until tender, about 5 minutes.

Spread the garlic over the bottom halves of the rolls. Spread the mayonnaise mixture on top of the garlic, and then top with the grilled mushrooms, tomato, basil and lettuce. Put the top half of each roll in place and serve.

Nutritional Analysis

Calories	215.01 Kcal	Protein	7.93 gm
Fat	4.30 gm	Carbohydrate	37.16 gm
Sodium	352.33 mg	Cholesterol	0.00 mg
Saturated fat	0.54 gm		

Steak Subs

Serves: 6

500g (1lb) boneless beef sirloin steak, all fat trimmed
shredded lettuce
1 loaf French bread, split lengthways
220g (7oz) bottled roasted red peppers, drained
salt and pepper to taste
125g (4oz) grated fat-free mozzarella cheese

Prepare a fire in a charcoal grill. Grill the steak until done to your liking. In the meantime, spread the lettuce over the bottom half of the split bread loaf. Spread the peppers over the lettuce. Carve the steak into thin slices, and season with salt and pepper. Spread the steak slices over the peppers; top with the cheese. Put

the top on the loaf, and cut into 6 portions. Serve at once.

Nutritional Analysis

Calories	339.02 Kcal	Protein	26.86 gm
Fat	6.35 gm	Carbohydrate	41.94 gm
Sodium	611.24 mg	Cholesterol	51.46 mg
Saturated Ffat	2.06 gm		

Lean, Juicy Burgers

Serves: 6

> 375g (12oz) lean top round beef, trimmed of fat and
>   minced
> 2 tbsp sunflower or safflower oil
> 125g (4oz) finely chopped onion
> 125g (4oz) finely chopped celery
> 2 tbsp seasoned dried breadcrumbs
> 1 tbsp Worcestershire sauce
> salt and pepper to taste
> 6 burger buns
> 60ml (2fl oz) low-fat mayonnaise
> 6 tomato slices
> 6 onion slices

Prepare a fire in a charcoal grill or preheat a grill.

In a large bowl, mix together the beef, oil, onion, celery, breadcrumbs, Worcestershire sauce and salt and pepper. Shape into 6 patties.

Place the patties on a grill rack or griddle pan. Grill, turning once, until done as desired, 7 to 8 minutes on each side for medium. Just before the burgers are ready, toast the buns on the grill or in the griddle. Spread the mayonnaise on the buns and top with the burgers. Place the tomato and

onion slices on the burgers and then the tops of the buns. Serve at once.

Nutritional Analysis

Calories	270.49 Kcal	Protein	17.96 gm
Fat	8.93 gm	Carbohydrate	28.09 gm
Sodium	440.78 mg	Cholesterol	35.59 mg
Saturated fat	1.55 gm		

Steak-Vegetable Pockets

Serves: 4

> 375g (12oz) top round beef
> 3 tbsp soy sauce
> 60ml (2fl oz) water
> 1¹/₂ tsp cornflour
> 375g (12oz) broccoli florets
> 1 small carrot, diced
> 1 small onion, chopped
> ¹/₂ green pepper, chopped
> 8 sugar snaps, halved crossways
> 6 mushrooms, sliced
> 1 small tomato, chopped
> 1 tbsp olive oil
> 4 pitta bread rounds, halved

Thinly slice the beef into bite-sized strips and set aside.

In a small bowl, stir together the soy sauce, water, and cornflour until the cornflour dissolves; set aside.

Spray a wok or large frying pan with nonstick cooking spray and place over high heat. Add

(continued)

Spicing up a Sandwich

For extra-tasty low-fat sandwiches, use spices. Use a spicy brown mustard on sliced turkey rather than mayonnaise. Sprinkle tomatoes in sandwiches with garlic powder and dried basil.

When making sandwiches, you can also experiment using different kinds of bread, such as wholemeal or cracked wheat, rye or pumpernickel. Special breads such as dill bread make great-tasting sandwiches. Pitta bread is good for really low-fat sandwiches and makes sandwich eating convenient, with no chance of the filling falling out while eating.

broccoli, carrot, onion and green pepper, and stir-fry until the carrot is tender, about 7 minutes. Add the sugar snaps, mushrooms and tomato, and stir-fry for 2 minutes. Remove the vegetables from the pan and set aside. Add the oil and heat over high heat. Add the beef and stir-fry until the beef is tender, about 3 minutes. Quickly stir the cornflour mixture and add it to the pan. Cook and stir until bubbling and the pan juices are thickening. Return the vegetables to the pan and heat through.

To serve, cut the pitta breads in half, forming 8 pockets. Spoon the vegetable-beef mixture into the pockets and serve.

Nutritional Analysis

Calories	405.91	Kcal	Protein	27.53	gm
Fat	12.86	gm	Carbohydrate	45.16	gm
Sodium	1165.82	mg	Cholesterol	51.92	mg
Saturated fat	3.73	gm			

Side Dishes

CHAPTER SIX

Amount Per Chapter

53 Recipes

% Daily Value

Easy to Prepare	**100%**
Low Fat/High Flavour	**100%**
Simple to Understand	**100%**

DELICIOUS, EASY, LOW-FAT RECIPES

Too many people regard side dishes as either a scoop of mashed potatoes or a spoonful of soggy green beans. It is no wonder that many diners tend to ignore the side dishes on their dinner plates in favour of the main course.

The great thing about cooking low-fat side dishes is that you learn to rely on the crunch and flavour of fresh vegetables and fruits in order to avoid the fat. Here are a number of delicious side dishes that depend on ingredients such as onion, garlic, apples and herbs to deliver taste with little fat.

Apple–Sweet Potato Bake

Serves: 4

3 Red Delicious apples, peeled, cored and sliced
1 tbsp lemon juice
1kg (2lb) sweet potatoes, peeled and sliced
80ml (2½fl oz) apple juice
1 tbsp butter, melted

Preheat oven to 180°C (350°F), gas mark 4.

In a bowl, toss the apple slices with the lemon juice. In a large flameproof baking dish, alternate layers of the sweet potatoes and apples. Pour the apple juice and the melted butter over the layers. Cover and bake until tender and juice is bubbling, about 1¼ hours.

Remove from the oven. Turn the oven to grill. Uncover the baking dish and slip in under the grill until top is lightly browned, about 5 minutes.

Nutritional Analysis

Calories	262.13	Kcal	Protein	2.88	gm
Fat	3.68	gm	Carbohydrate	56.54	gm
Sodium	51.91	mg	Cholesterol	7.76	mg
Saturated fat	1.91	gm			

Green Beans with Garlic

Serves: 6

500g (1lb) green beans
½ tbsp olive oil
1 small onion, chopped
1 tbsp chopped garlic
1 tbsp plain flour
500g (1lb) tinned chopped tomatoes, drained, liquid reserved

Steam the green beans until tender, about 5 minutes, then plunge them into cold water to cool. Drain and set aside.

In a medium nonstick saucepan, heat the oil over medium heat. Add the onion and garlic, and sauté for a few minutes. Stir in the flour and cook for 1 minute. Stir in the liquid from the tomatoes. Cook the mixture, stirring, until slightly thickened. Add the tomatoes and green beans, mixing well. Cook, stirring, over medium heat for a couple of minutes until the beans are done but still crisp and the flavours are blended.

Nutritional Analysis

Calories	62.91 Kcal	Protein	2.51 gm
Fat	1.43 gm	Carbohydrate	11.81 gm
Sodium	128.62 mg	Cholesterol	0.00 mg
Saturated fat	0.20 gm		

Risotto with Vegetables

Serves: 4

2 tbsp butter
1 onion, chopped
250g (8oz) basmati rice
1l (2pt) reduced-sodium, fat-free chicken stock, heated
250g (8oz) green beans, cut in 12mm (1/2in) lengths
250g (8oz) chopped courgette
90g (3oz) finely chopped fresh parsley
60g (2oz) grated Parmesan cheese
salt and pepper to taste

Melt 1 tablespoon of the butter in a large pan over medium heat. Add the onion and sauté until softened. Add the rice and stir to coat with the butter. Reduce the heat to low and add 125ml (4fl oz) of the stock. Cook, stirring, until it is absorbed. Add 375ml (12fl oz) more stock, 125ml (4fl oz) at a time, cooking and stirring until each addition is absorbed. Add the green beans and courgette, and cook for 2 minutes. Add the remaining stock, again 125ml (4fl oz) at a time. Simmer for about 15 minutes more. The risotto is done when the kernels are still slightly firm at the centre and the mixture is creamy. Add the parsley, Parmesan, remaining butter and salt and pepper.

(continued)

About Risotto

Although it may sound exotic, risotto is considered a simple rice dish in Italy. It is made by adding a hot stock in increments to uncooked rice in a saucepan over low heat. You must stir the rice continuously, and wait until the rice has absorbed all the stock before adding more. Risotto is typically creamy and served in a shallow puddle of stock. The average cooking time is about 25 minutes.

Nutritional Analysis

Calories	269.44 Kcal	Protein	9.59 gm
Fat	7.87 gm	Carbohydrate	40.07 gm
Sodium	718.72 mg	Cholesterol	19.47 mg
Saturated fat	4.53 gm		

Indian Rice

Serves: 8

1 tbsp butter
2 large onions, sliced
1l (2pt) reduced-sodium, fat-free chicken stock
500g (1lb) sliced mushrooms
300g (10oz) white rice
250g (8oz) brown lentils, soaked for 2 hours then
*   cooked for 30 minutes in water and drained*
1 tbsp peeled and finely chopped fresh ginger
1 tsp curry powder
1/4 tsp ground cinnamon
2 cloves garlic, crushed
125g (4oz) chopped fresh parsley
salt and pepper to taste

In a heavy frying pan, melt the butter over low heat. Add the onions and cook, stirring occasionally, until tender, about 20 minutes. Meanwhile, in a saucepan, combine the stock, mushrooms, rice, lentils, ginger, curry powder, cinnamon and garlic. Bring to the boil, reduce the heat to low, cover and cook until the rice and lentils are tender and the liquid is absorbed, about 30 minutes.

Uncover and mix in the parsley, salt and pepper. Serve at once.

Nutritional Analysis

Calories	257.76 Kcal	Protein	11.88 gm
Fat	2.08 gm	Carbohydrate	47.93 gm
Sodium	303.60 mg	Cholesterol	3.88 mg
Saturated fat	1.00 gm		

Vegetable Fried Rice

Serves: 6

1 tbsp peanut oil
500g (1lb) sliced courgette
250g (8oz) finely chopped celery
1kg (2lb) cold cooked rice
1 red pepper, diced
2 eggs, lightly beaten
500g (1lb) beansprouts
80ml (2 1/2fl oz) oyster sauce
1 onion, chopped

In a large, deep pan, heat the oil over medium-high heat. Add the courgette and celery, and stir-fry for 2 minutes. Add the rice and stir-fry for another minute. Add the pepper and stir-fry for another minute. Add the eggs and cook, stirring, for 30 seconds. Add the beansprouts and stir-fry for 1 minute longer, or until the eggs are set. Add the oyster sauce and stir until evenly distributed. Sprinkle with chopped onion and serve.

Nutritional Analysis

Calories	221.04 Kcal	Protein	8.34 gm
Fat	4.40 gm	Carbohydrate	37.30 gm
Sodium	672.15 mg	Cholesterol	70.83 mg
Saturated fat	0.98 gm		

Wild Rice Pilaf

Serves: 6

1 tbsp olive oil
1 onion, diced
750ml (1½pt) reduced-sodium, fat-free chicken stock
125g (4oz) wild rice
500g (8oz) white rice
60g (2oz) chopped fresh parsley
1 tsp dried basil, crumbled
salt and pepper to taste

In a large pan, heat the oil over medium heat for 1 minute. Add the onion and sauté until tender, about 5 minutes. Add the chicken broth, stir in wild rice, and bring to the boil for 10 minutes. Add the white rice. Reduce the heat to low, cover and cook until the rices are done, about 20 minutes. Mix in the parsley, basil, salt and pepper, and serve.

Nutritional Analysis

Calories	199.76 Kcal	Protein	6.05 gm
Fat	2.63 gm	Carbohydrate	37.39 gm
Sodium	285.00 mg	Cholesterol	0.00 mg
Saturated fat	0.37 gm		

Texan Rice

Serves: 6

250g (8oz) lean minced beef
1 medium onion, chopped
500g (8oz) hot cooked white rice
300g (10oz) tinned sweetcorn, drained and heated
125ml (4fl oz) barbecue sauce

In a large nonstick frying pan, cook the beef until brown, about 5 minutes. Drain off any fat. Add the onion and continue to cook until the onion is soft, about 8 minutes longer. Drain again.

Place the beef-onion mixture in a serving bowl. Add the rice, corn and barbecue sauce, and mix well.

Nutritional Analysis

Calories	195.81 Kcal	Protein	9.54 gm
Fat	6.06 gm	Carbohydrate	25.90 gm
Sodium	260.89 mg	Cholesterol	22.89 mg
Saturated fat	2.17 gm		

Indian Raita

Serves: 10

500ml (1pt) plain fat-free yogurt
2 medium cucumbers, chopped
1 clove garlic, crushed
2 tsp finely chopped fresh dill
1 tbsp olive oil
2 tsp distilled white vinegar

In a bowl, combine all the ingredients. Cover and chill for at least 1 hour before serving. Serve as a side dish with curry.

Nutritional Analysis

Calories	55.10 Kcal	Protein	3.58 gm
Fat	1.85 gm	Carbohydrate	6.26 gm
Sodium	44.37 mg	Cholesterol	1.13 mg
Saturated fat	0.31 gm		

Black Beans with Rice

Serves: 8

    1.18kg (2lb 6oz) tinned black beans, drained
    1kg (2lb) hot cooked white rice
    2 tsp ground cumin
    4 cloves garlic, crushed
    2 bay leaves
    2 tsp dried oregano, crumbled
    1 tsp salt
    1 medium onion, chopped
    1 green pepper, chopped
    2 tbsp lemon juice
    500g (1lb) tinned tomatoes, drained and cut up
    250g (8oz) shelled green peas, blanched
    250g (8oz) chopped fresh tomatoes
    2 spring onions, thinly sliced
    2 tbsp low-fat sour cream

In a large saucepan, combine the beans, cumin, garlic, bay leaves, oregano, salt, onion, pepper, lemon juice and tinned tomatoes. Bring to the boil, reduce the heat to medium, cover and cook until the vegetables are done, about 30 minutes.

    Discard the bay leaves. Mix the beans with the hot rice and stir in the green peas, fresh tomatoes, spring onions and sour cream, and serve.

Nutritional Analysis

Calories	259.96 Kcal	Protein	11.78 gm
Fat	1.97 gm	Carbohydrate	50.50 gm
Sodium	808.86 mg	Cholesterol	1.25 mg
Saturated fat	0.28 gm		

Baked Acorn Squash

Serves: 4

    1 acorn squash
    1 tbsp buttery light, reduced-fat margarine
    1 tsp brown sugar (optional)

Preheat oven to 200°C (400°F), gas mark 6.

    Cut the squash in half and scoop out the seeds. (Save and bake for snacks, if you like.) Bake the squash on an ungreased biscuit tray for 30 to 40 minutes, or until tender. Scoop out the pulp and mix with the margarine or butter and the brown sugar, if desired. (For a lower-calorie, lower-fat alternative, try a little ground cinnamon and nutmeg.) Return the mixture to the shells or place in a baking dish and heat thoroughly, about 15 minutes.

Nutritional Analysis

Calories	78.55 Kcal	Protein	1.03 gm
Fat	0.12 gm	Carbohydrate	17.08 gm
Sodium	31.80 mg	Cholesterol	0.00 mg
Saturated fat	0.51 gm		

Potato-Cheese Casserole

Serves: 6

    6 maris piper potatoes
    500g (1lb) low-fat cottage cheese
    2 tbsp olive oil
    1 onion, chopped
    2 tbsp plain flour
    1 tsp dried parsley flakes

1 tsp dried thyme, crumbled
¹⁄₈ tsp salt
pepper to taste
80ml (2¹⁄₂fl oz) skimmed milk
125g (4oz) fine dried breadcrumbs
2 tbsp grated Parmesan cheese
2 tbsp buttery light, reduced-fat margarine, cut
into bits

Place the potatoes in a saucepan with water to cover. Bring to the boil, reduce the heat to medium and simmer until tender, about 25 minutes. Drain and, when cool enough to handle, peel and slice.

Preheat oven to 180°C (350°F), gas mark 4. Grease a large baking dish.

In a bowl, beat together the cottage cheese and oil with a rotary beater until fluffy. Mix in the onion. In a small bowl, stir together the flour, parsley, thyme, salt and pepper. Make a layer of a third of the sliced potatoes in the prepared baking dish. Cover with a layer of half of the cottage cheese. Sprinkle with half of the seasoned flour. Repeat the layers, then end with a layer of potatoes. Pour the milk evenly over the potato-cheese layers. Mix the breadcrumbs with the Parmesan cheese and sprinkle over the potatoes. Dot with margarine.

Bake until cheese is lightly browned, about 30 minutes. Serve hot directly from the dish.

Adding Heat

Whenever I am making a dish that calls for Tabasco sauce and I know I will be serving it to guests, I don't add the Tabasco during cooking, and instead just place the bottle of sauce on the table.

People have different expectations of what constitutes 'hot' today. One person's hot is another person's tepid. Evidence of that fact is the difference between the hot curry I've encountered in the West End and the hot curry I might order in an Indian restaurant in Bradford.

In other words, play it safe. Let guests add their own heat.

(continued)

Calories	326.80 Kcal	Protein	15.16 gm
Fat	11.13 gm	Carbohydrate	41.37 gm
Sodium	527.74 mg	Cholesterol	4.58 mg
Saturated fat	2.30 gm		

Orangey Sweet Potatoes

Serves: 6

3 large sweet potatoes
60ml (2fl oz) orange juice
1 tbsp buttery light, reduced-fat margarine
1/8 tsp salt
1/4 tsp pepper
1/4 tsp ground ginger
3 oranges, peeled and cut into small pieces
60g (2oz) toasted almonds, slivered (optional)

Preheat oven to 200°C (400°F), gas mark 6.

Pierce potatoes with fork and bake until tender, about 1 hour. Remove from the oven and leave the oven set at 200°C. Halve the sweet potatoes lengthways and scoop out the pulp into a bowl, being careful to keep the skins intact. Put the skins aside. Mash the pulp, then add the orange juice, margarine, salt, pepper and ginger. Stir the orange pieces into the mixture. Spoon into the skins and place on a baking tray. Top with the almonds, if desired.

Bake until heated through, about 15 minutes. Serve hot.

Variations: use 250g (8oz) tinned crushed pineapple and its juice in place of the oranges and

orange juice. You may add 60g (2oz) raisins to either mixture. The sweet potato mixture can be baked in a baking dish instead of being stuffed into the skins. The mixture can be prepared up to a day in advance and refrigerated until ready to be heated.

Nutritional Analysis

Calories	171.23 Kcal	Protein	2.40 gm
Fat	2.37 gm	Carbohydrate	36.39 gm
Sodium	85.42 mg	Cholesterol	0.00 mg
Saturated fat	0.39 gm		

Asian Rice

Serves: 10

375ml (12fl oz) water
250ml (8fl oz) reduced-sodium, fat-free chicken stock
330g (11oz) washed long-grain white rice
1 tbsp buttery light, reduced-fat margarine
2 tbsp finely chopped onion
2 tbsp finely chopped green pepper
1/4 tsp ground sage
250g (8oz) finely chopped celery
250g (8oz) chopped pecans
125g (4oz) sliced water chestnuts
1/4 tsp ground nutmeg
1/8 tsp pepper

In a medium saucepan, bring the water and stock to the boil. Add the rice, stir, cover, reduce the heat to low and simmer for 20 minutes. Remove from the heat. Let stand covered until all the liquid is absorbed, about 5 minutes. Meanwhile, melt the

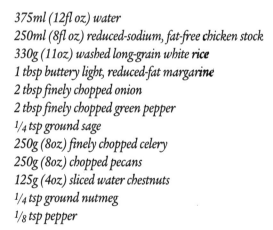

margarine in a large nonstick pan over medium heat. Add the onion, celery and peppers and sauté until tender, about 3 minutes. Stir in the pecans, water chestnuts, nutmeg and pepper, and heat through. Add the rice and fluff with a fork to distribute all the ingredients evenly, then serve.

Nutritional Analysis

Calories	145.42 Kcal	Protein	2.68 gm
Fat	4.98 gm	Carbohydrate	22.47 gm
Sodium	82.30 mg	Cholesterol	0.00 mg
Saturated fat	0.52 gm		

Wonderful Stuffed Potatoes

Serves: 8

4 baking potatoes
185g (6oz) low-fat cottage cheese
60ml (2fl oz) skimmed milk
2 tbsp buttery light, reduced-fat margarine
1 tsp dill weed, dried
3/4 tsp herb seasoning
4 to 6 drops Tabasco sauce
2 tsp grated Parmesan cheese

Preheat oven to 220°C (425°F), gas mark 7.

Prick the potatoes with a fork. Bake until easily pierced with a fork, about 1 hour. Remove from the oven and leave the oven set at 220°C. Halve the potatoes lengthways and scoop out the pulp into a bowl, leaving shells about 12mm (1/2in) thick. Mash the pulp, then mix in all the remaining ingredients except the Parmesan cheese. Spoon into the potato shells. Place on a

baking tray, and sprinkle the top of each with 1/4 teaspoon Parmesan cheese. Bake until tops are golden brown, 15 to 20 minutes.

Nutritional Analysis

Calories	130.95 Kcal	Protein	5.60 gm
Fat	3.38 gm	Carbohydrate	20.10 gm
Sodium	139.99 mg	Cholesterol	1.46 mg
Saturated fat	0.74 gm		

Lemony Asparagus and Carrots

Serves: 6

250g (8oz) baby carrots
250g (8oz) frozen asparagus spears
2 tbsp lemon juice
1 tsp lemon pepper

Steam the carrots until crisp tender, about 15 minutes, then plunge into cold water to cool. Drain and place in a bowl.

Meanwhile, cook the frozen asparagus spears according to the directions on the packet, then plunge into cold water to cool, and drain. Add to the carrots, cover and chill for 30 minutes.

To serve, arrange the carrots and asparagus on a platter. Sprinkle with a little lemon juice and lemon pepper.

(continued)

Nutritional Analysis

Calories	26.39 Kcal	Protein	1.62 gm
Fat	0.16 gm	Carbohydrate	5.69 gm
Sodium	87.46 mg	Cholesterol	0.00 mg
Saturated fat	0.02 gm		

Pineapple-Pear Mould

Serves: 6

2 envelopes unflavoured gelatin
625ml (1¹/₄pt) orange juice
600g (1 lb 4oz) tinned crushed pineapple
2 medium pears, cored, peeled and diced

In a small saucepan, soften the gelatin in 125ml (4fl oz) of the orange juice for 5 minutes. Place over low heat and stir until the gelatin dissolves. Stir in the undrained crushed pineapple and the remaining orange juice. Cover and chill until partially set, about 30 minutes.

Fold the pears into the pineapple mixture and transfer to a 1.5l (3 pint) mould.

Cover and chill until firm, about 30 minutes. To serve, dip the bottom of the mould in hot water for 10 seconds, then turn over onto a plate.

Nutritional Analysis

Calories	143.80 Kcal	Protein	3.29 gm
Fat	0.35 gm	Carbohydrate	34.36 gm
Sodium	6.54 mg	Cholesterol	0.00 mg
Saturated fat	0.02 gm		

Dijon Coleslaw

Serves: 6

1 small head cabbage, shredded
4 spring onions, chopped
1 small English onion, sliced
¹/₂ green pepper, sliced
2 carrots, grated or sliced
60g (2oz) golden or dark raisins
¹/₂ tsp celery seeds
125ml (4fl oz) low-fat mayonnaise
60ml (2fl oz) nonfat sour cream
125ml (4fl oz) nonfat buttermilk
1 tbsp Dijon or other prepared mustard
1 to 3 tbsp cider vinegar
2 tsp sugar

In a large bowl, combine the cabbage, spring onions, onion, pepper, carrots, raisins and celery seeds. In a small bowl, whisk together all the remaining ingredients. Add the mayonnaise mixture to the cabbage mixture and stir to combine. Chill for 15 minutes in the refrigerator (so liquid will drain to bottom). Pour off any liquid, mix well again and serve cold.

Nutritional Analysis

Calories	109.64 Kcal	Protein	3.69 gm
Fat	0.35 gm	Carbohydrate	23.56 gm
Sodium	264.67 mg	Cholesterol	1.41 mg
Saturated fat	0.02 gm		

Potato Gratin

Serves: 6

> *3 medium white potatoes, thinly sliced*
> *2 tbsp plain flour*
> *1 medium onion, thinly sliced into rings*
> *1/8 tsp cayenne pepper*
> *1 tsp paprika*
> *1/2 tsp pepper*
> *60g (2oz) grated Parmesan cheese*
> *1 small courgette, thinly sliced*
> *1/4 tsp nutmeg*
> *375g (12oz) evaporated milk*
> *2 tsp chopped fresh parsley*

Preheat oven to 200°C (400°F), gas mark 6.

Coat a 230mm (9in) pie dish or a similar-sized gratin dish with 3 sprays of cooking spray. Layer a third of the potatoes over the bottom of the prepared dish, overlapping the slices in a spiral pattern. Sprinkle 1 tablespoon of the flour over the potatoes and arrange the onion rings on top. Dust with the cayenne pepper and 1/2 teaspoon of the paprika. Layer another third of the potatoes, adding the remaining flour, all the black pepper and 2 tablespoons of the Parmesan cheese. Scatter the courgette over the top, and dust with the nutmeg. Top with a spiral layer of the remaining potatoes. Pour the evaporated milk evenly over the gratin and sprinkle on the remaining 1/2 teaspoon paprika and 2 tablespoons Parmesan cheese. Cover the dish with foil. Bake for 45 minutes. Uncover, reduce the oven temperature to 180°C (350°F), gas mark 4, and continue to bake until the top is golden brown, about 15 minutes longer. Remove from the oven and let cool for 10 minutes. Garnish with the parsley and serve.

Nutritional Analysis

Calories	196.52 Kcal	Protein	8.15 gm
Fat	6.54 gm	Carbohydrate	27.03 gm
Sodium	137.21 mg	Cholesterol	20.90 mg
Saturated fat	3.52 gm		

Herbed Rice Pilaf

Serves: 4

> *1 tbsp olive oil*
> *1 onion, chopped*
> *2 celery stalks, chopped*
> *1 clove garlic, crushed*
> *1 tsp dried thyme, crumbled*
> *1 bay leaf*
> *625ml (11/4pt) water*
> *250g (8oz) long-grain white rice*
> *1 fresh thyme sprig*

In a medium saucepan, heat the oil over medium heat. Add the onion, celery, garlic and thyme, and sauté until the onion is translucent, about 5 minutes. Add the bay leaf and water, bring to the boil and add the rice. Cover, reduce the heat to low and simmer until all the water is absorbed and the rice is tender, about 20 minutes.

Remove and discard the bay leaf. Spoon pilaf into a serving bowl. Garnish with the thyme sprig.

(continued)

Calories	221.24 Kcal	Protein	4.02 gm
Fat	3.79 gm	Carbohydrate	42.08 gm
Sodium	21.40 mg	Cholesterol	0.00 mg
Saturated fat	0.54 gm		

Risotto with Winter Squash

Serves: 6

1 tbsp olive oil
250g (8oz) finely chopped shallots or onions
1 tsp dried sage, crumbled
300g (12oz) basmati rice
1l (2pt) vegetable stock
1 small butternut squash, peeled, seeded and cut into 25mm (1in) cubes
1 tsp salt, or to taste
60ml (2oz) grated Parmesan cheese or balsamic vinegar to taste
pepper to taste
2 tbsp minced fresh parsley

Heat the oil in a pressure cooker over medium-high heat. Add the shallots and sauté, stirring frequently, for 1 minute. Add the sage and rice, and stir to coat the rice with the oil. Stir in 875ml (1.75 pints) of the stock and bring to the boil. Add the squash and salt. Secure the lid in place and bring to high pressure over high heat. Adjust the heat to maintain high pressure and cook for 5 minutes. Reduce the pressure with the quick-release method. Remove the lid, tilting it away from you to allow excess steam to escape.

If the risotto isn't creamy, stir in the remaining stock. Cook over medium heat, stirring constantly, until the rice achieves the desired consistency. Stir in the Parmesan cheese or vinegar, pepper and parsley. Serve immediately in shallow soup bowls.

Nutritional Analysis

Calories	246.13 Kcal	Protein	6.94 gm
Fat	3.83 gm	Carbohydrate	47.04 gm
Sodium	612.92 mg	Cholesterol	2.63 mg
Saturated fat	0.94 gm		

 ## Mediterranean Vegetable Couscous

Serves: 6

1 to 2 tbsp olive oil
2 tsp crushed garlic
250g (8oz) coarsely chopped onions
375ml (12fl oz) boiling water
1 small fennel bulb, cut into 12mm (1/2in) strips (chop and reserve fronds), or 2 large celery stalks, cut into 12mm (1/2in) thick slices, plus 1/2 tsp fennel seeds
1 large red pepper, thinly sliced
1 large carrot, cut on diagonal into 12mm (1/2in) wide slices
125g (4oz) mushrooms, halved
2 medium courgettes, cut into 38mm (11/2in) chunks
375g (12oz) coarsely chopped plum tomatoes

90g (3oz) pitted oil-cured black olives
1½ tsp dried basil leaves, crumbled
1½ tsp dried oregano leaves, crumbled
1 tsp salt or to taste
¼ tsp ground cinnamon
⅛ tsp pepper
1 to 3 tbsp balsamic vinegar or lemon juice
375g (12oz) instant wholewheat couscous
60g (2oz) finely chopped fresh basil or parsley

Heat 1 tablespoon oil in a pressure cooker over medium-high heat. Add the garlic and cook, stirring constantly, until just browned. Add the onions and cook, stirring frequently, for 1 minute. Add the water, fennel bulb strips or celery and fennel seeds, pepper, carrot, mushrooms, courgettes, tomatoes, olives, dried basil, oregano, salt, cinnamon and pepper.

Secure the lid in place and bring to high pressure over high heat. Adjust the heat to maintain high pressure and cook for 2 minutes. Reduce the pressure with the quick-release method. Remove the lid, tilting it away from you to allow excess steam to escape.

Stir in 1 tablespoon vinegar or lemon juice and the couscous. Replace the lid and let stand until couscous is tender, about 5 minutes. Add the fennel fronds, if using, the fresh basil or parsley, the remaining 1 tablespoon oil and additional vinegar or lemon juice to taste. Stir well and serve.

Note: leftovers are terrific at room temperature. Drizzle with olive oil and lemon juice and garnish with olives.

Nutritional Analysis

Calories	323.84 Kcal	Protein	10.99 gm
Fat	7.69 gm	Carbohydrate	57.88 gm
Sodium	707.99 mg	Cholesterol	0.00 mg
Saturated fat	0.80 gm		

Southwestern Succotash

Serves: 6

1 tbsp safflower or sunflower oil
¾ tsp cumin seeds
2 tsp finely chopped garlic
250g (8oz) coarsely chopped onions
1 medium red pepper, diced
1 or 2 jalapeño peppers, seeded and diced; 1 chipotle pepper, seeded and chopped into bits; or 1 generous pinch of red pepper flakes
250ml (8fl oz) water
2 tbsp tomato puree
1 medium butternut squash, halved, seeded, peeled and cut into 25mm (1in) pieces
500g (1lb) fresh or frozen corn kernels
salt to taste
500g (1lb) tinned small butter beans
90g (3oz) finely chopped fresh coriander

(continued)

Heat the oil in a pressure cooker over medium-high heat. Add the cumin seeds and let sizzle for 5 seconds. Add the garlic and cook, stirring frequently, until light brown, about 5 to 7 minutes. Add the onions, pepper and jalapeño or chipotle pepper and continue cooking, stirring frequently, for 1 minute.

Add water, tomato puree, squash, corn and salt. Secure the lid in place and bring to high pressure over high heat. Adjust the heat to maintain high pressure and cook for 2 minutes. Reduce the pressure with the quick-release method. Remove the lid, tilting it away from you to allow excess steam to escape. If the squash is not quite tender, replace but do not lock the lid; allow the squash to steam for a few more minutes in the residual heat.

Stir in the butter beans, cover and simmer until tender, 2 to 3 minutes. Stir in the coriander just before serving.

Nutritional Analysis

Calories	205.41 Kcal	Protein	7.53 gm
Fat	3.17 gm	Carbohydrate	41.17 gm
Sodium	79.08 mg	Cholesterol	0.00 mg
Saturated fat	0.27 gm		

Coriander Carrots

Serves: 6

1 tbsp oil
125g (4oz) chopped leeks or onions
250ml (8fl oz) water
60g (2oz) dried currants or raisins

1 tbsp ground coriander
1 bay leaf
1/2 tsp salt, or to taste
750g (1lb 8oz) carrots, cut on the diagonal into 12mm (1/2in) thick slices
1 to 2 tbsp lemon juice (optional)
1 tbsp finely chopped fresh parsley

Heat the oil in a pressure cooker over medium-high heat. Add the leeks or onions and cook, stirring frequently, for 1 minute. Add the water (use the amount recommended by the cooker manufacturer), currants or raisins, coriander, bay leaf, salt and carrots.

Secure the lid in place and bring to high pressure over high heat. Adjust the heat to maintain high pressure, and cook for 2 minutes. Reduce the pressure with the quick-release method. Remove the lid, tilting it away from you to allow excess steam to escape. If the carrots are not quite tender, replace but do not lock the lid. Let them continue to cook in residual steam for another minute or two.

Just before serving, stir in lemon juice, if desired, and the parsley.

Nutritional Analysis

Calories	92.31 Kcal	Protein	1.58 gm
Fat	2.52 gm	Carbohydrate	17.40 gm
Sodium	235.56 mg	Cholesterol	0.00 mg
Saturated fat	0.31 gm		

Indian-Style Rice

Serves: 6

500ml (1pt) water
2 tsp curry powder
½ tsp ground turmeric
¼ tsp ground cinnamon
250ml (8oz) long-grain white rice
275g (9oz) frozen green beans
1 onion, chopped
1 clove garlic, crushed
2 peaches, stoned, peeled and coarsely chopped
125g (4fl oz) plain low-fat yogurt
1 peach, stoned, peeled and sliced
60g (2oz) raisins

In a saucepan, combine the water, curry powder, turmeric and cinnamon. Bring to the boil, add the rice, cover, reduce the heat to low and cook until the liquid is absorbed and the rice is tender, about 20 minutes.

Meanwhile, place the frozen beans in a colander. Run hot water over them to thaw; drain well. Preheat oven to 190°C (375°F), gas mark 5.

When the rice is ready, mix the onion and garlic in it. Spoon half the rice into a medium baking dish. Scatter the chopped peaches and green beans over the rice. Top with the remaining rice mixture. Cover the dish with foil.

Bake for 30 minutes. Serve immediately. Serve the yogurt, sliced peaches and raisins at the table, if desired.

Exotic Rices

Although many of the rice recipes in this book can be made with ordinary white rice, you can easily add a bit of interest to these dishes by using an exotic rice, such as Arborio, jasmine, basmati or brown rice.

Arborio rice is from Italy and is used most often in risotto dishes. Jasmine is a faintly aromatic Thai white rice that cooks as easily as regular long-grain white rice and adds a bit of sweetness to your dish. Basmati is a Middle Eastern rice of long, slender grains that adds a hint of perfume to a dish. Finally, brown rice contains a good deal more fibre than white rice and has a nutty taste.

(continued)

Nutritional Analysis

Calories	199.45 Kcal	Protein	5.02 gm
Fat	0.77 gm	Carbohydrate	44.42 gm
Sodium	18.14 mg	Cholesterol	1.13 mg
Saturated fat	0.25 gm		

Mushroom-Pineapple Rice

Serves: 4

> *250g (8oz) tinned crushed pineapple, drained, with liquid reserved*
> *1 tsp salt*
> *250g (8oz) long-grain white rice*
> *1 tbsp butter*
> *60g (2oz) finely chopped spring onions*
> *125g (4oz) mushrooms, sliced*
> *2 tsp soy sauce*
> *1/2 tsp ground ginger*
> *60g (2oz) cashews*

Pour the pineapple liquid into a measuring pitcher and add enough water to measure just over 500ml (1 pint). Pour into a medium saucepan, add the salt and bring to the boil. Stir in the rice. Cover, reduce the heat to low and cook until the liquid is absorbed and the rice is tender, about 20 minutes.

Meanwhile, melt the butter in a frying pan over medium heat. Add the spring onions and mushrooms and sauté until tender, about 5 minutes. Stir in the soy sauce, ginger and pineapple, mixing well. Keep hot.

When the rice is ready, add the mushroom mixture and the nuts to it, stirring to distribute them evenly, then serve.

Nutritional Analysis

Calories	290.99 Kcal	Protein	5.75 gm
Fat	7.30 gm	Carbohydrate	51.38 gm
Sodium	790.07 mg	Cholesterol	7.76 mg
Saturated fat	2.65 gm		

Brown Rice with Pears

Serves: 8

> *3 tbsp lemon juice*
> *2 tsp finely chopped garlic*
> *1/4 tsp ground ginger*
> *1/4 tsp pepper*
> *2 William or comice pears, cored, peeled and diced*
> *750g (1lb 8oz) cooked brown rice, at room temperature*
> *125g (4oz) sliced spring onions*
> *125g (4oz) grated carrots*
> *125g (4oz) thinly sliced celery*
> *2 tbsp vegetable oil*

In a bowl, combine the lemon juice, garlic, ginger and pepper. Add the pears, toss to coat and set aside. In a separate bowl, combine all the remaining ingredients, mixing well. Gently fold in the pears. Cover and chill before serving.

Nutritional Analysis

Calories	158.23 Kcal	Protein	2.66 gm
Fat	4.36 gm	Carbohydrate	27.97 gm
Sodium	15.54 mg	Cholesterol	0.00 mg
Saturated fat	0.58 gm		

Rancho California Rice

Serves: 6

> 2 tbsp butter
> 250g (8oz) chopped onions
> 1kg (2lb) cooked white rice
> 250ml (8fl oz) low-fat sour cream
> 250g (8oz) low-fat cottage cheese
> 1 bay leaf, crumbled
> salt and pepper to taste
> 500g (1lb) tinned whole green chilli peppers, drained,
>   seeded and cut into strips
> 250g (8oz) grated fat-free cheddar cheese

Preheat oven to 190°C (375°F), gas mark 5.
Grease a large baking dish.

   In a large frying pan, melt the butter over low
heat. Add the onions and sauté until translucent,
about 5 minutes. Remove from the heat. Add the
rice, sour cream, cottage cheese, bay leaf, salt and
pepper. Mix well. Layer one-third of the rice
mixture in the prepared dish. Top with a layer of
the chillies and then 60g (2oz) of the cheddar
cheese. Repeat, ending with a layer of rice.

   Bake for 25 minutes. Top with the remaining
cheddar cheese and bake until cheese is lightly
browned, about 10 minutes longer. Serve hot.

Nutritional Analysis

Calories	310.44 Kcal	Protein	16.51 gm
Fat	7.99 gm	Carbohydrate	44.38 gm
Sodium	835.47 mg	Cholesterol	27.17 mg
Saturated fat	4.87 gm		

Wonderful Risotto

Serves: 2

> 2 tbsp butter
> 1 medium onion, diced
> 250g (8oz) Arborio risotto rice
> 430ml (14fl oz) reduced-sodium, fat-free chicken stock
> 125ml (4fl oz) sherry
> 125g (4oz) grated Parmesan cheese

In a large frying pan, melt butter over medium
heat. Add the onion and sauté until golden brown,
about 10 minutes. Add the rice and stir until the
rice turns yellow. Add the sherry then the stock,
ladle by ladle, bring to the boil, cover, reduce the
heat to low and cook until the liquid is absorbed
and the rice is tender, about 20 minutes. Stir in
the cheese and serve.

Nutritional Analysis

Calories	318.11 Kcal	Protein	9.33 gm
Fat	9.10 gm	Carbohydrate	44.55 gm
Sodium	496.57 mg	Cholesterol	23.42 mg
Saturated fat	5.56 gm		

Soulful Black-Eyed Peas

Serves: 8

> 1 tbsp olive oil
> 250g (8oz) chopped onion
> 2 cloves garlic, crushed
> 1l (2pt) water
> 1 tsp salt
> 1 tsp dried thyme, crumbled
> 2 bay leaves
> 1/4 tsp cracked red or black pepper
> 500g (1lb) dried black-eyed peas, picked over, soaked
>   in water to cover for 1 hour and drained

In a large, heavy saucepan, heat the oil over medium heat. Add the onion and sauté until almost browned, about 5 minutes. Stir in the garlic, water, salt, thyme, bay leaves and pepper. Bring to the boil, add the drained peas and return to the boil. Cover, reduce the heat to low and cook until the peas are tender, 45 minutes to 1 hour.

Nutritional Analysis

Calories	215.35	Kcal	Protein	13.62	gm
Fat	2.44	gm	Carbohydrate	36.25	gm
Sodium	301.18	mg	Cholesterol	0.00	mg
Saturated fat	0.40	gm			

Zesty Spanish Rice

Serves: 6

> 2 tbsp olive oil
> 1 bunch fresh parsley, finely chopped

> 1 large onion, finely chopped
> 1 tbsp finely chopped garlic
> 750ml (1 1/2pt) water
> 2 tbsp tomato puree
> 250g (8oz) peeled and chopped tomatoes
> 1/8 tsp salt
> 1/8 tsp pepper
> 300g (10oz) spinach, destemmed and chopped
> 250g (8oz) white rice, washed

In a large saucepan, heat the oil over medium-high heat. Add the parsley, onion and garlic, and sauté until translucent, 3 to 4 minutes. Add the water and bring to the boil. Add the tomato puree, chopped tomatoes, salt and pepper. Mix thoroughly. Add the spinach and rice, reduce the heat to low, and cook, covered, until the liquid is absorbed and the rice is tender, about 30 minutes. Serve at once.

Nutritional Analysis

Calories	189.26	Kcal	Protein	4.14	gm
Fat	5.00	gm	Carbohydrate	32.49	gm
Sodium	122.79	mg	Cholesterol	0.00	mg
Saturated fat	0.68	gm			

Wild Rice Casserole

Serves: 6

> 1 tbsp olive oil
> 250g (8oz) chopped onions
> 250g (8oz) sliced mushrooms
> 3 celery stalks, chopped

250g (8oz) wild rice
1 tsp seasoned salt
1l (2pt) reduced-sodium, fat-free chicken stock
salt and pepper to taste

Preheat oven to 190° (325°F), gas mark 5.

In a sauté pan, heat the oil over medium heat. Add the onions and sauté until translucent, about 5 minutes. Add the mushrooms and celery, and sauté until warmed through. Transfer to a large baking dish and add the rice, seasoned salt, stock, salt and pepper. Cover the dish with foil.

Bake until the rice is tender, about 1 hour. Serve hot.

Nutritional Analysis

Calories	142.58	Kcal	Protein	6.86	gm
Fat	2.63	gm	Carbohydrate	23.54	gm
Sodium	652.11	mg	Cholesterol	0.00	mg
Saturated fat	0.34	gm			

Glazed Baby Carrots

Serves: 8

1kg (2lb) baby carrots
1 tbsp butter
2 tbsp chopped fresh herbs (dill, parsley or rosemary)
1 bunch fresh mint, finely chopped
salt and pepper to taste

Place the carrots in a heavy saucepan and add water to barely cover. Add the butter, cover and

bring to the boil. Reduce the heat to low and cook until easy to pierce with a fork, about 15 minutes.

Remove the cover, bring to the boil and boil until the liquid has evaporated and the carrots are coated with butter, about 12 to 15 minutes. Watch the carrots carefully, as they burn easily. Add the herbs, season with salt and pepper and serve.

Nutritional Analysis

Calories	63.10	Kcal	Protein	1.28	gm
Fat	1.66	gm	Carbohydrate	11.79	gm
Sodium	55.49	mg	Cholesterol	3.88	mg
Saturated fat	0.92	gm			

'Creamed' Spinach

Serves: 6

300g (10oz) fresh spinach, chopped
1 small onion, finely chopped
1 tsp olive oil
3 tbsp plain flour
310ml (10fl oz) low-fat milk
1 tsp salt
1/2 tsp pepper

Place the spinach in a heavy pan over medium heat, cover and steam, stirring occasionally, until wilted, about 5 minutes. (There is no need to add water other than what clings to the leaves from washing.) Place in a sieve and press with the back of a spoon to remove as much moisture as possible.

(continued)

In a nonstick saucepan, sauté the onion in the olive oil over medium heat until translucent, about 7 to 10 minutes. Stir in the flour until a smooth paste forms. Gradually add milk, stirring constantly. Bring just to the boil, reduce the heat to low and simmer, stirring frequently until thickened, about 10 minutes. Add the salt and pepper. Grind the spinach finely in a blender or food processor and add to the cream sauce. Serve hot.

Nutritional Analysis

Calories	60.23 Kcal	Protein	3.64 gm
Fat	1.50 gm	Carbohydrate	8.79 gm
Sodium	451.78 mg	Cholesterol	2.03 mg
Saturated fat	0.45 gm		

Potato Parsnip Purée

Serves: 6

3 parsnips, peeled and quartered, hard core cut out
2 white potatoes, peeled and quartered
1/2 onion, cut into wedges
2 cloves garlic
1l (2pt) water
salt and pepper to taste

In a saucepan, combine the parsnips, potatoes, onion and garlic. Pour in the water, cover and bring to the boil. Reduce the heat to medium and cook until all the vegetables are tender, about 20 minutes. Drain the vegetables, then purée with a handheld blender or pass through a potato masher. Season with salt and pepper and serve immediately.

Yogurt: The Secret Weapon

One of the best tips for successfully pursuing a low-fat diet is to have a container of plain low-fat yogurt in your refrigerator at all times. Just a few spoonfuls of yogurt can add creaminess and a bit of zip to nearly any recipe.

You can forget about sugared, flavoured yogurts for the most part. If you yearn for a bit of variety, however, a cup of lemon-flavoured low-fat yogurt can add flavour and a lemony tang to rice or even Indian Raita.

Nutritional Analysis

Calories	93.19	Kcal	Protein	1.87	gm
Fat	0.28	gm	Carbohydrate	20.91	gm
Sodium	10.18	mg	Cholesterol	0.00	mg
Saturated fat	0.02	gm			

Sparkling Carrots

Serves: 8

2 tbsp buttery light, reduced-fat margarine
1 small onion, chopped
750g (1lb 8oz) carrots, thinly sliced
250ml (8fl oz) lemon-lime sparkling drink
salt and pepper to taste
1 tbsp sugar

In a large saucepan, melt the margarine over medium heat. Add the onion and sauté until translucent, about 5 minutes. Add the carrots and sparkling drink, and season with salt and pepper. Add the sugar, raise the heat to high and cook until the liquid is absorbed and the carrots are slightly glazed, 8 to 10 minutes. Serve hot.

Nutritional Analysis

Calories	72.79	Kcal	Protein	1.03	gm
Fat	1.68	gm	Carbohydrate	14.60	gm
Sodium	47.34	mg	Cholesterol	0.00	mg
Saturated fat	0.39	gm			

Steamed Sweet Potatoes with Yogurt-Herb Sauce

Serves: 8

750g (1lb 8oz) sweet potatoes, peeled and sliced 6mm
    (1/4in) thick
1 tbsp buttery light, reduced-fat margarine
250g (8oz) chopped onions
1 clove garlic, crushed
3/4 tsp dried dill, crumbled
3/4 tsp paprika
1/4 tsp salt
dash of pepper
125g (4oz) plain nonfat yogurt
1 tbsp lemon juice
dried parsley flakes

Steam the sweet potatoes until just tender, 6 to 10 minutes. Transfer to a warmed serving dish and keep hot. Meanwhile, melt the margarine in a small saucepan over medium heat. Add the onions, garlic, dill, paprika, salt and pepper. Sauté until the onions are tender, 6 to 8 minutes. Remove from the heat and stir in the yogurt and lemon juice. Return to low heat and cook until heated through, about 1 minute.

Pour the yogurt sauce over the potatoes and stir to coat. Sprinkle with the parsley and serve immediately.

(continued)

Nutritional Analysis

Calories	94.45 Kcal	Protein	2.12 gm
Fat	1.67 gm	Carbohydrate	18.11 gm
Sodium	108.26 mg	Cholesterol	0.28 mg
Saturated fat	0.28 gm		

Sesame Garlic Kasha

Serves: 4

1 tbsp sesame oil
185g (6oz) kasha
1 egg, lightly beaten
430ml (14fl oz) boiling water
1 clove garlic, crushed
1 tbsp soy sauce

In a saucepan, heat the sesame oil over medium heat. Add the kasha and sauté for 5 minutes. Add the egg and stir until the egg is cooked. Pour in the boiling water, stir well and cook, uncovered, for 3 minutes. Add the garlic and soy sauce, cover and cook over low heat until kasha is tender, about 10 minutes. Remove from the heat and let stand, covered, for 5 minutes before serving.

Nutritional Analysis

Calories	184.99 Kcal	Protein	6.63 gm
Fat	5.54 gm	Carbohydrate	29.12 gm
Sodium	276.78 mg	Cholesterol	53.12 mg
Saturated fat	0.86 gm		

Orange Pilaf

Serves: 4

125g (4oz) raisins
90g (3oz) slivered blanched almonds
grated zest and juice of 1 orange
½ tbsp sesame oil
60g (2oz) bulgur
1 small onion, chopped
375ml (12fl oz) water

Combine the raisins, nuts, orange zest and orange juice in a blender. Blend for 5 seconds.

In a nonstick saucepan, heat the oil over medium heat. Add the bulgur and onion, and sauté for 3 minutes. Reduce the heat to low and add the orange mixture. Add the water. Cover and cook until the bulgur is tender, 15 to 20 minutes. Fluff with a fork before serving.

Nutritional Analysis

Calories	248.80 Kcal	Protein	6.60 gm
Fat	8.10 gm	Carbohydrate	41.75 gm
Sodium	8.90 mg	Cholesterol	0.00 mg
Saturated fat	0.88 gm		

Pesto Potatoes

Serves: 3

12 red potatoes
2 tbsp pesto, homemade or commercially prepared
salt and pepper to taste

Steam the potatoes until tender, about 15 minutes. Remove from the steamer, place in a bowl and add the pesto. Toss well, season with salt and pepper, and serve.

Nutritional Analysis

Calories	173.83 Kcal	Protein	3.89 gm
Fat	5.26 gm	Carbohydrate	28.00 gm
Sodium	84.80 mg	Cholesterol	1.66 mg
Saturated fat	0.83 gm		

Ginger Carrots

Serves: 3

60ml (2oz) distilled white vinegar
1 tbsp honey
1 tbsp water
1 tbsp soy sauce
1 tbsp peeled and grated fresh ginger
2 carrots, cut into thin strips

In a bowl, stir together the vinegar, honey, water, soy sauce and ginger. Add the carrots and toss thoroughly to coat.

Nutritional Analysis

Calories	49.07 Kcal	Protein	0.85 gm
Fat	0.10 gm	Carbohydrate	12.49 gm
Sodium	360.44 mg	Cholesterol	0.00 mg
Saturated fat	0.01 gm		

Fresh Ginger

Fresh ginger is readily available these days, and it's so tangy and tasty that I don't know why everyone isn't using it.

One of my favourite ways to use grated fresh ginger is to add it to ice cream. People aren't expecting to taste it in their dessert bowls, and they immediately discover what a great taste it gives.

Ginger is also an effective breath freshener. A former landlady of mine always chewed fresh ginger before she went out ballroom dancing – she never wanted for partners, so I guess it must have worked.

Sesame Oil

Sesame oil, which is widely available in supermarkets, is not like the big bottles of vegetable oils that line the shelves. Because sesame oil is generally used only in small amounts, it is typically available in glass bottles that hold 300g (10oz) or less.

Sesame oil is made from roasted seeds, and it has an intense nutty taste that brings out the earthy flavour of brown rice or wild rice. Indeed, whenever you want to add a nutty taste to a dish without using nuts that are rich in fats, choose sesame oil. You'll get robust flavour with a minimum of fat and calories.

Curried Cauliflower

Serves: 4

1 cauliflower, cut into florets
250g (8oz) peeled and sliced potato
1l (2pt) low-fat milk
1 tbsp butter
1 tsp salt
1 tsp curry powder
1 tsp ground cumin
2 tbsp finely chopped onion

In a large saucepan, combine the cauliflower, potato and milk. Bring to the boil, cover, reduce the heat to medium and cook until the cauliflower is tender, about 20 minutes.

Remove from the heat and, working in batches if necessary, purée in a food processor. Add the butter, salt, curry powder and cumin, mixing well. Pour into a bowl, cover and chill overnight. Adjust the seasonings before serving. Garnish with the onion.

Nutritional Analysis

Calories	184.21	Kcal	Protein	10.77	gm
Fat	5.81	gm	Carbohydrate	23.70	gm
Sodium	750.58	mg	Cholesterol	17.52	mg
Saturated Fat	3.42	gm			

Open Sesame Carrots

Serves: 6

1 tbsp sesame seeds
60ml (2fl oz) orange juice

1 tbsp peeled and grated fresh ginger
1 tsp sesame oil
1 tsp soy sauce
500g (1lb) carrots, cut into thin strips
salt and pepper to taste

In a small pan, heat the sesame seeds over medium heat, stirring occasionally until golden brown, about 1 minute. Transfer to a plate. In a small bowl, mix together the orange juice, ginger, sesame oil and soy sauce; set aside.

Steam the carrots until tender, about 5 to 8 minutes. Transfer to a bowl and add the sesame seeds and ginger mixture. Toss well, season with salt and pepper, and serve.

Nutritional Analysis

Calories	53.70 Kcal	Protein	1.16 gm
Fat	1.63 gm	Carbohydrate	9.36 gm
Sodium	84.13 mg	Cholesterol	0.00 mg
Saturated fat	0.22 gm		

Roast Potatoes with Rosemary and Garlic

Serves: 8

1kg (2lb) red potatoes, sliced
2 tbsp olive oil
3 cloves garlic, crushed
2 tsp dried rosemary
salt and pepper to taste

Preheat oven to 170°C (325°F), gas mark 3.

In a large baking dish, toss the potatoes with the oil, garlic, rosemary, salt and pepper. Bake until the potatoes are tender when pierced with a fork, about 1 hour. Serve at once.

Nutritional Analysis

Calories	124.12 Kcal	Protein	2.25 gm
Fat	3.62 gm	Carbohydrate	20.92 gm
Sodium	9.05 mg	Cholesterol	0.00 mg
Saturated fat	0.47 gm		

Buttermilk Mashed Potatoes

Serves: 12

1.5kg (3lb) potatoes, peeled and quartered
500ml (1pt) buttermilk, heated
2 tbsp butter
1 onion, chopped
pinch of ground nutmeg
salt and pepper to taste

Place the potatoes in a large saucepan with water to cover. Bring to the boil, cover, reduce the heat to medium and cook until tender, about 20 minutes. Drain, return to the pan and mash until smooth. Gradually add the buttermilk, stirring constantly. Stir in the butter, then add the onion, nutmeg, salt and pepper. Serve immediately.

Nutritional Analysis

Calories	105.94 Kcal	Protein	3.29 gm
Fat	2.36 gm	Carbohydrate	18.47 gm
Sodium	67.91 mg	Cholesterol	6.80 mg
Saturated fat	1.43 gm		

Oven-Baked Chips

Serves: 6

4 large potatoes, chipped
1 tbsp vegetable oil
½ tsp paprika
½ tsp chilli powder

Preheat oven to 220°C (475°F), gas mark 7.

In a medium bowl, toss together the potatoes, oil, paprika and chilli powder. Spread out on a baking tray. Bake, turning occasionally, until golden, about 30 minutes. Serve hot.

Nutritional Analysis

Calories	132.87 Kcal	Protein	3.35 gm
Fat	2.48 gm	Carbohydrate	25.33 gm
Sodium	12.74 mg	Cholesterol	0.00 mg
Saturated fat	0.32 gm		

Sweet Potato and Apple Purée

Serves: 12

1.5kg (3lb) sweet potatoes, peeled and cubed
2 large apples, cored, peeled and chopped
125ml (4fl oz) water
1 tbsp butter
ground nutmeg to taste
salt and pepper to taste
2 tbsp sunflower seeds, toasted

In a medium saucepan, combine the potatoes with water to cover. Cover, bring to the boil,

reduce the heat to medium and cook until tender, about 15 minutes. Drain.

Meanwhile, in a small saucepan, combine the apples with 125ml (4fl oz) water. Bring to a simmer over medium heat and cook until tender, about 5 minutes. Transfer the potatoes and undrained apples to a food processor and purée until smooth. Transfer to a warmed serving bowl. Add the butter, nutmeg, salt and pepper, and stir to mix and melt the butter. Sprinkle with the sunflower seeds and serve.

Nutritional Analysis

Calories	114.97 Kcal	Protein	1.72 gm
Fat	1.99 gm	Carbohydrate	23.28 gm
Sodium	20.41 mg	Cholesterol	2.58 mg
Saturated fat	0.71 gm		

Macaroni Cheese

Serves: 8

500g (1lb) macaroni
1 onion, chopped
500ml (1pt) low-fat milk
2 tbsp cornflour
1 tsp dry mustard
250g (8oz) grated fat-free cheddar cheese
250g (8oz) grated low-fat mozzarella cheese
salt and pepper to taste
125g (4oz) seasoned dried breadcrumbs
2 tbsp grated Parmesan cheese
1 tbsp butter, melted

In a large pot, bring water to the boil. Add the macaroni and cook for 5 minutes. Add the onion and cook for another 5 minutes, or until the macaroni is nearly al dente. Drain and set aside.

Preheat oven to 180° (350°F), gas mark 4.

In a large saucepan, combine the milk, cornflour and mustard, stirring to dissolve the cornflour and mustard. Place over medium heat and cook, stirring, until thickened. Add the cheddar and mozzarella cheeses and cook, stirring, until the cheeses melt. Add the cooked macaroni, and season with salt and pepper. Pour into a 230 x 330mm (9 x 13in) baking dish. In a small bowl, stir together the breadcrumbs, Parmesan cheese and butter. Scatter over the macaroni. Bake until bubbling, about 20 minutes. Serve hot.

Nutritional Analysis

Calories	244.24 Kcal	Protein	15.67 gm
Fat	5.40 gm	Carbohydrate	32.90 gm
Sodium	440.90 mg	Cholesterol	17.02 mg
Saturated fat	3.06 gm		

Tomato Potatoes

Serves: 8

1 tbsp olive oil
1 tsp butter
2 onions, chopped
6 cloves garlic, crushed
1kg (2lb) tinned tomatoes, well drained and diced
salt and pepper to taste
2 tbsp finely chopped fresh parsley

1 tsp dried basil, crumbled
1 tsp dried oregano, crumbled
1.25kg (2lb 8oz) maris piper potatoes, thinly sliced
125g (4oz) grated Parmesan cheese

Preheat oven to 170°C (325°F), gas mark 3. Spray a large baking dish with nonstick cooking spray.

In a frying pan, heat the oil and the butter over medium heat. Add the onions and garlic, and sauté for 1 minute. Cover, reduce the heat to low and cook until the onions are translucent, about 5 minutes. Remove from the heat and add the tomatoes, salt, pepper, parsley, basil and oregano. Mix well.

Spread a third of the onion mixture in the prepared dish. Spread half the sliced potatoes on top. Sprinkle salt and pepper and 60g (2oz) of the Parmesan over the potatoes. Repeat the layers. Top with the remaining onion mixture. Cover with foil.

Bake for 1¼ hours. Uncover and continue to bake until the potatoes are tender, about 30 minutes longer. Serve hot.

Nutritional Analysis

Calories	205.27 Kcal	Protein	6.56 gm
Fat	4.80 gm	Carbohydrate	35.30 gm
Sodium	312.97 mg	Cholesterol	5.24 mg
Saturated fat	1.64 gm		

Spicy Sweet Potato Salad

Serves: 8

1kg (2lb) sweet potatoes
1 small onion, chopped
2 celery stalks, finely chopped
125g (4oz) chopped fresh parsley
1 tbsp olive oil
2 tbsp lemon juice
1 tsp soy sauce
pepper to taste

In a saucepan, combine the sweet potatoes with water to cover. Cover, bring to the boil, reduce the heat to medium and cook until tender, 30 to 40 minutes. Drain and let cool.

Peel and dice the sweet potatoes and place in a large bowl. Add the onion, celery and parsley, and stir to mix. In a small bowl, whisk together the olive oil, lemon juice, soy sauce and pepper to form a dressing. Add the dressing to the potato mixture, toss gently and serve warm.

Nutritional Analysis

Calories	110.10 Kcal	Protein	1.69 gm
Fat	1.97 gm	Carbohydrate	21.97 gm
Sodium	64.93 mg	Cholesterol	0.00 mg
Saturated fat	0.26 gm		

Spring Onion Tabbouleh

Serves: 8

250g (8oz) bulgur
500ml (1pt) boiling water

125g (4oz) chopped fresh parsley
185g (6oz) raisins
250g (8oz) chopped spring onions
80ml (2½fl oz) lime juice
2 tbsp olive oil
salt and pepper to taste

In a medium bowl, mix together the bulgur and boiling water. Allow to stand for up to 1 hour, or until tender. Drain the bulgur in a colander to remove excess moisture, then transfer to a serving bowl. Add the parsley, raisins and spring onions. Toss to mix well. In a small bowl, stir together the lime juice, oil, salt and pepper. Add to the bulgur mixture, toss well and serve.

Nutritional Analysis

Calories	133.48 Kcal	Protein	2.86 gm
Fat	3.70 gm	Carbohydrate	24.71 gm
Sodium	9.50 mg	Cholesterol	0.00 mg
Saturated fat	0.50 gm		

Dilled Summer Green Beans

Serves: 6

500g (1lb) green beans
3 cloves garlic, crushed
12 fresh dill sprigs, chopped
1 tsp red pepper flakes
½ tsp dry mustard
250ml (8fl oz) cider vinegar
250ml (8fl oz) water
2 tbsp sugar
½ tsp salt

Steam the beans until tender, about 5 minutes, then immediately plunge in cold water to cool. Drain.

Place beans in a bowl. Add the garlic, dill, red pepper flakes and mustard. Combine the vinegar, water, sugar and salt in a small saucepan, bring to the boil and then reduce the heat. Pour the hot marinade over the beans and let cool. Cover and chill overnight before serving.

Eyes on the Potato

Whenever you cook potatoes, try not to peel them if there is a choice. Potato skins can add a nice crunch to the overall texture of a dish, and in addition they carry valuable dietary fibre and vitamins.

If you're in a hurry and need precooked potato chunks for a recipe, cut them into thin slices. They'll cook faster than larger pieces.

Nutritional Analysis

Calories	48.85 Kcal	Protein	1.56 gm
Fat	0.21 gm	Carbohydrate	12.51 gm
Sodium	199.92 mg	Cholesterol	0.00 mg
Saturated fat	0.01 gm		

Baked Butter Bean Casserole

Serves: 6

1 tbsp olive oil
1 onion, chopped
1 large apple, peeled, cored and chopped
185g (6oz) tomato puree
1/2 tsp dry mustard
3 tbsp red wine vinegar
1 tsp dried oregano, crumbled
3 tbsp honey
300g (10oz) tinned butter beans, drained

Preheat oven to 180°C (350°F), gas mark 4. Spray a medium baking dish with nonstick cooking spray.

(continued)

Don't Forget the Herbs

When preparing side dishes, don't forget fresh herbs and spices. Use fresh herbs whenever possible, and use a mortar and pestle to grind them for the freshest and fullest flavour. Add dried herbs such as ginger, thyme, rosemary and marjoram to dishes for a stronger taste, but use them sparingly. You can also add, for example, chives, garlic, ginger, dill, onion, pimiento or saffron for mouth-watering potatoes.

In a frying pan, heat the oil over medium heat. Add the onion and apple, and sauté until the onion is translucent, about 5 minutes. Transfer to the prepared dish and add all the remaining ingredients, mixing well. Cover with tinfoil. Bake until beans are tender, about 30 minutes. Serve hot.

Nutritional Analysis

Calories	154.35 Kcal	Protein	4.52 gm
Fat	3.00 gm	Carbohydrate	29.92 gm
Sodium	252.67 mg	Cholesterol	0.00 mg
Saturated fat	0.37 gm		

Baked Sweet Potatoes with Lime

Serves: 6

6 sweet potatoes
juice of 1 to 2 limes, to taste

Preheat oven to 180°C (350°F), gas mark 4.

Prick the sweet potatoes with a fork. Place on a baking tray and bake until tender when pierced with a fork, about 45 minutes. Remove from the oven and slice in half lengthways almost all the way through. Sprinkle with the lime juice. Cover and chill overnight.

To serve, reheat in a 180°C (350°F), gas mark 4 oven for 30 minutes.

Nutritional Analysis

Calories	173.68 Kcal	Protein	2.72 gm
Fat	0.49 gm	Carbohydrate	40.37 gm
Sodium	21.31 mg	Cholesterol	0.00 mg
Saturated fat	0.09 gm		

Pasta Dishes

CHAPTER SEVEN

Amount Per Chapter
41 Recipes

	% Daily Value
Easy to Prepare	**100%**
Low Fat/High Flavour	**100%**
Simple to Understand	**100%**

DELICIOUS, EASY, LOW-FAT RECIPES

Conventional wisdom tells us that pasta is a natural low-fat food – the fat is in the sauce. For once, conventional wisdom is right – a 60g (2oz) portion, the recommended serving size, has only 211 calories and 1 gram of fat. Even if 125g (4oz) is a more realistic helping, pasta is a calorie and fat bargain. To keep sauces in the same category needs some care. But with a few common-sense techniques, sauces can be kept low-fat without sacrificing taste and texture.

It is also good to remember that the pasta itself is delicious – nutty, chewy and pleasantly filling. Digging into a hot dish of noodles with just a touch of olive oil, salt and garlic is so satisfying that forgoing more fattening ingredients really isn't difficult at all.

Penne with Chicken, Broccoli and Rosemary

Serves: 4

1 tbsp olive oil
1 clove garlic, crushed
2 shallots, finely chopped
½ tsp dried rosemary, crumbled
185 (6oz) skinless chicken breast meat, cut into bite-sized strips
500g (1lb) broccoli florets, separated into bite-sized pieces
125ml (4fl oz) reduced-sodium, fat-free chicken stock
60ml (2fl oz) dry white wine
2 tbsp fresh parsley, chopped
250g (8oz) penne
salt and pepper to taste
2 tbsp grated Parmesan cheese

In a large, deep pan, heat the oil over medium heat. Add the garlic, shallots and rosemary, and cook for 1 minute. Add the chicken and sauté, tossing well, until lightly browned, about 3 minutes. Add the broccoli, stock, wine and parsley. Simmer to heat through.

Meanwhile, cook the penne in boiling salted water until al dente. Drain.

Add the penne to the skillet with the chicken. Raise the heat to high and boil, stirring, until the liquid reduces enough to glaze the pasta lightly. Season with salt and pepper. Transfer to a warmed platter, sprinkle with the Parmesan and serve.

Nutritional Analysis

Calories	382.67 Kcal	Protein	30.69 gm
Fat	6.43 gm	Carbohydrate	47.03 gm
Sodium	496.50 mg	Cholesterol	51.34 mg
Saturated fat	1.38 gm		

Summer Vegetable Spaghetti

Serves: 8

500g (1lb) small onions, cut into eighths
500g (1lb) peeled and chopped tomatoes
250g (8oz) thinly sliced yellow courgettes
250g (8oz) thinly sliced green courgettes
375g (12oz) green beans, cut in 12mm (1/2in) lengths
180ml (6fl oz) water
2 tbsp finely chopped fresh parsley
1 clove garlic, crushed
1/2 tsp chilli powder
1/4 tsp salt
1/8 tsp pepper
185g (6z) tomato puree
500g (1lb) spaghetti
125g (4oz) grated Parmesan cheese

In a large saucepan, combine all the ingredients except the tomato puree, spaghetti and cheese. Place over low heat and cook, stirring frequently, for 10 minutes, then stir in the tomato puree. Cover and cook gently, stirring occasionally, until the vegetables are tender, about 15 minutes. Meanwhile, cook the spaghetti in boiling unsalted water until al dente. Drain and place in a large bowl. Spoon the sauce over the spaghetti and then sprinkle the Parmesan over the top. Serve immediately.

Nutritional Analysis

Calories	289.00 Kcal	Protein	11.71 gm
Fat	2.86 gm	Carbohydrate	54.96 gm
Sodium	539.61 mg	Cholesterol	3.95 mg
Saturated fat	1.13 gm		

Broccoli-Pasta Toss

Serves: 6

500g (1lb) broccoli florets
125g (4oz) eggless fettuccine, broken up
1 tbsp olive oil
3 tbsp grated Parmesan cheese
1 tsp sesame seeds, toasted
1/8 tsp garlic powder
pepper to taste

In a large saucepan, cook the broccoli and pasta in boiling salted water until the pasta is al dente, stirring once or twice. Drain and place in a bowl.

Add the oil to the pasta mixture and toss well. Add the cheese, sesame seeds, garlic powder and pepper. Toss gently to coat. Serve immediately.

Nutritional Analysis

Calories	117.84 Kcal	Protein	4.98 gm
Fat	3.76 gm	Carbohydrate	16.53 gm
Sodium	130.94 mg	Cholesterol	1.97 mg
Saturated fat	0.87 gm		

Those Pasta Names!

Ruote! Radiatori! Capellini!

You don't need a degree in Italian to tell the different types of pasta apart in the supermarket, and serving these more unusual shapes is a great way to liven up a dish of pasta – in addition to using garlic, that is. Learn by studying the packets, and have some fun when you tell your family you're serving little radiators (radiatori), angel hair (capellini) or wagon wheels (ruote).

Stuffed Pasta Triangles

Serves: 8

Pasta Triangles:
4 eggs
2 tsp oil
1/2 tsp salt
500g (1lb) 00-type flour

Tomato Sauce:
2 tbsp olive oil
1 medium onion, finely chopped
5 cloves garlic, crushed
875g (1lb 12oz) tinned plum tomatoes, undrained
8 fresh basil sprigs
2 tsp salt
pepper to taste
1 tbsp sugar

Filling:
750g (1lb 8oz) part-skimmed ricotta cheese
375g (12oz) spinach, cooked, chopped and well drained
1 tsp ground nutmeg
4 eggs, lightly beaten
60ml (2oz) grated Parmesan cheese
salt and pepper to taste

1 tbsp olive oil
2 tbsp grated Parmesan cheese

To make the pasta, combine the eggs, oil and salt in a large bowl and whisk until well blended. Add the flour, a little at a time, beating after each addition. Turn out onto a well-floured work surface

and knead for several minutes until the dough is firm and smooth but not dry. Add more flour if necessary to reduce stickiness. Cover and let stand at slightly warm temperature for about 30 minutes to ripen.

Cut the dough into 50mm (2in) portions. Flatten each portion slightly with a rolling pin so it will fit easily into the pasta machine. Working with one portion at a time and with the pasta machine set at its widest setting, roll the dough through the machine. Continue rolling out the dough while gradually narrowing the setting on the machine until the dough has passed through the next-to-finest setting. The pasta will be very thin (expansion takes place during cooking). Place on a floured work surface and sprinkle lightly with flour. Repeat until all the dough is rolled out into strips. Cut the strips into 100mm (4in) squares and let rest for 10 minutes before cooking and filling.

To make the sauce, in a large pan, heat the oil over medium-high heat. Add the onion and garlic and sauté until golden, about 5 minutes. Add the undrained tomatoes, basil, salt and pepper. Bring to the boil and simmer about 15 minutes. Add the sugar at the last minute.

To make the filling, in a bowl, combine the ricotta cheese, spinach, nutmeg, eggs and Parmesan and mix well. Season with salt and pepper.

Preheat oven to 200°C (400°F), gas mark 6.

Bring a large pot of generously salted water to a boil. Add 1 tablespoon oil. Drop the plain pasta squares, a few at a time, into the boiling water and cook just until they float to the surface, 3 to 4 minutes. Remove at once and plunge into a bowl filled with iced water; let stand for 1 minute. Transfer the squares to a clean kitchen towel to prevent sticking. Place 1 tablespoon filling in the centre of each pasta square. Fold the square into a triangle, then again into a smaller triangle. Press the edges together to seal.

Spoon a layer of the tomato sauce into a large baking dish. Arrange the pasta triangles on the sauce in rows, slightly overlapping them. Cover with the remaining sauce and sprinkle with additional Parmesan cheese.

Bake, uncovered, until the cheese is lightly browned, 5 to 7 minutes. Serve hot.

 Nutritional Analysis

Calories	397.20	Kcal	Protein	25.90	gm
Fat	13.13	gm	Carbohydrate	40.45	gm
Sodium	1453.00	mg	Cholesterol	215.45	mg
Saturated fat	3.22	gm			

Pasta Shells with Courgettes
Serves: 4

2 tsp butter
1 clove garlic, crushed
4 courgettes, sliced
1 tsp dried rosemary, crumbled
salt and pepper to taste
500g (1lb) large pasta shells
2 tbsp chopped fresh parsley
90g (3oz) grated Parmesan cheese

(continued)

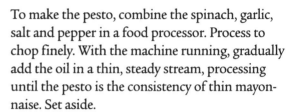

In a large frying pan or shallow saucepan, melt the butter over medium heat. Add the garlic and courgettes and cook until crisp-tender, about 5 to 7 minutes. Add the rosemary and season with salt and pepper. Raise the heat and cook for a few minutes to blend. Remove from the heat.

Meanwhile, cook the pasta in boiling salted water until al dente. Drain thoroughly and add to the courgette mixture. Return the pan to the heat and toss until the shells are well coated with sauce, 2 to 3 minutes. Add the parsley and cheese, and toss again. Serve at once.

Nutritional Analysis

Calories	494.58 Kcal	Protein	19.32 gm
Fat	5.95 gm	Carbohydrate	90.47 gm
Sodium	544.04 mg	Cholesterol	10.39 mg
Saturated fat	2.77 gm		

Corkscrew Pasta with Spinach Pesto

Serves: 4

Pesto:
300g (10oz) spinach, destemmed
4 cloves garlic, cut
salt and pepper to taste
2 tbsp olive oil

Pasta:
500g (1lb) corkscrew pasta
125g (4fl oz) low-fat mayonnaise
2 tbsp olive oil
2 tbsp pine nuts
diced pimiento

To make the pesto, combine the spinach, garlic, salt and pepper in a food processor. Process to chop finely. With the machine running, gradually add the oil in a thin, steady stream, processing until the pesto is the consistency of thin mayonnaise. Set aside.

Cook the pasta in boiling salted water until al dente. Drain, then transfer to a large bowl. Add the mayonnaise and olive oil. Mix well. Add the pesto, and stir and toss until well mixed. Cover and chill before serving. Garnish with the pine nuts and pimiento.

Nutritional Analysis

Calories	630.66 Kcal	Protein	17.28 gm
Fat	19.75 gm	Carbohydrate	96.47 gm
Sodium	717.36 mg	Cholesterol	0.00 mg
Saturated fat	2.46 gm		

California Fettuccine

Serves: 4

250g (8oz) eggless fettuccine
1/2 avocado, pitted, peeled and cut into
*   chunks*
250g (8oz) tinned marinated artichoke hearts,
*   drained*
1 large tomato, diced
2 cloves garlic, crushed
1 tbsp olive oil
2 spring onions, thinly sliced
250g (8oz) cooked prawns
2 tbsp grated Parmesan cheese

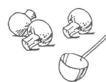

Cook the fettuccine in boiling salted water until al dente. Drain and place in a bowl. Add all the remaining ingredients except the Parmesan cheese, and toss well. Serve warm or chilled. Top with the Parmesan just before serving.

Variations: Chopped fresh basil or coriander or toasted sesame seeds are nice additions to this dish.

Nutritional Analysis

Calories	418.93 Kcal	Protein	22.69 gm
Fat	13.98 gm	Carbohydrate	52.41 gm
Sodium	672.48 mg	Cholesterol	112.63 mg
Saturated fat	2.42 gm		

Italian-Style Pistachio Pasta

Serves: 4

1 tbsp butter or buttery light, reduced-fat margarine
1 onion, cut into thin wedges
60g (2oz) finely diced green pepper
60g (2oz) finely diced yellow pepper
60g (2oz) finely diced red pepper
2 tbsp crushed garlic
125g (4oz) prosciutto, sliced 3mm (1/8in) thick and then diced
250g (8oz) pistachios, coarsely chopped
1 1/2 tsp dried rosemary, crumbled
3 tbsp extra-virgin olive oil
500g (1lb) penne

In a frying pan, melt the butter or margarine over low heat. Add the onion and sauté until nearly

tender. Add all the peppers, garlic, prosciutto, pistachios, rosemary and olive oil. Continue to cook, stirring, until thoroughly heated.

Meanwhile, cook the penne in boiling salted water until al dente. Drain and place in a bowl. Spoon the hot sauce over the top and serve.

Nutritional Analysis

Calories	816.16 Kcal	Protein	30.08 gm
Fat	34.81 gm	Carbohydrate	99.47 gm
Sodium	953.85 mg	Cholesterol	30.78 mg
Saturated fat	6.54 gm		

Savoury Pastitsio

Serves: 10

1 tsp olive oil
1 large onion, finely chopped
750g (1lb 8oz) lean minced beef or minced turkey
250ml (8fl oz) water
180ml (6fl oz) dry white wine
185g (6oz) tomato puree
125g (4oz) bulgur
3/4 tsp cinnamon
3/4 tsp nutmeg
3/4 tsp allspice
1 1/2 tsp salt, plus more to taste
1/2 tsp black pepper, plus more to taste
500g (1lb) low-fat cottage cheese
2 tbsp plain flour
250ml (8fl oz) reduced-sodium, fat-free chicken stock
375ml (12fl oz) evaporated skim milk
185g (6oz) plus 2 tbsp freshly grated Parmesan cheese

(continued)

500g (1lb) macaroni
1 tsp olive oil
2 tbsp chopped fresh parsley (optional)

In a large nonstick frying pan, heat oil over medium heat; add onion and sauté until softened, about 5 minutes. Add minced meat and cook, breaking it up with a wooden spoon, until no longer pink, about 5 minutes. Drain off fat. Add water, wine, tomato puree, bulgur, spices, 1 teaspoon of the salt and $1/2$ teaspoon of the pepper. Simmer, uncovered, over low heat, stirring occasionally, until the bulgur is tender, about 20 minutes. Taste and adjust seasonings.

In a food processor or blender, purée the cottage cheese until completely smooth. Set aside. In a small bowl, stir together flour and 60ml (2fl oz) cold chicken stock until smooth. In a medium-sized heavy saucepan, combine evaporated skim milk and the remaining chicken stock. Heat over medium heat until scalding. Stir the flour mixture into the hot milk mixture and cook, stirring constantly, until thickened, about 2 minutes. Remove from the heat and whisk in the puréed cottage cheese and 90g (3oz) of grated cheese. Season with salt and a generous grinding of pepper to taste. To prevent a skin from forming, place greaseproof paper or cling film directly over the surface and set aside.

In a large pot of boiling salted water, cook the macaroni until al dente, 8 to 10 minutes. Drain and return to the pot. Toss with 90g (3oz) of the grated cheese, oil and $1/2$ teaspoon of the salt.

Preheat oven to 180° (350°F), gas mark 4. Spray a 230 x 330mm (9 x 13in) baking dish with nonstick cooking spray. Spread half of the pasta mixture over the bottom of the prepared dish. Top with a third of the cream sauce. Spoon all the meat sauce over, spreading evenly. Cover with another third of the cream sauce. Top with the remaining pasta mixture and cover with the remaining cream sauce. Sprinkle with the remaining 2 tablespoons of grated cheese. Bake for 40 to 50 minutes, or until bubbling and golden. Sprinkle with parsley, if using, and serve.

Nutritional Analysis

Calories	470.06 Kcal	Protein	31.98 gm
Fat	14.49 gm	Carbohydrate	51.94 gm
Sodium	1086.83 mg	Cholesterol	51.28 mg
Saturated fat	5.91 gm		

Pasta with Sautéed Artichokes

Serves: 1

1 artichoke
1 lemon, halved
2 tbsp olive oil
250g (8oz) sliced mushrooms
2 tbsp dry white wine
60g (2oz) thinly sliced spring onions
$1/2$ tsp dried basil, crumbled

salt to taste
125g (4oz) pasta of your choice
1 tbsp grated Parmesan cheese
cracked pepper to taste

Bend back the outer leaves of the artichoke until they snap off easily near base. Edible portions of the leaf should remain on the artichoke base or heart. Continue to snap off and discard the thick, dark leaves until a central core of pale green leaves is reached. Cut off the top 50mm (2in) of artichoke; discard. Cut off the stem; reserve. Using a paring knife, trim the dark green outer layer from the artichoke bottom and the stem. Rub all cut surfaces with a lemon half to prevent discolouring. Quarter the artichoke lengthways. Scoop or cut out the prickly centre petals and discard. Rub again with a lemon half. Cut the artichoke and stem lengthways into very thin slices.

In a large frying pan, heat the oil over medium heat. Add the artichoke and mushrooms and sauté for 2 minutes. Add the wine, spring onions and basil; cover and simmer until the liquid has evaporated and the artichokes are tender, about 5 minutes. Season with salt. Cook the pasta in boiling salted water until al dente. Drain and place in a bowl. Spoon the sauce over the pasta and sprinkle with Parmesan and pepper.

Nutritional Analysis

Calories	790.78 Kcal	Protein	22.78 gm
Fat	30.83 gm	Carbohydrate	104.37 gm
Sodium	617.49 mg	Cholesterol	3.95 mg
Saturated fat	4.94 gm		

Fusilli with Chicken and Coriander Pesto

Serves: 4

2 whole chicken breasts, halved
90g (3oz) fresh coriander
4 cloves garlic, cut
125g (4oz) slivered blanched almonds
4 chilli peppers, seeded
2 tbsp olive oil
250ml (8fl oz) low-fat mayonnaise
500g (1lb) fusilli, cooked, drained and chilled

Preheat oven to 190° (375°F), gas mark 5.

Place the chicken breasts in a baking pan. Bake until cooked through and tender, 15 to 20 minutes. Remove from the oven and let cool. Remove and discard the skin and bones, and mince the meat. Place in a bowl, cover and chill.

In a food processor or blender, combine the coriander, garlic, almonds and chillies. Process until finely chopped. With the motor running, add the oil in a thin, steady stream, processing until the pesto is the consistency of a thick paste. Place the pesto in a bowl, then whisk in the mayonnaise.

In a large bowl, combine the chilled pasta, minced chicken and pesto. Stir to mix well. Cover and chill for 1 hour before serving.

Nutritional Analysis

Calories	833.08 Kcal	Protein	45.44 gm
Fat	24.60 gm	Carbohydrate	106.10 gm
Sodium	1027.79 mg	Cholesterol	73.10 mg
Saturated fat	2.87 gm		

Pasta Salad Niçoise

Serves: 4

> 60ml (2fl oz) low-fat Italian dressing
> chopped fresh basil
> 2 cloves crushed garlic
> 1/4 tsp red pepper flakes
> 500g (1lb) small shell pasta, cooked, drained and
> chilled
> 185g (6oz) tinned water-packed albacore tuna,
> drained and flaked
> 185g (6oz) diced tomato
> 1/2 avocado, peeled and diced
> 60g (2oz) thinly sliced red onion
> 2 tbsp chopped black olives
> 4 lettuce leaves

In a small bowl, stir together the dressing, basil, garlic and red pepper flakes to form a dressing. In a large bowl, combine the pasta, tuna, tomato, avocado, red onion and olives. Add dressing and toss well. Line 4 plates with the lettuce leaves. Spoon the pasta mixture on the lettuce, dividing evenly. Serve at once.

Nutritional Analysis

Calories	236.73 Kcal	Protein	14.57 gm
Fat	5.82 gm	Carbohydrate	22.94 gm
Sodium	370.63 mg	Cholesterol	16.61 mg
Saturated fat	0.97 gm		

Pistachio Pasta Salad Florentine

Serves: 4

> 375g (12oz) frozen peas
> 60g (2oz) small tubular pasta
> 2 tbsp honey
> 2 1/2 tbsp Dijon mustard
> 3 tbsp red wine vinegar
> 1 egg white
> 1 1/2 tsp dried oregano, crumbled
> 1/2 tsp garlic powder
> 500g (1lb) spinach leaves, torn
> 500g (1lb) halved cherry tomatoes
> 125g (4oz) pistachio nuts

Place the peas in a sieve and rinse with running hot water to thaw; drain well and set aside. Cook the pasta in boiling salted water until al dente.

Meanwhile, in a small bowl, stir together the honey, mustard, vinegar, egg white, oregano and garlic powder to form a dressing.

When the pasta is ready, drain and place in a bowl. Add the spinach, tomatoes, peas, pistachios and dressing. Toss well and serve warm.

Nutritional Analysis

Calories	358.43 Kcal	Protein	13.76 gm
Fat	8.90 gm	Carbohydrate	56.20 gm
Sodium	475.65 mg	Cholesterol	0.00 mg
Saturated fat	1.14 gm		

Jumbo Shells Stuffed with Cheese

Serves: 6

12 jumbo pasta shells
2 tbsp grated Parmesan cheese
¼ tsp chilli powder
375g (12oz) low-fat cheddar cheese, grated
2 cloves garlic, crushed
1 tbsp chopped fresh parsley
60ml (2fl oz) low-fat sour cream
60g (2oz) chopped black olives

Cook the pasta shells in a large pot of boiling salted water until al dente. Drain into a colander and let stand for at least 10 minutes, or until completely drained. (Shells may be prepared in advance and stored in a covered container in the refrigerator.)

In a shallow bowl, mix together the Parmesan cheese and chilli powder. Roll the pasta shells in the mixture. In a mixing bowl, combine the cheddar cheese, garlic, parsley, sour cream and olives. Mix well. Stuff the shells with the cheese mixture. The shells can be eaten as they are, or you can bake them. To do the latter, preheat an oven to 200°C (400°F), gas mark 6. Arrange the shells on a baking tray, propping their open ends up with crumpled tinfoil so the filling won't run out during baking. Bake until the cheese is melted, 8 to 10 minutes. Serve hot.

Nutritional Analysis

Calories	154.37 Kcal	Protein	13.95 gm
Fat	2.11 gm	Carbohydrate	20.58 gm
Sodium	378.06 mg	Cholesterol	7.64 mg
Saturated fat	0.93 gm		

A Pasta Fallacy

It seems that nearly every pasta recipe I see – whether it's on the side of a pasta package or in another cookbook – instructs the cook to add up to a tablespoon of oil to the pasta cooking water to prevent the pasta strands from sticking together.

I conducted an experiment in which I cooked two pots of pasta side by side, using the same amount of pasta and water in each pot and adding the oil to only one of the pots. I did not notice any difference between the two. If you've been cooking your pasta with oil in the water, I therefore think it's safe to say that you can cut down on the fat in your pasta dishes by eliminating the oil.

Garden Pasta

Serves: 6

> 5 tomatoes, peeled and chopped
> 2 carrots, chopped
> 2 celery stalks, chopped
> 1 medium onion, chopped
> 8 spring onions, chopped
> 1 tsp dried basil, crumbled
> 1/2 tsp salt
> 1/2 tsp dried oregano, crumbled
> 1/4 tsp garlic powder
> 1/2 tsp pepper
> 1 tbsp olive oil
> 500g (1lb) spaghetti

In a large saucepan, combine the tomatoes, carrots, celery, onions and spring onions. Cover tightly and cook over medium heat, stirring occasionally, for 10 minutes. Add the basil, salt, oregano, garlic powder and pepper. Cover and cook over medium-low heat for 5 minutes. Add the oil and simmer until the carrots are tender, about 30 minutes.

Meanwhile, cook the spaghetti in boiling salted water until al dente. Drain and place in a bowl. Add the sauce and toss well, then serve.

Nutritional Analysis

Calories	351.98 Kcal	Protein	11.53 gm
Fat	3.89 gm	Carbohydrate	68.13 gm
Sodium	489.33 mg	Cholesterol	0.00 mg
Saturated fat	0.52 gm		

Linguine Stir-Fry with Asparagus and Garlic

Serves: 4

> 500g (1lb) linguine
> 2 tbsp olive oil
> 500g (1lb) skinless chicken breast meat, slivered
> 500g (1lb) asparagus, trimmed and cut on the diagonal into 25mm (1in) lengths
> 2 red peppers, diced
> 4 cloves garlic, crushed
> 60ml (2fl oz) teriyaki sauce
> 250ml (8fl oz) reduced-sodium, fat-free chicken stock

Cook the linguine in boiling salted water until it is al dente.

Once the water is put on to boil, in a wok or large, deep frying pan, heat 1 tablespoon of the oil over high heat. Add the chicken and stir-fry until firm and cooked through, about 4 minutes. Remove the chicken and set aside. Add the remaining tablespoon of oil to the pan. When it is hot, add the asparagus and pepper and stir-fry until crisp-tender, about 5 minutes. Add the garlic and stir-fry for 30 seconds. Stir in the teriyaki sauce and the stock.

As the pasta finishes cooking, return the chicken to the wok and heat through. Drain the pasta, and toss with the chicken and sauce. Transfer to a warmed platter and serve at once.

Nutritional Analysis

Calories	658.90 Kcal	Protein	45.79 gm
Fat	10.21 gm	Carbohydrate	94.35 gm
Sodium	1302.60 mg	Cholesterol	65.83 mg
Saturated fat	1.58 gm		

Curried Tonnarelli and Vegetables

Serves: 4

1 tbsp vegetable or peanut oil
1 small onion, diced
6 spring onions, thinly sliced
1 tbsp chopped garlic
1 jalapeño pepper, seeded, if desired, and finely chopped
1 tbsp curry powder, or to taste
1 large tomato, cut into 12mm (1/2in) cubes
1 tbsp soy sauce
125g (4oz) grated carrots
125g (4oz) diced courgette
125g (4oz) broccoli florets
125g (4oz) shelled peas
375g (12oz) tonnarelli or penne pasta
2 tbsp honey
125g (4oz) raisins

In a large frying pan, heat the oil over medium heat. Add the onion, spring onions, garlic and jalapeño pepper, and sauté until the onion is wilted and begins to brown, about 4 minutes. Stir in the curry powder and cook for 1 minute. Add the tomato and soy sauce, reduce the heat to low and cook until the tomato begins to give off liquid, about 12 to 15 minutes. Stir in the carrots, courgette, broccoli and peas, and cook until crisp-tender, 3 to 5 minutes. Remove from heat.

Meanwhile, cook the pasta in boiling salted water until al dente. Just before it is ready to drain, scoop out 60ml (2fl oz) of the cooking water and stir it into the curry mixture. Return the pan to low heat and cook until heated through.

Drain the pasta and transfer to a warmed bowl. Add the curry mixture and stir well to coat with the sauce. Fold in the honey and raisins and serve at once.

Nutritional Analysis

Calories	502.66 Kcal	Protein	15.17 gm
Fat	5.46 gm	Carbohydrate	101.11 gm
Sodium	580.53 mg	Cholesterol	0.00 mg
Saturated fat	0.82 gm		

Pasta with Yellow Courgette and Roasted Garlic

Serves: 4

8 cloves garlic
1/2 tsp dried thyme, crumbled
1/2 tsp dried basil, crumbled
2 tbsp olive oil
500g (1lb) rotini or fusilli
3 yellow courgettes, coarsely grated
salt and pepper to taste

Preheat oven to 230° (450°F), gas mark 8. Place the whole garlic cloves in the centre of a large piece of tinfoil. Sprinkle with the thyme and basil. Pour the oil over the garlic and herbs. Fold the tinfoil to form a well-sealed packet and place in the centre of the oven. Bake until the garlic is soft, 20 to 30 minutes.

Meanwhile, cook the pasta in boiling salted water until al dente. About 2 minutes before it is ready, add the courgette to the pasta cooking water. When the pasta is ready, scoop out 125ml (4fl oz) of the cooking water. Drain the pasta and courgette, and place in a warmed bowl.

(continued)

Open the tinfoil and, in a small bowl, mash the garlic lightly with a spoon. Add up to 125ml (4fl oz) of the reserved pasta water and stir to form a thick, slightly liquid sauce. Pour over the pasta and courgette, toss well, season with salt and pepper, and serve immediately.

Nutritional Analysis

Calories	514.87 Kcal	Protein	16.10 gm
Fat	8.88 gm	Carbohydrate	92.12 gm
Sodium	399.24 mg	Cholesterol	0.00 mg
Saturated fat	1.23 gm		

Capellini with Super Low-Fat Tomato Sauce

Serves: 4

875g (1lb 12oz) tinned plum tomatoes, undrained
125g (4oz) diced onion
2 cloves garlic, finely chopped
1 tsp dried basil, crumbled
1 tsp dried parsley, crumbled
1 tsp dried oregano, crumbled
¹/₄ to ¹/₂ tsp red pepper flakes
salt to taste
500g (1lb) capellini

In a medium-large saucepan, combine the tomatoes, onion, garlic, basil, parsley, oregano and red pepper flakes. Bring to the boil, reduce the heat to medium and simmer until the liquid is reduced by half, 10 to 20 minutes. Season with salt. In a food processor or blender, purée the sauce, in batches, to the desired consistency. Use quick on-off pulses for

a chunky sauce, and a steady action for a smoother sauce. Reheat to serving temperature, if necessary.

Meanwhile, cook the pasta in boiling salted water until al dente. Drain and transfer to a warmed bowl. Toss with the sauce and serve.

Nutritional Analysis

Calories	473.28 Kcal	Protein	16.77 gm
Fat	2.35 gm	Carbohydrate	96.05 gm
Sodium	720.17 mg	Cholesterol	0.00 mg
Saturated fat	0.33 gm		

Southwestern Radiatore

Serves: 4

3 medium tomatoes, minced
3 spring onions, thinly sliced
125ml (4fl oz) lime juice
1 tsp salt
2 tsp olive oil
2 cloves garlic, crushed
1 small red onion, chopped
1 jalapeño pepper, seeded and finely chopped
1 large red pepper, cut into thin strips
1 large green pepper, cut into thin strips
¹/₂ tsp ground cumin
¹/₂ tsp chilli powder
500g (1lb) radiatore
2 tbsp fresh coriander leaves, chopped

Place the tomatoes and spring onions in a large bowl. Stir in the lime juice and salt.

In a large, deep frying pan, heat the oil over medium heat. Add the garlic and cook until soft-

ened. Add the red onion and jalapeño pepper, and sauté until softened, 2 to 3 minutes. Add the peppers and sauté until crisp-tender, about 5 minutes. Add the tomato mixture, cumin and chilli powder, and cook until the sauce thickens slightly, about 10 minutes.

Meanwhile, cook the pasta in boiling salted water until al dente. Drain.

Add the pasta to the sauce in the pan and toss well. Transfer to a warmed bowl, sprinkle with the coriander and serve.

Nutritional Analysis

Calories	501.17	Kcal	Protein	16.69	gm
Fat	4.64	gm	Carbohydrate	98.88	gm
Sodium	1001.28	mg	Cholesterol	0.00	mg
Saturated fat	0.60	gm			

Fettuccine with Light Alfredo Sauce

Serves: 4

500g (1lb) eggless fettuccine
250ml (8fl oz) evaporated skimmed milk
125g (4oz) grated Parmesan cheese
125g (4oz) finely chopped fresh parsley
white pepper to taste
pinch of red pepper flakes (optional)

Cook the fettuccine in boiling salted water until al dente.

While the pasta is cooking, heat the evaporated milk in a deep saucepan over medium heat. Bring to a simmer, but do not boil. Add the Parmesan

cheese and parsley. As soon as the cheese has melted and the sauce is thick and creamy, remove from the heat. Drain the pasta and place in a warmed bowl. Add the sauce and toss well. Season with white pepper and red pepper flakes, if using. Serve immediately.

Nutritional Analysis

Calories	519.34	Kcal	Protein	23.63	gm
Fat	4.93	gm	Carbohydrate	92.98	gm
Sodium	658.01	mg	Cholesterol	10.45	mg
Saturated fat	2.23	gm			

Ziti with Chicken, Pineapple and Mint

Serves: 4

500g (1lb) skinless chicken breast meat
1 tbsp vegetable oil
60ml (2fl oz) dry white wine
1/4 tsp cayenne pepper
6 spring onions, cut on the diagonal into 25mm (1in) lengths
375ml (12fl oz) pineapple juice
1 tbsp soy sauce
1 tbsp peeled and grated fresh ginger
1 tbsp honey
1 tablespoon orange juice
1 tbsp buttery light, reduced-fat margarine, melted
250g (8oz) ziti
300g (10oz) tinned mandarin oranges, drained
1 tbsp chopped fresh mint

(continued)

Ricotta Cheese

I've always considered ricotta cheese one of the most delicious dairy products I've ever tasted. In fact, I will sometimes use the semi-skimmed type as a substitute for yogurt, mixing honey, coconut, and fruit into it to make a great lunch.

Most people are familiar with ricotta as a primary ingredient in lasagna and stuffed shells, and although nonfat ricotta is available, it detracts from the dish. Choose semi-skimmed instead, and beat in a few egg whites to give it volume and texture.

Preheat oven to 180°C (350°F), gas mark 4. Place the chicken in a baking dish and brush with the oil. Sprinkle with wine, and season with the cayenne pepper. Cover with tinfoil and bake until cooked through and tender, about 15 minutes. Do not overcook. During the last 2 to 3 minutes, add the spring onions to the pan. Remove from the oven, let cool slightly and cut the chicken into bite-sized pieces. Reserve the spring onions.

While the chicken is cooking, combine the pineapple juice, soy sauce, ginger and honey in a small saucepan. Bring to a boil over medium-high heat and cook until reduced by half, about 20 minutes. Add the orange juice. Remove from the heat and whisk in the margarine.

Meanwhile, cook the pasta in boiling salted water until al dente. Drain and transfer to a large warmed bowl. Top with the spring onions, pour the sauce over the pasta and toss well. Fold in the mandarin oranges and mint. Serve at once.

Nutritional Analysis

Calories	512.80 Kcal	Protein	34.91 gm
Fat	8.70 gm	Carbohydrate	73.13 gm
Sodium	572.52 mg	Cholesterol	65.83 mg
Saturated fat	1.39 gm		

Fusilli with Fresh Herbs and Ricotta
Serves: 4

475g (15oz) semi-skimmed ricotta cheese
180ml (6fl oz) low-fat milk
60g (2oz) grated Parmesan cheese
1 tbsp olive oil

185g (6oz) chopped onion
4 cloves garlic, crushed
125g (4oz) chopped fresh basil leaves
125g (4oz) chopped fresh chives
125g (4oz) chopped fresh parley
salt and pepper to taste
500g (1lb) fusilli

In a food processor or blender, combine the ricotta cheese, milk and Parmesan. Process until smooth. In a large, deep frying pan, heat the oil over medium heat. Add the onion and sauté until nearly brown, about 10 minutes. Add the garlic and cook until softened.

Add the ricotta mixture and fold in the basil, chives and parsley. Cook until heated through. Season with salt and pepper.

Meanwhile, cook the pasta in boiling salted water until al dente. Drain and add to the frying pan. Toss well so that the pasta is coated with the sauce. Transfer to a warmed bowl and serve.

Nutritional Analysis

Calories	614.45 Kcal	Protein	27.42 gm
Fat	11.50 gm	Carbohydrate	96.43 gm
Sodium	606.82 mg	Cholesterol	31.29 mg
Saturated Fat	4.49 gm		

Vermicelli with Tuna, Anchovies and Capers

Serves: 4

2 tbsp olive oil
125g (4oz) chopped onion
1 clove garlic, crushed

500g (1lb) tinned plum tomatoes, drained
150g (5oz) anchovy fillets, finely chopped
2 tbsp buttery light, reduced-fat margarine, softened
500g (1lb) vermicelli
3 tbsp capers
185g (6oz) tinned water-packed tuna, drained and flaked
2 tbsp chopped fresh parsley

In a large, deep frying pan, heat the oil over medium heat. Add onion and sauté until soft, about 5 to 7 minutes. Add the garlic and sauté briefly. Add the tomatoes, break them up with a wooden spoon, cover and simmer until soft, about 10 minutes.

Place the anchovies in a small bowl and mash them with a spoon. (Alternatively, process them in a mini food processor.) Add the margarine to the anchovies and mash together with a fork.

Meanwhile, cook the pasta in boiling salted water until al dente. Scoop out 125ml (4fl oz) of the cooking water. Drain the pasta.

Stir enough of the reserved cooking water into the anchovy butter to make it thick and smooth and no longer a paste. Add the capers to the frying pan and stir to blend. Add the tuna fish and heat through over medium heat. Add the pasta to the sauce and toss until the pasta is coated. Transfer to a warmed bowl, sprinkle with the parsley and serve.

(continued)

Calories	623.37 Kcal	Protein	28.35 gm
Fat	14.83 gm	Carbohydrate	92.51 gm
Sodium	1165.01 mg	Cholesterol	17.81 mg
Saturated fat	2.22 gm		

Radiatore with Aubergine and Tomatoes

Serves: 4

2 tbsp olive oil
185g (6oz) chopped onion
3 cloves garlic, crushed
1 large aubergine, peeled and cut into 12–25mm
    (1/2–1in) cubes
2 tbsp balsamic vinegar
125ml (4fl oz) reduced-sodium, fat-free chicken stock
500g (1lb) tinned plum tomatoes, undrained
1 tbsp tomato puree
1/2 tsp dried oregano, crumbled
2 tbsp chopped fresh basil
dash of red pepper flakes
salt to taste
375g (12oz) radiatore

In a large, deep frying pan, heat the oil over medium heat. Add the onion and sauté until soft, about 5 minutes. Add the garlic and sauté briefly. Add the aubergine, vinegar and stock. Cover and cook until the aubergine is tender, about 10 minutes. Add the tomatoes and break them up with a wooden spoon. Stir in the tomato puree and oregano. Cook, uncovered, until the sauce

thickens slightly, about 15 minutes. Stir in the basil and red pepper flakes, and season with salt.

Meanwhile, cook the pasta in boiling salted water until al dente. Drain and transfer to a large warmed bowl. Add the sauce and toss well. Serve immediately.

Calories	438.50 Kcal	Protein	13.76 gm
Fat	8.52 gm	Carbohydrate	77.32 gm
Sodium	588.51 mg	Cholesterol	0.00 mg
Saturated fat	1.15 gm		

Turkey and Spinach Fettuccine Casserole

Serves: 4

2 tsp olive oil
375g (12oz) mushrooms, sliced
375g (12oz) boneless, skinless turkey breast, cut into
    12mm (1/2in) strips
125ml (4fl oz) dry white wine
3 tbsp plain flour
500ml (1pt) skimmed milk
1/2 tsp dried marjoram, crumbled
125g (4oz) grated Parmesan cheese
salt and pepper to taste
250g (8oz) eggless spinach fettuccine
3 tbsp slivered blanched almonds

Preheat oven to 200°C (400°F), gas mark 6.

In a large, deep frying pan, heat the oil over medium heat. Add the mushrooms and sauté until

they begin to soften, about 5 minutes. Add the turkey and sauté until just browned, about 10 minutes. Add the wine and cook for 3 minutes. Stir in the flour, mixing thoroughly. Gradually add the milk, stirring constantly, and cook until the mixture thickens slightly, about 10 minutes. Stir in the marjoram and 60g (2oz) of the Parmesan cheese until blended. Season with salt and pepper.

Meanwhile, cook the pasta in boiling salted water until nearly al dente. Drain and combine with the turkey mixture, tossing well. Then transfer the contents of the skillet to a 280 x 180mm (11 x 7in) baking dish. Top with the remaining Parmesan and sprinkle with almonds.

Bake until heated through and the top is lightly browned, about 20 minutes. Serve at once.

Nutritional Analysis

Calories	502.83 Kcal	Protein	40.33 gm
Fat	11.66 gm	Carbohydrate	58.49 gm
Sodium	508.78 mg	Cholesterol	65.55 mg
Saturated fat	3.66 gm		

Baked Ziti with Meat

Serves: 4

2 tbsp olive oil
250g (8oz) chopped onion
4 cloves garlic, crushed
250g (8oz) lean minced beef
125ml (4fl oz) dry white wine
875g (1lb 12oz) tinned crushed tomatoes
1/2 tsp dried basil, crumbled

1/2 tsp dried oregano, crumbled
1 tbsp tomato paste
2 tbsp plain flour
125ml (4fl oz) low-fat milk
salt and pepper to taste
375g (12oz) ziti
250g (8oz) grated low-fat mozzarella cheese
125g (4oz) grated romano cheese

Preheat oven to 200°C (400°F), gas mark 6.

In a large frying pan, heat the oil over medium heat. Add the onion and sauté until soft, about 10 minutes. Add the garlic and sauté briefly. Stir in the beef, breaking it up with a wooden spoon and browning well. Drain off the oil from the pan. Stir in the white wine and scrape the bottom of the pan as it cooks. Add the tomatoes, basil, oregano and tomato puree, stirring to blend. Cook for 3 minutes. Add the flour and stir well until combined. Gradually add the milk and cook until slightly thickened, about 10 minutes. Season with salt and pepper.

Meanwhile, cook the pasta in boiling salted water until nearly al dente. Drain and place in a large warmed bowl. Add the meat mixture to the pasta, tossing well. Transfer to a large baking dish.

Bake until heated through, about 15 minutes. Distribute the mozzarella evenly over the top and sprinkle with the romano cheese. Return to the oven and bake until the cheese melts and the top has browned lightly, about 15 minutes.

Serve immediately.

(continued)

Calories	690.85 Kcal	Protein	36.89 gm
Fat	23.52 gm	Carbohydrate	82.54 gm
Sodium	1007.50 mg	Cholesterol	58.01 mg
Saturated fat	8.56 gm		

Salmon with Fettucine

Serves: 4

250ml (8fl oz) reduced-sodium, fat-free chicken stock
125ml (4fl oz) dry white wine
500g (1lb) salmon fillets, skinned and cut into 12mm
    (1/2in) pieces
1 tbsp vegetable oil
3 shallots, finely chopped
6 spring onions, thinly sliced
500g (1lb) tinned plum tomatoes, drained
2 tbsp tomato puree
125ml (4fl oz) evaporated nonfat milk
125g (4oz) snipped fresh dill
375g (12oz) eggless fettuccine
4 fresh dill sprigs

In a large pan, bring the stock and wine to the boil. Reduce the heat to a simmer and add the salmon. Cover and cook until the fish is opaque, about 5 minutes. Remove the fish with a slotted spoon. Set aside; cover to keep warm. Reserve 125ml (4fl oz) of the cooking liquid.

In a frying pan, heat the oil over medium heat. Add the shallots and spring onions and cook until soft, about 5 minutes. Add the tomatoes, breaking them up with a wooden spoon.

Stir in the tomato puree, evaporated milk, reserved cooking liquid and dill. Simmer until the sauce thickens, about 10 minutes. Return the fish to the pan and heat through.

Meanwhile, cook the pasta in boiling salted water until al dente. Drain and place in a large warmed bowl. Pour the sauce over the pasta and toss gently. Serve on warmed individual plates. Garnish with dill sprigs.

Calories	622.74 Kcal	Protein	38.16 gm
Fat	17.49 gm	Carbohydrate	76.51 gm
Sodium	725.41 mg	Cholesterol	68.23 mg
Saturated fat	3.17 gm		

Orecchiette with Summer Tomato Sauce and Olives

Serves: 4

750g (1lb 8oz) tomatoes, peeled, seeded and chopped
    into 12mm (1/2in) pieces
1 tsp crushed garlic
3 tbsp olive oil
2 tbsp shredded fresh basil leaves
pepper to taste
500g (1lb) orecchiette or round or shell-shaped pasta
90g (3oz) Kalamata or other brine-cured black olives,
    pitted

In a large bowl, combine the tomatoes, garlic, oil, basil and pepper. Stir to mix well. Set aside at room temperature for at least 30 minutes.

Cook the pasta in boiling salted water until al dente. Drain. Stir the olives into the tomatoes, add the pasta, toss well and serve immediately.

Nutritional Analysis

Calories	578.61	Kcal	Protein	15.93	gm
Fat	15.40	gm	Carbohydrate	93.84	gm
Sodium	610.28	mg	Cholesterol	0.00	mg
Saturated fat	2.06	gm			

Sweet-and-Sour Chicken with Ruote

Serves: 4

250g (8oz) tinned pineapple chunks in unsweetened juice
1¹/₂ tbsp tomato puree
2 tbsp cider vinegar
2 tbsp soy sauce
1 tbsp sugar
2 tsp cornflour
2 tbsp vegetable oil
500g (1lb) skinless chicken breast meat, cut into 12mm (¹/₂in) wide slices
3 cloves garlic, crushed
2 tsp peeled and grated fresh ginger
125g (4oz) chopped onion
125g (4oz) chopped green pepper
500g (1lb) thinly sliced pak choi or Chinese cabbage
4 spring onions, thinly sliced
250g (8oz) ruote
2 tbsp chopped fresh coriander

(continued)

Fresh or Dried Pasta?

Most of us grew up eating dried spaghetti that came out of a packet. If you've ever eaten fresh pasta, it may actually seem mushy to you.

Fresh pasta can be heavenly in taste and texture, but since it is fresh, it needs only a minute or two of cooking, just to heat through. Nowadays, you can buy freshly made pasta in the supermarket, and although it's more expensive than the dried variety, you can look at it as a special treat. Read the label, however; many fresh pastas contain more egg than dried pastas do.

Drain the pineapple, saving 125ml (4fl oz) of the juice. Pour the juice into a small bowl. Add the tomato paste, vinegar, soy sauce, sugar and cornflour. Stir well and reserve.

In a wok or large, deep frying pan, heat the oil over medium heat. Add the chicken and stir-fry until firm and lightly browned, about 10 minutes. Add the garlic, ginger, onion and pepper. Sauté until they soften, about 5 minutes. Add the cabbage and stir-fry until crisp-tender, about 3 minutes.

Stir the tomato-pineapple mixture and add to the pan, mixing well. Add the pineapple and stir constantly so that the sauce coats the contents as it thickens. Add the spring onions and toss to mix.

Meanwhile, cook the pasta in boiling salted water until al dente. Drain. Transfer to a large warmed bowl. Pour the sauce over the pasta and toss to combine completely. Sprinkle with the coriander and serve immediately.

Nutritional Analysis

Calories	482.24 Kcal	Protein	35.66 gm
Fat	9.34 gm	Carbohydrate	63.24 gm
Sodium	861.81 mg	Cholesterol	65.83 mg
Saturated fat	1.37 gm		

Shells with Scallops and Sun-Dried Tomato Pesto

Serves: 4

250ml (8fl oz) water
125g (4oz) dry-packed sun-dried tomatoes
1 clove garlic, peeled

2 tbsp pine nuts
2 tbsp grated Parmesan cheese
2 tbsp olive oil
1/4 tsp salt
60ml (2fl oz) dry white wine
2 tsp cornflour
500g (1lb) scallops
125ml (4fl oz) reduced-sodium, fat-free chicken stock
375g (12fl oz) medium pasta shells
2 tbsp chopped fresh parsley

In a medium saucepan, bring the water to the boil. Add the sun-dried tomatoes and cook until softened, about 10 minutes. Add the garlic and cook for another 2 minutes. Pour the mixture into a food processor or blender. Add the pine nuts, Parmesan cheese, 1 tablespoon of oil and salt. Process until smooth pesto forms. Reserve. In a small bowl, combine the wine and cornflour, mixing well. Set aside.

In a large, deep frying pan, heat the remaining oil over medium heat. Add the scallops and cook until slightly firm, about 5 minutes. Add the stock and cook for 1 minute. Stir in the tomato pesto. Heat through. Stir the cornflour-wine mixture and add to the skillet. Cook, stirring constantly, until the sauce thickens slightly, about 1 minute.

Meanwhile, cook the pasta in boiling salted water until al dente. Drain. Add the shells to the pan and toss to glaze the pasta with the sauce. Transfer to a warmed bowl. Sprinkle with the parsley and serve immediately.

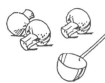

Nutritional Analysis

Calories	558.64 Kcal	Protein	34.48 gm
Fat	11.98 gm	Carbohydrate	74.64 gm
Sodium	750.95 mg	Cholesterol	39.42 mg
Saturated fat	2.01 gm		

Rich Low-Fat Lasagna

Serves: 8

1 tbsp olive oil
2 garlic cloves, crushed
1 red onion, finely chopped
425g (14oz) tinned kidney beans, drained
1l (2pt) tomato passata
1 tsp dried oregano, crumbled
1 tsp dried basil, crumbled
pepper to taste
500g (1lb) lasagna noodles, cooked
500g (1lb) semi-skimmed ricotta cheese
250g (8oz) low-fat mozzarella cheese, thinly sliced
60g (2oz) grated Parmesan cheese

Preheat oven to 180°C (350°F), gas mark 4.

In a saucepan, heat the oil over medium heat. Add the garlic and onion, and sauté until soft, about 5 minutes. Add the beans, and cook for 5 more minutes. Add the passata, oregano, basil and pepper. Bring to the boil, reduce the heat to medium, and cook for 5 minutes to blend the flavours together.

Spoon some of the sauce onto the bottom of a 230 x 330mm (9 x 13in) baking dish. Arrange a layer of noodles on top and then some of the ricotta and mozzarella. Repeat the layers, using up the ricotta, mozzarella, noodles and sauce. Finish off with a layer of noodles topped with sauce. Sprinkle with the Parmesan cheese and cover with tinfoil.

Bake until the top is bubbling, about 45 minutes. Let stand for 10 minutes before serving.

Nutritional Analysis

Calories	471.29 Kcal	Protein	30.25 gm
Fat	8.73 gm	Carbohydrate	69.13 gm
Sodium	1116.24 mg	Cholesterol	24.03 mg
Saturated fat	3.89 gm		

Artichoke Lasagna

Serves: 10

375g (12z) dried or 500g (1lb) fresh lasagne noodles
90g (3oz) plus 1 tsp plain flour
1.25l (1½pt) low-fat milk
3 tbsp reduced-fat cream cheese
250g (8oz) freshly grated Parmesan cheese
1 tbsp chopped fresh thyme or 1 tsp dried thyme leaves
2 tsp fresh lemon juice
1 tsp salt, plus more to taste
¼ tsp freshly ground black pepper, plus more to taste
2 tsp olive oil
375g (12oz) chopped onions
375g (12oz) finely chopped carrots
2 cloves garlic, crushed

(continued)

A Pasta Rainbow

Today, pasta comes in as many shades as there are colours in the rainbow. Many of these pastas contain exotic ingredients, from squid ink to pesto to sun-dried tomatoes.

I think the exotic ingredients should be *on* the pasta, not *in* it. Some of these colourful additions add to the cost of the pasta without adding much flavour. Dried spinach pasta is always available if you want to try the 'exotic' without spending much money.

500g (1lb) frozen artichoke hearts, thawed and coarsely chopped, or 500g (1lb) tinned artichoke hearts, drained, squeezed dry and coarsely chopped
125ml (4fl oz) reduced-sodium, fat-free chicken stock

In a large pot of boiling salted water, cook the noodles until barely tender (8 minutes for dried, 1 minute for fresh). Drain and rinse under cold water. Spread the noodles on clean kitchen towels, cover with cling film and set aside.

Place 90g (3oz) of the flour in a small bowl and gradually whisk in 125ml (4fl oz) of the milk until smooth. Set aside. In a large saucepan, heat the remaining milk over medium heat until the milk is steaming. Whisk the flour and milk mixture into the hot milk and stir constantly over the heat until the sauce comes to a simmer and thickens. Lower the heat. Continue cooking and stirring for 1 minute. Remove from the heat. Whisk in cream cheese, then 125g (4oz) of the Parmesan, thyme, lemon juice, 1 teaspoon salt, and pepper. Set the cheese sauce aside.

In a large nonstick frying pan, heat the oil over medium-high heat. Add onions and carrots and cook, stirring, until they begin to brown and soften, about 5 minutes. Add garlic and stir for 1 minute longer. Add the artichoke hearts and sprinkle with the remaining flour and chicken stock. Stir well and cook until the liquid is thick and simmering, about 3 minutes. Remove from the heat and season with salt and pepper.

Preheat oven to 200°C (400°F), gas mark 6. Lightly oil a 230 x 330mm (9 x 13in) baking dish, or coat it with nonstick cooking spray. Smear the

bottom of the prepared dish with 125ml (4fl oz) of the cheese sauce. Line the bottom with a single layer of noodles. Spread half of the artichoke mixture over the noodles. Spoon on another 125ml (4fl oz) cheese sauce and use a spatula to spread it evenly. Add another layer of noodles, and spread another 125ml (4fl oz) sauce on top. Add a third layer of noodles, the remaining artichoke mixture, and spread this with 125ml (4fl oz) sauce. Finish with the remaining noodles and sauce. Sprinkle with the remaining Parmesan.

Lightly oil a large piece of tin foil or spray it with nonstick cooking spray, and use it to tightly cover the dish. Bake the lasagne for 30 minutes. Uncover and bake for about 15 minutes more, or until the top is lightly browned. Let stand for 10 minutes before serving.

Nutritional Analysis

Calories	275.82	Kcal	Protein	13.67	gm
Fat	6.57	gm	Carbohydrate	40.67	gm
Sodium	646.71	mg	Cholesterol	13.63	mg
Saturated fat	3.20	gm			

Szechuan Noodle Salad

Serves: 4

500g (1lb) thin spaghetti
60ml (4fl oz) white wine vinegar
60ml (4fl oz) water
2 tbsp soy sauce
2 tbsp peeled and finely chopped fresh ginger
1 tbsp sesame oil
2 cloves garlic, crushed
1 tsp sugar

1 tsp Tabasco sauce
250g (8oz) grated carrot
250g (8oz) frozen peas, thawed
1 red pepper, cut into narrow strips
500g (1lb) beansprouts
60g (2oz) chopped fresh parsley

Cook the spaghetti in boiling salted water until al dente. Drain.

Meanwhile, in a large bowl, stir together the vinegar, water, soy sauce, ginger, oil, garlic, sugar and Tabasco. Add the warm, cooked noodles and toss. Add the carrot, peas, pepper, beansprouts and parsley. Toss well and serve.

Nutritional Analysis

Calories	527.65	Kcal	Protein	19.07	gm
Fat	5.52	gm	Carbohydrate	100.23	gm
Sodium	972.92	mg	Cholesterol	0.00	mg
Saturated fat	0.78	gm			

Pad Thai

Serves: 4

125g (4oz) dried rice noodles
2 tsp peanut oil
3 cloves garlic, crushed
1 egg, lightly beaten
250g (8oz) small prawns, peeled and deveined
500g (1lb) mung beansprouts
125g (4oz) sliced spring onion tops
3 tbsp rice vinegar
2½ tbsp fish sauce
2 tbsp sugar

(continued)

1 tsp Chinese chilli paste with garlic
3 tbsp chopped dry-roasted peanuts

In a large bowl, soak the rice noodles in warm water to cover until they are limp and white, about 20 minutes. In a wok or large deep frying pan, heat oil over high heat until very hot. Add the garlic and stir-fry until golden, about 10 seconds. Add the egg and cook, stirring, until scrambled, about 30 seconds. Add the prawns and stir-fry until they curl and turn pink, about 2 minutes.

Drain the noodles and add to the wok, tossing with tongs until they soften and curl, about 1 minute. Add beansprouts, spring onion tops, vinegar, fish sauce, sugar and chilli paste. Toss until the prawns are fully cooked and the noodles are heated through, 1 to 2 minutes. Sprinkle with peanuts and serve immediately.

Nutritional Analysis

Calories	292.64	Kcal	Protein	16.06	gm
Fat	8.88	gm	Carbohydrate	38.13	gm
Sodium	545.53	mg	Cholesterol	123.85	mg
Saturated fat	1.64	gm			

Linguine with White Clam Sauce

Serves: 4

1 tbsp olive oil
3 cloves garlic, crushed
300g (10oz) finely chopped tinned clams, drained with
    liquid reserved
1 tsp red pepper flakes

1 tsp dried oregano, crumbled
1 tsp dried basil, crumbled
2 tbsp fresh chopped parsley
125ml (4fl oz) dry white wine
500g (1lb) linguine

In a large frying pan, heat the oil over medium heat. Add the garlic and sauté until soft, about 3 minutes. Add the clams, red pepper flakes, oregano, basil, parsley, wine and reserved clam liquid. Cook over medium heat about 15 minutes.

Meanwhile, cook the linguine in boiling salted water until al dente. Drain and place in a warmed bowl. Add the sauce, toss well and serve.

Nutritional Analysis

Calories	533.63	Kcal	Protein	24.39	gm
Fat	6.00	gm	Carbohydrate	88.46	gm
Sodium	439.67	mg	Cholesterol	24.69	mg
Saturated fat	0.79	gm			

Chicken and Seafood Pasta

Serves: 4

1 whole chicken breast, split, boned and skinned
2 tbsp olive oil
60g (2oz) plain flour
125g (4oz) jumbo prawns, peeled and deveined
125g (4oz) scallops
4 cloves garlic, crushed
250ml (8fl oz) reduced-sodium, fat-free chicken stock
250g (8oz) stemmed spinach leaves
10 dry-packed, sun-dried tomatoes, chopped

1 tsp dried basil, crumbled
salt and pepper to taste
250g (8oz) radiatore

Using a meat mallet, tenderize the chicken to create thin cutlets. In a frying pan, heat 1 tablespoon of the oil over high heat. Add the chicken and cook, turning once, for 5 minutes. Remove from the pan and set aside. Lightly flour the shrimp and scallops. Return the pan to medium heat. Add the prawns and scallops and sauté until the prawns turn pink, 3 to 4 minutes. Remove from the pan and set aside.

To the same pan, add the remaining oil and the garlic; heat until the garlic is brown, about 5 minutes. Return the chicken, prawns and scallops to the pan and add the stock. Add the basil, oregano, salt and pepper to taste. Add the sundried tomatoes and the spinach. Cook for 4 minutes and remove from the heat.

While the sauce is cooking, cook the pasta in boiling salted water until al dente. Drain and place in a large warmed bowl. Spoon the chicken and seafood mixture on top, and serve immediately.

Nutritional Analysis

Calories	444.71 Kcal	Protein	33.72 gm
Fat	9.13 gm	Carbohydrate	54.89 gm
Sodium	473.83 mg	Cholesterol	78.08 mg
Saturated fat	1.33 gm		

Angry Ziti

Serves: 4

500g (1lb) ziti
1 tbsp olive oil
1 onion, chopped
4 cloves garlic, crushed
2 chilli peppers
250g (8oz) sliced mushrooms
250g (8oz) chopped fresh plum tomatoes
2 tsp dried basil, crumbled
60ml (2fl oz) dry white wine
875g (1lb 12oz) tinned chopped tomatoes
salt and pepper to taste
60g (2oz) grated Parmesan cheese

Cook the pasta in boiling salted water until al dente.

Meanwhile, in a large frying pan, heat the oil over medium heat. Add the onions and garlic, and sauté until translucent, about 5 minutes. Add the hot peppers and mushroom, and sauté for 2 minutes. Add the plum tomatoes, basil, white wine, chopped tomatoes, salt and pepper, and sauté until blended, about 2 minutes.

Drain the pasta and add to the pan with the cheese. Cook, stirring and tossing, for 1 minute, then serve.

Nutritional Analysis

Calories	562.75 Kcal	Protein	20.09 gm
Fat	7.44 gm	Carbohydrate	102.26 gm
Sodium	820.12 mg	Cholesterol	3.95 mg
Saturated fat	1.77 gm		

Quick Lasagna

Serves: 8

60g (2oz) grated Parmesan cheese
250g (8oz) semi-skimmed ricotta cheese
250g (8oz) grated fat-free mozzarella cheese
875g (1lb 12oz) readymade spaghetti sauce
375g (12oz) no-cook lasagna noodles

Preheat oven to 180°C (350°F), gas mark 4.

In a medium bowl, stir together the Parmesan cheese, ricotta cheese and mozzarella. Grease a 230 x 330mm (9 x 13in) baking dish. Spread some of the sauce in the bottom. Layer the noodles on top of the sauce. Spread a third of the cheese mixture over the noodles. Repeat the layers until the ingredients are used up, ending with sauce. Cover with tin foil.

Bake until heated through, about 45 minutes. Remove from the oven and let cool for 10 minutes before serving.

Nutritional Analysis

Calories	443.39 Kcal	Protein	21.42 gm
Fat	11.70 gm	Carbohydrate	65.86 gm
Sodium	909.55 mg	Cholesterol	17.34 mg
Saturated fat	3.54 gm		

Linguine Fra Diavolo

Serves: 4

250g (8oz) linguine
2 tbsp olive oil
3 cloves garlic, crushed

500g (1lb) tomatoes, peeled and chopped
250g (8oz) finely chopped fresh basil
salt and pepper to taste
125g (4oz) scallops
125g (4oz) prawns, peeled and deveined
125g (4oz) haddock fillet, cut into 25mm (1in) chunks
8 mussels, well scrubbed and debearded

Cook the linguine in boiling salted water until al dente.

Meanwhile, in a large frying pan, heat the oil over medium-high heat. Add the garlic and sauté until soft, about 5 minutes. Add the tomatoes, basil, salt and pepper, and cook, stirring occasionally, for 2 minutes. Add the scallops, prawns, haddock and mussels, and cook until the haddock is translucent, about 3 minutes.

Drain the linguine and place in a warmed bowl. Pour the sauce over the top, toss well and serve.

Nutritional Analysis

Calories	388.43 Kcal	Protein	25.42 gm
Fat	9.26 gm	Carbohydrate	50.28 gm
Sodium	352.59 mg	Cholesterol	64.51 mg
Saturated fat	1.27 gm		

Fettuccine with Spinach Tomato Sauce

Serves: 4

375g (12oz) eggless fettuccine
1 tbsp olive oil
1 onion, chopped
2 cloves garlic, crushed
300g (10oz) frozen chopped spinach
1/4 tsp salt
1 large tomato, chopped
250g (8oz) semi-skimmed ricotta cheese
60g (2oz) grated Parmesan cheese
salt and pepper to taste

Cook the fettuccine in boiling salted water until al dente.

Meanwhile, in a large frying pan, heat the oil over medium heat. Add the onion and sauté until translucent, about 4 minutes. Add the garlic, spinach and salt, and cook for 5 minutes. Add the tomato and cook until soft, about 5 minutes longer. Drain the fettuccine and add to the pan with the ricotta cheese. Toss and cook until heated through, 1 to 2 minutes. Add the Parmesan, salt and pepper, then toss well again. Transfer to a warmed bowl and serve immediately.

Nutritional Analysis

Calories	500.60 Kcal	Protein	23.06 gm
Fat	11.52 gm	Carbohydrate	76.52 gm
Sodium	668.67 mg	Cholesterol	23.01 mg
Saturated fat	4.68 gm		

Pasta Is Low-Fat

250g (8oz) of cooked spaghetti or macaroni, without salt or oil, has 0.1g of saturated fat, 0mg cholesterol and only 4 calories from fat with a total number of 197 calories. That's something to think about when choosing a quick, low-fat meal. Spice up pasta by sprinkling garlic powder and fresh or dried basil on the hot pasta; or, for a really tangy pasta dish, add chopped hot peppers. Remember, though, that a little hot pepper goes a long way.

Fish and Shellfish Dishes

CHAPTER EIGHT

Amount Per Chapter

23 Recipes

	% Daily Value
Easy to Prepare	**100%**
Low Fat/High Flavour	**100%**
Simple to Understand	**100%**

DELICIOUS, EASY, LOW-FAT RECIPES

Fish are winners when it comes to a low-fat diet. High in protein and low in fat, fish provides low-fat diners with a tasty way to eat a filling, delicious main course without the fat of a piece of chicken or beef of comparable weight.

A wide variety of fish from all over the world is now available in fish markets and supermarkets. This new bounty has convinced cooks and diners that dishes made from these fresh- and saltwater denizens are wonderful alternatives to heartier, traditional meat or poultry recipes.

To my mind, the only things a piece of fish usually needs are a sprinkling of crushed garlic and a squeeze of juice from a lemon half. But the following recipes don't require much more effort than my garlic-and-lemon treatment, and they are certain to win raves – even from people who insist that they don't like fish.

Seafood Rice

Serves: 8

> 2 tbsp olive oil
> 6 spring onions, thinly sliced
> 1 large onion, finely chopped
> 1 clove garlic, chopped
> 250g (8oz) scallops
> 250g (8oz) prawns, peeled and deveined
> 250ml (8fl oz) dry white wine, plus more if needed
> 125ml (4fl oz) bottled clam juice
> 1 tbsp tomato puree
> 1kg (2lb) mussels, well scrubbed and debearded
> 375g (12oz) washed white or brown rice
> 250g (8oz) finely chopped fresh parsley
> pepper to taste
> lemon wedges

In a large saucepan, heat the oil over medium heat for 1 minute. Add the spring onions, onion and garlic, and sauté until soft, about 5 minutes.

Transfer to a bowl. In the same pan, add the scallops and prawns, and cook, stirring, for a few minutes until the prawns turn pink. Transfer the seafood to the bowl holding the spring onion mixture. Keep warm.

Add 250ml (8fl oz) wine, the clam juice and tomato puree to the pan over medium heat, stirring. Add the mussels, cover and bring to the boil over high heat. Cook until the mussels open, about 5 minutes. Remove the mussels from the pan with a slotted spoon, reserving the sauce in the pan. When the mussels are cool enough to handle, discard any that did not open. Remove the meat from the opened shells and discard the shells. Add the mussels to the bowl with the seafood-onion mixture; continue to keep warm.

Measure the liquid left in the pan and, if necessary, add wine to make 750ml (1½ pints). Return the liquid to the pan and bring to the boil. Add the rice, stir, cover, reduce the heat to low and

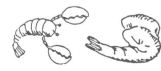

cook until all the liquid is absorbed and the rice is tender, about 20 minutes for white rice and 30 minutes for brown rice.

Add the seafood mixture, parsley and pepper to the cooked rice. Fluff with a fork and serve with lemon wedges.

Nutritional Analysis

Calories	254.85 Kcal	Protein	16.71 gm
Fat	5.02 gm	Carbohydrate	34.32 gm
Sodium	231.49 mg	Cholesterol	53.93 mg
Saturated fat	0.74 gm		

French Country Mussels

Serves: 6

1 tbsp olive oil
1 large onion, chopped
2 tbsp crushed garlic
500g (1lb) tinned peeled tomatoes, drained
125g (4oz) finely chopped fresh parsley
pepper to taste
250ml (8fl oz) dry white wine
2kg (4lb) mussels, scrubbed and debearded

In a large pot, heat the oil over medium heat. Add the onion and garlic, and sauté until browned, about 10 minutes. Add the tomatoes, breaking them up with a wooden spoon. Add the parsley and pepper. Raise the heat to high, and cook for about 2 minutes. Add the wine, and cook for another 2 minutes.

Add the mussels, tossing them to coat well with the tomato mixture. Cover and cook, stirring occasionally, until the mussels open, about 5 minutes. Discard any mussels that did not open. Serve immediately.

Nutritional Analysis

Calories	158.20 Kcal	Protein	11.92 gm
Fat	4.47 gm	Carbohydrate	11.48 gm
Sodium	379.85 mg	Cholesterol	24.57 mg
Saturated fat	0.71 gm		

Tuna-Noodle Casserole, Italian Style

Serves: 6

375g (12oz) tinned water-packed albacore or yellow-fin tuna
3 tbsp vegetable oil
250g (8oz) chopped celery
125g (4oz) chopped onion
500g (1lb) tinned tomatoes, drained
185g (6oz) tomato puree
125ml (4fl oz) water
1/2 tsp garlic powder
1 tsp dried oregano, crumbled
1/2 tsp dried basil, crumbled
1/4 tsp fennel seeds
250g (8oz) egg noodles
2 tbsp grated Parmesan cheese

Drain the tuna. In a frying pan, heat the oil over medium heat. Add the celery and onion, and sauté until soft, about 10 minutes. Add the

(continued)

151

tomatoes, tomato puree, water, garlic powder, oregano, basil and fennel seeds. Mix well, cover and simmer over low heat, about 20 minutes. Add the tuna.

Preheat oven to 180°C (350°F), gas mark 4. Spray a large baking dish with nonstick spray.

Cook the noodles in boiling salted water until nearly al dente. Drain. Layer half the noodles in the prepared baking dish. Top with half the tuna mixture and 1 tablespoon of the cheese. Repeat the layers.

Bake until firm, about 30 minutes. Serve immediately.

Nutritional Analysis

Calories	331.35 Kcal	Protein	22.66 gm
Fat	10.30 gm	Carbohydrate	37.79 gm
Sodium	726.23 mg	Cholesterol	59.93 mg
Saturated fat	1.62 gm		

Tomato-Seafood Stew

Serves: 6

1 tbsp olive oil
250g (8oz) chopped onion
2 cloves garlic, crushed
500g (1lb) tinned chopped tomatoes, juice reserved
250ml (8fl oz) tomato sauce
1 potato, peeled and diced
1 green pepper, chopped
1 celery stalk, chopped
1 carrot, grated
1 tsp dried thyme, crumbled
1/4 tsp pepper

4 dashes of Tabasco sauce
250g (8oz) prawns, peeled, deveined and halved lengthways
625g (1lb 4oz) tinned whole baby clams, drained
2 tbsp snipped fresh parsley

In a large saucepan, heat the oil over medium heat. Add the onion and garlic, and sauté until soft, about 10 minutes.

Stir in the tomatoes and their juice, tomato sauce, potato, pepper, celery, carrot, thyme, pepper and Tabasco sauce. Bring to the boil, cover, reduce the heat to low and simmer until the vegetables are tender, 20 to 25 minutes.

Stir in the prawns, clams and parsley. Bring to the boil, cover, reduce the heat to low and simmer until the prawns turn pink, about 2 minutes. Spoon into serving bowls and serve immediately.

Nutritional Analysis

Calories	191.20 Kcal	Protein	21.16 gm
Fat	4.08 gm	Carbohydrate	17.72 gm
Sodium	466.35 mg	Cholesterol	80.07 mg
Saturated fat	0.52 gm		

Quick Crab Cakes

Serves: 4

12 crackers, crushed
2 eggs, lightly beaten
2 tbsp low-fat mayonnaise
1 tsp Worcestershire sauce
2 tsp barbecue seasoning

¹⁄₄ tsp red pepper flakes
500g (1lb) lump crabmeat, picked over for shells

In a large bowl, combine the crushed crackers, eggs, mayonnaise, Worcestershire sauce, barbecue seasoning and red pepper flakes. Mix well.

Add the crabmeat and, using a rubber spatula, fold the mixture together. Form into 4 patties.

Spray a large frying pan with nonstick cooking spray and heat over medium heat. Add the patties and cook, turning once, until brown and heated through, 12 to 15 minutes. Serve at once.

Nutritional Analysis

Calories	207.92 Kcal	Protein	26.93 gm
Fat	6.31 gm	Carbohydrate	9.04 gm
Sodium	879.74 mg	Cholesterol	219.75 mg
Saturated fat	2.92 gm		

Prawn-Pear Pasta Salad

Serves: 4

250ml (8fl oz) plain low-fat yogurt
2 tsp Dijon mustard
¹⁄₂ tsp dried dill, crumbled
Tabasco sauce to taste
250g (8oz) fusilli, cooked and drained
2 William or comice pears, cored and sliced
125g (4oz) chopped red pepper
125g (4oz) chopped green pepper
2 spring onions, chopped
125g (4oz) prawns, peeled, deveined and cooked
1 small head butter lettuce, leaves separated

In a small bowl, stir together the yogurt, mustard, dill and Tabasco sauce to form a dressing. In a large bowl, combine the fusilli, pears, peppers, spring onions and prawns. Stir to mix. Add the dressing, and stir and toss to coat evenly.

Line a platter or individual plates with the lettuce leaves, and spoon the pasta mixture on top. Serve at once.

Nutritional Analysis

Calories	339.25 Kcal	Protein	17.23 gm
Fat	2.50 gm	Carbohydrate	61.83 gm
Sodium	364.61 mg	Cholesterol	58.73 mg
Saturated fat	0.78 gm		

 ## Crab Surprise

Serves: 4

60ml (2fl oz) olive oil
3 tbsp plain flour
180ml (6fl oz) reduced-sodium, fat-free chicken stock
180ml (6fl oz) low-fat milk
60ml (2fl oz) tomato ketchup
2 tsp Worcestershire sauce
1 tsp paprika
3 drops of Tabasco sauce
1 tbsp lemon juice
875g (1lb 12oz) shelled crab claws
750g (1lb 8oz) hot cooked white rice

In a saucepan, heat the oil over low heat. Add the flour and cook, stirring, for 2 minutes. Whisk in the stock and milk, and simmer over low heat until thickened slightly, about 10 minutes.

(continued)

Whisk in the ketchup, Worcestershire sauce, paprika, Tabasco sauce and lemon juice, and continue to simmer for 2 more minutes. Add the crabmeat and simmer until it is cooked, about 10 minutes.

Spoon the rice onto individual plates, top with the crab mixture, and serve.

Nutritional Analysis

Calories	537.53	Kcal	Protein	46.17	gm
Fat	17.95	gm	Carbohydrate	44.95	gm
Sodium	876.76	mg	Cholesterol	200.25	mg
Saturated fat	2.63	gm			

Steamed Fish and Spinach

Serves: 4

1 tbsp olive oil
125g (4oz) chopped onion
1 clove garlic, crushed
125ml (4fl oz) dry white wine
1/4 tsp dried tarragon or basil, crumbled
1/8 tsp salt
1/8 tsp pepper
300g (10oz) frozen chopped spinach, thawed and drained
500g (1lb) fish fillet such as haddock or cod, divided into 4 equal pieces
1 green pepper, cut into long, narrow strips

Prepare a fire in a charcoal grill.

In a small frying pan, heat the oil over medium heat. Add the onion and garlic, and sauté until soft, about 10 minutes. Remove from the heat.

Stir in the wine, tarragon or basil, salt and pepper. Return to heat, bring to the boil and cook gently until most of the liquid has evaporated, about 2 minutes. Remove from the heat and set aside.

Cut four 305 x 406mm (12 x 18in) pieces of tin foil. Divide the spinach in half, and distribute one half evenly among the pieces of tin foil. Place a piece of fish on each portion of spinach. Spoon the onion mixture evenly over the fish. Top with the remaining spinach, again dividing evenly, and then the pepper strips. Bring up the long edges of tin foil and, leaving a little space for steam expansion, seal tightly with a double fold. Then fold the short ends to seal.

Place the tin-foil packets on the grill rack, seam side up, directly over medium-hot coals. Grill, turning the packets twice, until the fish flakes easily when tested with a fork, about 20 minutes. Serve at once.

Nutritional Analysis

Calories	160.26	Kcal	Protein	23.98	gm
Fat	4.45	gm	Carbohydrate	6.16	gm
Sodium	204.77	mg	Cholesterol	64.69	mg
Saturated fat	0.62	gm			

Citrus Prawns and Scallops

Serves: 4

250g (8oz) sea scallops
12 large prawns, peeled and deveined
1 tsp finely grated orange zest
125ml (4fl oz) orange juice
1 tsp peeled and grated fresh ginger

¹/₄ tsp cayenne pepper
2 tbsp soy sauce
1 clove garlic, crushed
12 fresh or frozen mangetouts
1 orange, cut into 8 wedges

Halve any large scallops. Place the scallops and prawns in a resealable plastic bag set in a deep bowl. In a small bowl, stir together the orange zest, orange juice, ginger, cayenne pepper, soy sauce and garlic. Pour over the seafood. Seal the bag. Marinate in the refrigerator for 30 minutes.

Prepare a fire in a charcoal grill.

Drain the seafood, reserving the marinade. If using fresh mangetouts, cook in boiling water for about 2 minutes, then drain. If using frozen mangetouts, thaw and drain well. Wrap 1 mangetout around each prawn. Thread the prawns onto four 255 to 305mm (10 to 12in) long skewers alternately with the scallops and orange wedges.

Place the skewers on the grill rack and grill over medium-hot coals for 5 minutes. Turn, brush with the reserved marinade and grill until the prawns turn pink and the scallops are opaque, 5 to 7 minutes longer. Brush the kebabs occasionally with the marinade as they cook. (These kebabs can also be grilled about 100mm/4in from the heat source. Cook for 4 minutes on the first side and 4 to 6 minutes on the second side.)

Cooking Fish

In most cases, fish requires only a few minutes of cooking time on each side. A white-fleshed fish such as sole or halibut takes less time than a firm steak-like fish such as salmon or tuna. In most cases, the fish is done when the flesh is opaque and can be flaked easily with a fork.

(continued)

Nutritional Analysis

Calories	141.49 Kcal	Protein	20.20 gm
Fat	1.33 gm	Carbohydrate	11.38 gm
Sodium	675.47 mg	Cholesterol	89.45 mg
Saturated fat	0.20 gm		

Baked Sole with Breadcrumb Topping

Serves: 4

> 750g (1lb 8oz) sole fillets
> 250g (8oz) fresh breadcrumbs
> 1/2 medium onion, finely chopped
> 1 tbsp lemon juice
> 1/2 tsp dried marjoram, crumbled
> 1/2 tsp salt
> 1 tsp pepper
> 2 tbsp butter, melted
> 1 tomato, coarsely chopped
> 2 tbsp grated Parmesan cheese

Preheat oven to 200°C (400°F), gas mark 6. Grease or spray a large baking dish in which all the fillets fit snugly with nonstick cooking spray.

Arrange the sole in a single layer in the prepared baking dish. In a small dish, stir together the breadcrumbs, onion, lemon juice, marjoram, salt, pepper and butter. Spread the mixture over the fish. Top with the tomato and sprinkle with the Parmesan cheese.

Bake until the fish is opaque throughout and flakes easily when tested with a fork, about 15 minutes. Serve immediately.

Nutritional Analysis

Calories	367.30 Kcal	Protein	37.77 gm
Fat	11.44 gm	Carbohydrate	26.57 gm
Sodium	759.91 mg	Cholesterol	101.01 mg
Saturated fat	5.17 gm		

Stuffed Fillet of Sole

Serves: 4

> 185g (6oz) seasoned dried breadcrumbs
> 250g (8oz) cooked crabmeat, flaked
> 180ml (6fl oz) dry sherry
> 1 tsp lemon juice
> 4 sole fillets, 125g (4oz) each
> paprika

Preheat oven to 180°C (350°F), gas mark 4. Lightly grease a small baking dish with olive oil.

In a bowl, stir together the breadcrumbs, crabmeat, sherry and lemon juice. Place a quarter of the stuffing on each fillet, and roll up the fillet. Secure with toothpicks. Place the rolls in the prepared baking dish, seam side down. Sprinkle with paprika.

Bake until the fish flakes easily when tested with a fork, about 10 minutes. Serve at once.

Nutritional Analysis

Calories	310.60 Kcal	Protein	36.02 gm
Fat	4.05 gm	Carbohydrate	17.76 gm
Sodium	850.68 mg	Cholesterol	111.18 mg
Saturated fat	0.75 gm		

Prawn Scampi

Serves: 6

> *16 jumbo prawns, peeled and deveined*
> *500g (1lb) eggless fettuccine*
> *1 tbsp olive oil*
> *60g (2oz) butter*
> *3 cloves garlic, crushed*
> *16 clams, well scrubbed*
> *250ml (8fl oz) dry white wine*
> *1 tsp dried oregano, crumbled*
> *1 tsp dried basil, crumbled*

Split each prawn along the back from the tail to the head, but not all the way through.

Cook the fettuccine in boiling salted water until al dente. Drain the fettuccine, place in a warmed bowl and toss with the olive oil. Meanwhile, melt the butter in a large frying pan over medium heat. Add the garlic and sauté until soft and translucent, about 10 minutes. Add the prawns, clams, wine, oregano and basil. Cook until the prawns are pink and the clams have opened, 5 to 10 minutes. Discard any clams that did not open. Toss the prawns and clams with the pasta, and serve.

Nutritional Analysis

Calories	473.53 Kcal	Protein	23.68 gm
Fat	12.23 gm	Carbohydrate	59.02 gm
Sodium	429.58 mg	Cholesterol	99.14 mg
Saturated fat	5.41 gm		

Baked Boston Haddock

Serves: 4

> *4 haddock fillets, about 250g (8oz) each*
> *salt and pepper to taste*
> *2 tbsp lemon juice*
> *375ml (12fl oz) dry white wine*
> *250g (8oz) seasoned dried breadcrumbs*

Preheat oven to 180°C (350°F), gas mark 4. Lightly grease a baking pan with olive oil.

Place the haddock in the prepared pan and sprinkle with the salt, pepper and lemon juice, and add the wine.

Bake until the fish is opaque throughout and flakes easily when tested with a fork. Remove the pan from the oven. Preheat the grill. Sprinkle the breadcrumbs over the fish. Grill until light brown, 2 to 3 minutes. Serve immediately.

Nutritional Analysis

Calories	367.97 Kcal	Protein	44.79 gm
Fat	3.44 gm	Carbohydrate	22.31 gm
Sodium	923.59 mg	Cholesterol	97.61 mg
Saturated fat	0.65 gm		

Poached Cod with Spicy Buttermilk Sauce

Serves: 6

> *750g (1lb 8oz) cod fillets*
> *3/4 tsp ground turmeric*
> *pepper to taste*

(continued)

750ml (1½pt) buttermilk
1 tbsp lemon juice
½ tsp salt
2 tsp ground cumin

Sprinkle the cod fillets with the turmeric and pepper. Pour the buttermilk into a heavy frying pan and bring to a simmer. Slip the fish into the pan, cover and poach over low heat for 5 minutes.

Remove the fish from the pan. Add the lemon juice and salt to the buttermilk, raise the heat to high, and boil for 5 minutes to blend the flavours and reduce the sauce. Stir in the cumin, reduce the heat to low and return the fish to the pan. Cook until the fish is done, another 5 to 10 minutes. Spoon the sauce over the fish to serve.

Nutritional Analysis

Calories	146.10	Kcal	Protein	24.40	gm
Fat	1.99	gm	Carbohydrate	6.49	gm
Sodium	384.69	mg	Cholesterol	53.70	mg
Saturated fat	0.81	gm			

Curried Prawns and Vegetables with Brown Rice

Serves: 6

1 tbsp olive oil
1 large onion, sliced
3 cloves garlic, crushed
1 tbsp curry powder
½ tsp ground cinnamon
½ tsp salt, if desired
375ml (12fl oz) water

2 large carrots, sliced
2 large potatoes, peeled and cubed
1 large courgette, sliced
500g (1lb) tinned chopped tomatoes, juice reserved
500g (1lb) prawns, peeled and deveined
1kg (2lb) hot cooked brown rice

In a large frying pan, heat the oil over medium heat. Add the onion and garlic, and sauté until translucent, about 5 minutes. Add the curry powder, cinnamon, salt and water. Bring to the boil and add the carrots and potatoes. Reduce the heat, cover and cook for 10 minutes. Add the courgette, tomatoes with their juices and prawns, re-cover, and cook until the prawns are pink, about 10 minutes longer. Spoon the hot rice onto individual plates and then top with the prawns and vegetables.

Nutritional Analysis

Calories	329.19	Kcal	Protein	19.08	gm
Fat	5.02	gm	Carbohydrate	52.81	gm
Sodium	431.58	mg	Cholesterol	93.16	mg
Saturated fat	0.80	gm			

Lemon and Tarragon Sole

Serves: 4

60ml (2fl oz) plain low-fat yogurt
1 tsp plain flour
1 tsp dried tarragon, crumbled
1 tsp grated lemon zest
500g (1lb) sole fillets

Preheat grill. Spray a baking tray with nonstick cooking spray.

In a small bowl, combine the yogurt, flour, tarragon and lemon zest. Place the sole fillets on the prepared baking tray. Spread the yogurt mixture on the fish. Place under the grill until the fish is done, 5 to 10 minutes. Serve immediately.

Nutritional Analysis

Calories	117.86 Kcal	Protein	22.27 gm
Fat	1.83 gm	Carbohydrate	1.76 gm
Sodium	102.13 mg	Cholesterol	55.33 mg
Saturated fat	0.45 gm		

Baked Sole Almandine

Serves: 4

1 egg
60ml (2fl oz) low-fat milk
250g (8oz) seasoned dried breadcrumbs
1 tsp dried basil, crumbled
salt and pepper to taste
500g (1lb) sole fillets
2 tbsp lemon juice
2 tbsp water
1 tbsp butter, melted
3 tbsp blanched slivered almonds
3 spring onions, chopped

Preheat oven to 220°C (425°F), gas mark 7. Spray a baking tray with nonstick cooking spray.

In a shallow dish, stir together the egg and milk until blended. On a separate plate, mix together the breadcrumbs, basil, salt and pepper.

Dip the sole fillets first in the egg mixture and then in the crumbs. Place on the prepared baking tray. In a small bowl, mix together the lemon juice, water and butter. Sprinkle over the fish. Scatter the almonds over the top.

Bake until the fish flakes easily when tested with a fork, about 10 minutes. Sprinkle with the spring onions and serve.

Nutritional Analysis

Calories	308.75 Kcal	Protein	29.30 gm
Fat	10.03 gm	Carbohydrate	24.69 gm
Sodium	943.71 mg	Cholesterol	115.97 mg
Saturated fat	3.09 gm		

Seafood Pasta Salad

Serves: 4

250g (8oz) ziti
250g (8oz) sea scallops
150g (5oz) mangetouts
250ml (8fl oz) plain low-fat yogurt
2 cloves garlic, crushed
1 tsp dried oregano, crumbled
250g (8oz) medium prawns, cooked and peeled
125g (4oz) crabmeat, picked over for bones and flaked
1 red pepper, diced
1 onion, chopped
salt and pepper to taste

Cook the ziti in boiling salted water until al dente. Drain and set aside.

(continued)

Cleaning Mussels

When you first open a bag of mussels, throw away any with cracked shells or those that do not close to the touch. With the rest, scrape off the beards with a sharp knife, and scrub well with a stiff brush under running water. Place in a large pot and add cold water to cover. Let stand for 20 to 30 minutes. Drain the mussels, and then rinse them once more before cooking.

Steam the scallops until opaque throughout, about 3 minutes. Remove from the steamer and set aside. Steam the mangetouts until barely tender, about 1 minute. Set aside as well.

In a small bowl, stir together the yogurt, garlic and oregano. In a large bowl, combine the ziti, scallops, mangetouts, prawns, crabmeat, pepper, onion and yogurt mixture. Toss to coat all the ingredients evenly. Season with salt and pepper, and serve.

Nutritional Analysis

Calories	421.56	Kcal	Protein	39.15	gm
Fat	3.49	gm	Carbohydrate	56.10	gm
Sodium	538.52	mg	Cholesterol	161.15	mg
Saturated fat	0.97	gm			

Seafood Louisiana Style

Serves: 4

2 cloves garlic, crushed
2 shallots
60ml (2fl oz) dry white wine
10 large sea scallops
1 whole lobster, cooked and shelled
4 jumbo prawns, peeled and deveined
8 clams, well scrubbed
8 mussels, well scrubbed and debearded
1 tomato, chopped
500g (1lb) hot cooked white rice

In a large soup pot, sauté the garlic and shallots in the white wine over medium heat until the garlic softens, about 5 minutes. Add the scallops, lobster and prawns, and sauté for 5 minutes. Add the clams, mussels and tomato, and cook until the clams and mussels open, about 7 minutes. Discard any clams or mussels that do not open. Spoon the rice onto individual plates and top with the seafood mixture.

Nutritional Analysis

Calories	312.27 Kcal	Protein	38.76 gm
Fat	2.20 gm	Carbohydrate	28.89 gm
Sodium	489.88 mg	Cholesterol	116.31 mg
Saturated fat	0.33 gm		

Quick Sole Florentine in the Microwave

Serves: 4

500g (1lb) sole fillets
salt and pepper to taste
1/2 tsp paprika
500g (1lb) destemmed spinach leaves

On a large microwave-safe plate, arrange the fillets. Season the fillets with salt, pepper and paprika. Cover the plate with cling film. Cut a small slit in the film. Microwave on the high setting for 5 minutes. Remove the cling film. Drain off the juices and sprinkle spinach leaves over fillets. Serve at once.

Nutritional Analysis

Calories	110.26 Kcal	Protein	22.22 gm
Fat	1.47 gm	Carbohydrate	1.13 gm
Sodium	114.14 mg	Cholesterol	54.48 mg
Saturated fat	0.32 gm		

Scallop-and-Pepper Stir-Fry

Serves: 4

1 tbsp olive oil
500g (1lb) scallops
1 green pepper, chopped
1 red pepper, chopped
1 red onion, chopped
1 tsp red pepper flakes
500g (1lb) cold cooked white rice
salt and pepper to taste

In a large frying pan or wok, heat the oil over medium-high heat. Add the scallops, peppers, onion and red pepper flakes. Stir-fry until the scallops are cooked and tender, about 5 minutes. Add the rice and cook, stirring, until heated through. Season with salt and pepper, and serve.

Nutritional Analysis

Calories	252.61 Kcal	Protein	22.05 gm
Fat	4.61 gm	Carbohydrate	29.63 gm
Sodium	188.84 mg	Cholesterol	37.45 mg
Saturated fat	0.60 gm		

Curried Cod with Apricots

Serves: 4

60g (2oz) finely chopped fresh parsley
1 small onion, chopped
3 cloves garlic, crushed
250ml (8fl oz) dry white wine
2 tsp curry powder
1/4 tsp dried thyme, crumbled
1 bay leaf
500g (1lb) cod fillets
60g (2oz) dried apricots, cut into strips

Coat a frying pan with nonstick cooking spray and place over medium heat. Add the parsley, onion and garlic, and sauté for 2 minutes. Add the wine, curry powder, thyme and bay leaf and bring to the boil. Reduce the heat to medium, add the fish and cook for 5 minutes. Turn the fish over and continue to cook until the fish flakes easily when tested with a fork, about 5 minutes longer. Transfer the fillets to a warmed platter.

Add the apricots to the pan and cook over high heat until they plump up slightly, about 2 minutes. Discard the bay leaf. Spoon the apricots and pan juices over the fish, and serve immediately.

Nutritional Analysis

Calories	174.05	Kcal	Protein	21.23	gm
Fat	1.26	gm	Carbohydrate	9.75	gm
Sodium	68.37	mg	Cholesterol	48.80	mg
Saturated fat	0.14	gm			

Paella

Serves: 6

500ml (1pt) chicken stock
1/4 tsp saffron threads, crushed, or 1/4 tsp powdered
*   saffron*
1 1/2 tbsp olive oil
250g (8oz) medium prawns, peeled and deveined
250g (8oz) boneless, skinless chicken breast, trimmed
*   of fat and cut into 12mm (1/2in) thick strips*
salt and pepper to taste
1 onion, chopped
2 cloves garlic, crushed
425g (14oz) tinned tomatoes, undrained
1/8 tsp red pepper flakes
250g (8oz) arborio rice
250g (8oz) artichoke hearts, tinned in water or frozen
*   and thawed*
250g (8oz) frozen peas, thawed
90g (3oz) roasted red pepper, cut into strips
90g (3oz) dry-packed smoked mussels

In a small saucepan, combine the chicken stock and saffron and bring to a simmer. Remove from the heat and set aside.

In a large nonstick frying pan, heat 1 teaspoon of the oil over high heat. When the pan is hot, add the prawns and sauté until pink and curled, 3 to 4 minutes. Remove from the pan and set aside. Add 1 teaspoon of oil to the pan. Add the chicken and sauté until lightly browned on the outside and opaque inside, 3 to 4 minutes. Remove from the pan. Season the prawns and chicken with salt and pepper and set aside.

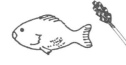

Reduce heat to medium and add the remaining oil to the pan. Stir in the onions and garlic. Sauté until softened, 3 to 5 minutes. Add 1 to 2 teaspoons of water if they become too dry. Stir in the undrained tomatoes and red-pepper flakes and simmer, uncovered, for 3 minutes, breaking up tomatoes with a wooden spoon. Add the rice and stir to coat well with the tomato mixture. Stir in the reserved chicken stock and bring to a simmer. Cover and cook over low heat for 20 minutes.

Gently stir the artichoke hearts, peas, roasted red pepper, smoked mussels and reserved prawns and chicken into the rice mixture. Cover and cook for 5 to 10 minutes longer, or until the rice is tender and the prawns and chicken are heated through. (Stir occasionally to prevent scorching, if necessary.) Taste and season with salt and pepper. Serve immediately.

Nutritional Analysis

Calories	309.75 Kcal	Protein	23.30 gm
Fat	5.81 gm	Carbohydrate	40.21 gm
Sodium	462.30 mg	Cholesterol	79.14 mg
Saturated fat	1.04 gm		

Spicing up Low-Fat Cooking

Cooking low-fat style doesn't have to be tasteless. A creative cook can make low-fat cooking exciting and tantalizing. Experiment with seasonings: for fish and seafood, use spices such as allspice, basil, cayenne, curry powder, cumin, fennel, garlic, green pepper, fresh lemon juice, marjoram, mint, dry mustard powder, paprika, saffron, sage, sesame seeds, tarragon, thyme and turmeric. And for a real zing, add fresh hot peppers to your dishes – remember to remove the membrane and the seeds before chopping finely, and always bear in mind that a little goes a long way.

Meat Dishes

CHAPTER NINE

Amount Per Chapter
15 Recipes

% Daily Value

Easy to Prepare	**100%**
Low Fat/High Flavour	**100%**
Simple to Understand	**100%**

DELICIOUS, EASY, LOW-FAT RECIPES

When many people begin to consider a low-fat diet, the first thing they cross off their list of approved foods is meat. That's a shame, because if you get into the habit of choosing the leanest cuts of beef, pork or lamb, you'll get a healthy dose of muscle-building protein as well as a lower-than-average fat content.

Start to think about meat as a condiment or as an occasional treat when you eat out. And remember that even if you eat a succulent filet mignon, you won't be forced to go on a water-and-carrot diet for the rest of the week. In addition, once you get into the habit of eating less meat and meat with a lower fat content, you'll start to crave it less. The following recipes use meat as a healthy and tasty part of your everyday low-fat diet.

Steak Stroganoff

Serves: 4

500g (1lb) boneless rump steak
3 tbsp buttery light, reduced-fat margarine
125g (4oz) chopped onions
250g (8oz) mushrooms, sliced
2 tbsp tomato puree
2 tbsp water
1/2 tsp dried basil, crumbled
1 tbsp cornflour
250ml (8fl oz) plain low-fat yogurt
60ml (2fl oz) sherry or beef stock
750g (1lb 8oz) hot cooked noodles

Trim any visible fat from the beef, then slice the beef into narrow strips.

In a frying pan, melt 2 tablespoons of the margarine over medium heat. Add the onion and sauté until soft, about 5 minutes. Add the beef and cook, stirring occasionally, until brown, about 5 minutes. Remove the beef to a plate and keep warm. Add the remaining 1 tablespoon margarine to the pan, melt over medium heat and add the mushrooms. Sauté until mushrooms are soft, about 8 minutes. Stir in the tomato puree, water and basil. Return the meat to the pan and simmer briefly.

In a small saucepan, mix together the corn-flour with 1 tablespoon of the yogurt until thoroughly combined. Then stir in the remaining yogurt and cook over medium heat until thickened, about 10 minutes. Add to the meat mixture and heat through. Thin the sauce with the sherry or stock. Serve over cooked noodles.

Nutritional Analysis

Calories	475.54 Kcal	Protein	36.34 gm
Fat	15.25 gm	Carbohydrate	43.47 gm
Sodium	373.43 mg	Cholesterol	107.69 mg
Saturated fat	3.65 gm		

Hearty Meat Loaf

Serves: 6

500g (1lb) lean rump beef, trimmed of fat and minced
125g (4oz) seasoned dried breadcrumbs
2 egg whites or egg substitute equal to 2 eggs
1 tbsp sunflower oil (optional)
250g (8oz) chopped onion
250g (8oz) chopped celery with leaf top
1/2 tsp Worcestershire sauce
salt and pepper to taste
250ml (8fl oz) ketchup

Preheat oven to 190°C (375°F), gas mark 5.

In a large bowl, mix together the minced meat, breadcrumbs, egg whites or egg substitutes, oil (if using), onion, celery, Worcestershire sauce, salt and pepper. Mix well. Press the meat into a standard nonstick loaf pan. Spread the ketchup on top.

Bake until cooked through when tested with a knife, 1 to 1¼ hours. Serve hot or cold.

Variations: if you like, you can 'stuff' the meat loaf. Put half the meat mixture in the bottom of the loaf pan. Top with 375g (12oz) sliced red, green or yellow peppers; 375g (12oz) carrots cut into thin strips; 250g (8oz) chopped black olives; 4 hard-cooked egg whites, slivered; or 375g (12oz) cooked sliced mushrooms. Then press the remaining meat on top and cover with the ketchup. Bake as directed.

Nutritional Analysis

Calories	198.15	Kcal	Protein	21.72	gm
Fat	2.95	gm	Carbohydrate	21.39	gm
Sodium	834.90	mg	Cholesterol	43.13	mg
Saturated fat	0.94	gm			

Quick Pressure-Cooked Pot Roast

Serves: 8

1.2kg (2lb 8oz) roasting beef, all fat trimmed
plain flour for dredging
salt and pepper to taste
1 tbsp vegetable oil
1 large onion, cut into chunks
3 celery stalks, cut into chunks
1 tsp dried thyme, crumbled
1 tsp dried rosemary, crumbled
3 tbsp honey
2 tbsp cider vinegar
125ml (4fl oz) dry red wine
500ml (1pt) vegetable juice cocktail, such as
*   V8 brand*

Dust the beef roast with flour that has been seasoned liberally with salt and pepper. In the bottom of a large pressure cooker, heat the oil over high heat. Brown the meat on all sides and transfer to a plate. Reduce the heat to medium. Add the onion and celery, and cook until soft, about 1 minute, stirring frequently. Add the

(continued)

thyme, rosemary, honey, vinegar and wine. Bring to the boil. Add the vegetable juice and heat just until the mixture simmers. Adjust seasoning with salt and pepper.

Return the beef to the pot. Secure the lid in place. Bring to high pressure over high heat. Adjust the heat to maintain high pressure and cook for **40** minutes. Remove from the heat and let stand for **10** minutes, then release the remaining steam through escape valve. Remove the lid, tilting it away from you to allow any excess steam to escape. Transfer the pot roast to a plate.

Slice the meat and serve with the juices from the cooker.

Nutritional Analysis

Calories	261.08 Kcal	Protein	29.13 gm
Fat	8.95 gm	Carbohydrate	14.85 gm
Sodium	326.82 mg	Cholesterol	75.48 mg
Saturated fat	2.65 gm		

Caribbean Beef

Serves: 10

1 tbsp vegetable oil
1.5kg (3lb) fillet of beef, cut into cubes
600g (1lb 4oz) tinned pineapple chunks
250ml (8fl oz) water
180ml (6fl oz) vinegar
125ml (4fl oz) brown sugar, packed
4 tbsp cornflour
1 tsp salt
2 tbsp reduced-sodium soy sauce

250g (8oz) thinly sliced green peppers
250g (8oz) thinly sliced onions
2kg (4lb) hot cooked white rice
10 tomato wedges, for garnish
20 green pepper strips, for garnish

Heat the oil in a frying pan over medium-high heat. Add cubed beef and brown the meat slowly on all sides.

Drain the pineapple, reserving the syrup. In a large saucepan, combine water, vinegar, brown sugar, cornflour, salt, soy sauce and the pineapple syrup. Cook over medium heat until thickened. Add meat and cover. Cook over low heat until meat is tender, approximately 45 minutes.

Add green pepper, onions and pineapple chunks. Simmer for 30 minutes. Serve over hot rice. Garnish with tomato wedges and green pepper strips.

Nutritional Analysis

Calories	299.85 Kcal	Protein	30.57 gm
Fat	7.37 gm	Carbohydrate	27.42 gm
Sodium	433.55 mg	Cholesterol	73.54 mg
Saturated fat	2.19 gm		

Spicy Beef in Lettuce Cups

Serves: 4

375g (12oz) rump beef steak
125ml (4fl oz) orange juice
2 tbsp hoisin sauce
2 tbsp reduced-sodium soy sauce
2 tbsp rice vinegar

1 tsp cornflour
1 tsp vegetable oil
1 tbsp grated, peeled fresh ginger
¼ tsp red pepper flakes
300g (10oz) grated cabbage
425g (14oz) grated carrots
3 spring onions, cut into 6mm (¼in) pieces
4 medium-size cos or romaine lettuce leaves

With a sharp knife, trim all fat from the steak. Cut the steak lengthways in half, then cut each half across into 3mm (⅛in) thick slices.

In a small bowl, combine the orange juice, hoisin sauce, soy sauce, vinegar and cornflour. Heat the oil in a 305mm (12in) nonstick pan over medium-high heat. Add ginger and crushed red pepper and cook for 20 seconds; add the beef and cook until it just loses its pink colour. Transfer the beef to the bowl; keep warm. Add the orange-juice mixture, cabbage, carrots, and half the spring onions to the pan and cook, stirring constantly, until the sauce thickens slightly, about 1 minute. Return the beef to the pan; heat through.

Line 4 plates with the lettuce leaves. Spoon the beef mixture into the leaves and sprinkle with the remaining spring onions. Serve immediately.

Nutritional Analysis

Calories	213.88 Kcal	Protein	23.44 gm
Fat	4.50 gm	Carbohydrate	19.96 gm
Sodium	536.04 mg	Cholesterol	48.52 mg
Saturated fat	1.16 gm		

Orangey Beef and Broccoli Stir-Fry

Serves: 6

3 oranges
3 tbsp reduced-sodium soy sauce
1 tbsp rice wine or dry sherry
1 tbsp cornflour
½ tsp sugar
3 tsp sesame oil
500g (1lb) lean beef sirloin, trimmed of fat and sliced
    against the grain into 3mm (⅛in) slices
2 tbsp crushed garlic
2 tbsp finely chopped fresh ginger
6 to 8 small dried red chillies
1kg (2lb) broccoli, broken into very small florets
80ml (2½fl oz) water
1 red pepper, seeded and sliced
125g (4oz) sliced spring onion tops

With a small sharp knife or vegetable peeler, carefully pare wide strips of zest from one of the oranges. Cut the zest into 25mm (1in) lengths and set aside. Squeeze the juice from all the oranges into a small bowl. Add soy sauce, rice wine (or sherry), cornflour and sugar; stir to combine and set aside.

In a wok or large frying pan, heat 1 teaspoon of the oil over high heat until almost smoking. Add the beef and stir-fry just until no longer pink on the outside, about 1 minute. Transfer to a plate lined with paper towels and set aside.

(continued)

Add the remaining oil to the pan and heat until very hot. Add the garlic, ginger, chillies and reserved orange peel. Stir-fry until fragrant, about 30 seconds. Add the broccoli and water. Cover and simmer, stirring occasionally, until the water has evaporated and the broccoli sizzles, about 3 minutes. Add the peppers and stir-fry for 1 minute.

Stir the reserved orange sauce and pour into the wok. Bring to the boil, stirring; cook until the sauce has thickened slightly, 1 to 2 minutes. Add the spring onion tops and reserved beef, toss to coat with sauce, and heat through.

Nutritional Analysis

Calories	229.51 Kcal	Protein	22.21	gm
Fat	6.53 gm	Carbohydrate	23.04	gm
Sodium	387.07 mg	Cholesterol	46.15	mg
Saturated fat	1.60 gm			

Thai-Style Beef Salad

Serves: 4

3 tbsp soy sauce
1½ tbsp brown sugar
2 tbsp water
375g (12oz) rump steak, trimmed of fat and cut into strips 50mm (2in) long by 6mm (¼in) wide by 6mm (¼in) thick
2 tbsp seasoned rice vinegar
1 tbsp lemon juice
1 large clove garlic, crushed
1 tsp sesame oil

¼ tsp red pepper flakes
1kg (2lb) shredded Chinese cabbage or iceberg lettuce
375g (12oz) coarsely grated carrots
250g (8oz) thinly sliced spring onions
250g (8oz) cooked spaghetti
60ml (2oz) loosely packed fresh coriander leaves

In a small bowl, combine 1 tablespoon of the soy sauce, 1 tablespoon of the brown sugar and the water. Place the beef in a shallow bowl and pour the soy mixture over it. Toss to coat. Marinate for 30 minutes. Drain the beef, discarding the marinade. In a nonstick frying pan, stir-fry the beef over high heat until brown, about 3 minutes. Remove from the pan and let cool to room temperature.

In a small bowl, stir together the remaining soy sauce and the remaining brown sugar with the vinegar, lemon juice, garlic, sesame oil and red pepper flakes. In a large bowl, combine the beef, cabbage or lettuce, carrots, spring onions, spaghetti and coriander leaves. Toss to mix. Pour on the dressing, toss well and serve.

Nutritional Analysis

Calories	233.19 Kcal	Protein	23.52	gm
Fat	4.44 gm	Carbohydrate	24.82	gm
Sodium	960.95 mg	Cholesterol	48.52	mg
Saturated fat	1.19 gm			

Beef Stew

Serves: 4

1 tsp olive oil
500g (1lb) extra-lean stewing beef, cut into 25mm
   (1in) cubes
1 large onion, sliced
salt and pepper to taste
310ml (10fl oz) water
4 small potatoes, cubed
250g (8oz) green beans, cut into 12mm (1/2in) pieces
4 small carrots
250g (8oz) chopped tomatoes
1 tbsp plain flour

In the bottom of a pressure cooker, heat the oil over high heat. Add the meat and brown on all sides. Add the onion, salt, pepper and 250ml (8fl oz) of the water to the cooker. Place the potatoes, green beans, carrots and tomatoes on top of the meat. Secure the lid in place. Bring to high pressure over high heat. Adjust the heat to maintain high pressure and cook for 8 minutes. Reduce the pressure with the quick-release method. In a small bowl, make a paste of the flour and the remaining water. Remove the cooker lid, tilting it away from you to allow excess steam to escape. Place the cooker over medium heat and stir in the flour paste to thicken the juices.

Serve the meat and vegetables with the pan juices spooned over them.

Nutritional Analysis

Calories	340.62 Kcal	Protein	26.29 gm
Fat	10.09 gm	Carbohydrate	36.27 gm
Sodium	122.45 mg	Cholesterol	73.77 mg
Saturated fat	3.34 gm		

Burgundy-Style Beef

Serves: 8

1kg (2lb) rump steak
salt and pepper to taste
3 onions, chopped
4 cloves garlic, crushed
1/2 tsp dried thyme, crumbled
1 bay leaf
90g (3oz) finely chopped fresh parsley
310ml (10fl oz) dry red wine
2 tbsp plain flour
250ml (8fl oz) beef stock
375g (12oz) mushrooms, sliced

Cut the meat into 50mm (2in) cubes and place in a dish. Season with salt and pepper. Spread a third of the onions and all the garlic over the meat. Add the thyme, bay leaf and parsley. Pour in the wine. Cover and marinate for at least 2 hours at room temperature or longer in the refrigerator, turning occasionally.

In a large frying pan, heat the oil over medium heat. Add the rest of the onions and sauté until soft, about 5 minutes. Drain the meat, reserving the marinade, and dredge in the flour. Add to the pan and sauté for several minutes with the

(continued)

171

onions. Add the marinade, stir well and add the stock. Bring to the boil, cover, reduce the heat to low and simmer until the meat is tender, 1½ hours. Add the mushrooms during the last 10 minutes of cooking, then serve.

Nutritional Analysis

Calories	207.22 Kcal	Protein	27.40 gm
Fat	5.84 gm	Carbohydrate	10.52 gm
Sodium	150.01 mg	Cholesterol	65.83 mg
Saturated fat	1.92 gm		

Spicy Chinese Beef

Serves: 12

1 tbsp peanut oil
2 onions, sliced
4 cloves garlic, crushed
4 tsp peeled and finely chopped fresh ginger
500g (1lb) extra-lean beef, thinly sliced
2 tomatoes, cut into chunks
2 green peppers, cut into long, narrow strips
60ml (2fl oz) oyster sauce
2 tbsp soy sauce
2 tsp chilli paste
500g (1lb) beansprouts
1kg (2lb) cold cooked white rice
3 tbsp peanuts
5 spring onions, chopped

In a wok or large, deep frying pan, heat the oil over high heat for 30 seconds. Add the onions and stir-fry for 2 minutes. Add the garlic, ginger and beef,

and stir-fry until the beef is brown, another 2 minutes. Add the tomatoes, peppers, oyster sauce, soy sauce and chilli paste. Stir-fry for another 2 minutes. Add the beansprouts and stir well. Add the rice and toss with the beef mixture. Sprinkle with the peanuts and spring onions, and serve.

Nutritional Analysis

Calories	173.86 Kcal	Protein	12.19 gm
Fat	4.39 gm	Carbohydrate	21.42 gm
Sodium	459.88 mg	Cholesterol	21.94 mg
Saturated fat	1.01 gm		

Pork Pinwheels with Apricot Stuffing

Serves: 6

1 pork tenderloin, about 500g (1lb)

Stuffing:
180ml (6fl oz) reduced-sodium, fat-free chicken stock, heated
90g (3oz) snipped dried apricots
2 tbsp chopped celery
1 small onion, chopped
1 tbsp buttery light, reduced-fat margarine
1/8 tsp ground cinnamon
dash of pepper
300g (10oz) wholemeal bread cubes

Sauce:
1½ tsp cornflour
dash of ground nutmeg
250g (8oz) apricot conserve

Preheat the grill.

Split the tenderloin lengthways, but do not cut all the way through. Open it out flat, as if it were a book. Pound the meat lightly with a meat mallet to a 255 x 100mm (10 x 6in) rectangle.

To make the stuffing, place the apricots in a small bowl and pour the stock over them. Let stand for 5 minutes. In a small pan, melt the margarine over medium heat. Add the celery and onion and sauté until soft but not brown, about 5 minutes. Remove from the heat and stir in the cinnamon and pepper. In a large bowl, mix together the bread cubes, onion mixture and apricot mixture; toss lightly to moisten.

Spread the stuffing evenly over the tenderloin. Roll up roulade style, starting from the short side. Secure the roll with wooden toothpicks or tie with kitchen string at 25mm (1in) intervals. Cut the meat roll across into six 25mm (1in) thick slices. Place the meat slices on a grill pan, cut side down. Slip under the grill about 100mm (4in) from the heat source and grill for 12 minutes. Turn the slices over and heat until the meat is cooked through, 11 to 12 minutes. Remove the toothpicks or string, and transfer the meat slices to a serving platter.

Meanwhile, to make the sauce, combine the cornflour and nutmeg in a small saucepan. Stir in the apricot conserve and place over medium heat. Cook, stirring, until bubbling, then cook and stir for 2 minutes more. Serve the sauce with meat slices.

Nutritional Analysis

Calories	188.18	Kcal	Protein	17.05	gm
Fat	3.69	gm	Carbohydrate	19.83	gm
Sodium	179.19	mg	Cholesterol	46.23	mg
Saturated fat	1.53	gm			

Pork Chops Dijon

Serves: 4

500g (1lb) boneless lean pork chops
1 onion, chopped
3 tbsp Dijon mustard
2 tbsp low-fat Italian dressing
1/4 tsp pepper

Spray a large frying pan with nonstick cooking spray and place over medium-high heat. Add the chops and brown on both sides, turning once. Transfer the chops to a plate and set aside. Add the onions to the pan and cook and stir over medium heat until soft, about 3 minutes. Push the onions to the side of the pan and return the chops to the pan. In a small bowl, quickly stir together the mustard, dressing and pepper. Spread the mixture over the chops. Cover and cook over medium-low heat until the meat is tender, about 15 minutes. Serve immediately.

Nutritional Analysis

Calories	211.64	Kcal	Protein	24.80	gm
Fat	6.72	gm	Carbohydrate	4.24	gm
Sodium	391.28	mg	Cholesterol	66.90	mg
Saturated fat	2.22	gm			

Pork and Wild Rice Salad with Plums

Serves: 4

> 185g (6oz) white and wild rice mix
> 60ml (2fl oz) herb vinegar
> 1 tbsp Dijon mustard
> 1 tbsp crushed garlic
> 1 tbsp honey
> 2 tsp cornflour
> 250ml (8fl oz) water
> 2 tbsp diced spring onions
> 2 tsp dried parsley flakes
> 1/4 tsp red pepper flakes
> 500g (1lb) mixed salad greens
> 500g (1lb) thinly sliced carrots
> 375g (12oz) slivered sugar snaps
> 300g (10oz) roast pork, trimmed and thinly sliced
> 8 plums, stoned and sliced

Cook white and wild rice mix as directed on the packet. Set aside.

In a saucepan over medium heat, combine the vinegar, mustard, garlic, honey and cornflour. Stir in the water and cook, stirring, until thickened, about 5 minutes. Remove from the heat and stir in the spring onions, parsley and red pepper flakes. Let cool, cover and chill.

In a bowl, toss together the salad greens, carrots and sugar snaps. Divide among individual salad plates. Spoon the rice into the centre of the plates, and top with the pork and plums. Drizzle with the dressing and serve.

Nutritional Analysis

Calories	504.91 Kcal		Protein	29.04 gm
Fat	10.71 gm		Carbohydrate	73.83 gm
Sodium	701.54 mg		Cholesterol	63.75 mg
Saturated fat	4.24 gm			

Pork and Chick Pea Curry

Serves: 4

> 500g (1lb) pork fillets, cut into 25mm (1in) chunks
> 1 tbsp olive oil
> 2 cloves garlic, crushed
> 1 onion, chopped
> 2 tsp peeled and finely chopped fresh ginger
> 1 tbsp plain flour
> 1 tsp curry powder
> 1/2 tsp ground coriander
> 1/2 tsp ground cumin
> salt and pepper to taste
> 2 carrots, grated
> 2 white potatoes, peeled and cubed
> 125ml (4fl oz) water
> 625g (1lb 4oz) tinned chick peas, drained and rinsed
> 1 apple, peeled, cored and chopped

In a frying pan, brown the pork in olive oil over medium heat for 5 minutes. Add the garlic, onion and ginger, and cook for 2 minutes. Stir in the flour, curry powder, coriander, cumin, salt and pepper. Add the carrots, potato and water, and bring to the boil. Reduce the heat to low, cover and cook for 10 minutes, adding the water if the mixture begins to dry out. Add the chick peas and apple, cover and cook over medium heat until the

vegetables are cooked through, about 10 minutes longer. Serve immediately.

Nutritional Analysis

Calories	400.22 Kcal	Protein	30.78 gm
Fat	12.08 gm	Carbohydrate	41.74 gm
Sodium	232.05 mg	Cholesterol	77.18 mg
Saturated fat	2.71 gm		

Veal Scaloppine Dijon

Serves: 4

4 dry-packed unsalted sun-dried tomato halves
500g (1lb) veal cutlets
1/4 tsp salt
1/4 tsp coarse black pepper
3 medium cucumbers
1 medium leek
3 tbsp low-fat milk
1 tbsp Dijon mustard
3/4 tsp cornflour
3 tsp light corn oil spread
3/4 tsp instant low-fat chicken bouillon
185ml (6fl oz) water

Place sun-dried tomato halves in small bowl with 250ml (8fl oz) boiling water. Let stand 15 minutes to soften.

Meanwhile, with a meat mallet tenderize the veal cutlets to 3mm (1/8in) thickness. Cut each veal cutlet across in half. Sprinkle with salt and pepper. With a vegetable peeler, remove several strips of peel from each cucumber. Cut the cucumbers into 38mm (1½in) chunks. Cut off the roots and trim

the leaf ends of the leek. Separate leek into leaves and rinse with running cold water to remove sand. Cut leaves across into 75mm (3in) pieces, then cut lengthways into 6mm (1/4in) thick strips. Drain and thinly slice the sun-dried tomato halves.

In a small bowl, mix the milk, mustard and cornflour until smooth. Set aside.

Melt 1 teaspoon of the light corn-oil spread in a 305mm (12in) nonstick frying pan over medium-high heat. Place cucumbers and 1/2 teaspoon salt in the pan, stir frequently and sauté until golden and tender-crisp. Place the cucumbers in a bowl. Keep warm.

In the same pan over medium-high heat, melt the remaining light corn-oil spread. Add the veal cutlets, half at a time. Cook about 2 minutes, turning once, until veal just loses its pink colour. Remove the veal cutlets to a plate as they are done.

In the same pan, bring the leek, low-fat chicken bouillon and water to the boil. Reduce heat to low. Cover and simmer until the leek is tender, 3 to 5 minutes. Stir in the cornflour mixture and dried tomatoes. Over medium-high heat, bring to the boil for 1 minute. Add the veal with any juices in the plate to the sauce in the pan. Heat through. Serve the veal with sauce and cucumbers.

Nutritional Analysis

Calories	204.61 Kcal	Protein	26.41 gm
Fat	2.42 gm	Carbohydrate	14.45 gm
Sodium	545.73 mg	Cholesterol	88.98 mg
Saturated fat	1.23 gm		

Poultry Dishes

CHAPTER TEN

Amount Per Chapter
45 Recipes

	% Daily Value
Easy to Prepare	**100%**
Low Fat/High Flavour	**100%**
Simple to Understand	**100%**

DELICIOUS, EASY, LOW-FAT RECIPES

I can't think of any meat-eater I know who doesn't like chicken. No doubt that's because it's tasty and easy to cook, plus it's low in fat and cholesterol if you remove the skin and trim away any visible fat.

Chicken is also versatile – the main reason why I like it so much. You can spread a grilled chicken breast with a bit of pesto, place it between two slices of bread with some lettuce and tomato, and you have a quick lunch. On the other hand, you can go all-out and create a dish that will fit in with a gourmet dinner, and it will still be low in fat.

The following recipes underscore the versatility and wonderful flavour of chicken, so let the cooking begin.

Chicken Marsala

Serves: 4

1 tbsp buttery light, reduced-fat margarine
4 skinless, boneless chicken breast halves
⅛ tsp salt
⅛ tsp pepper
2 tbsp shallots or spring onions, finely chopped
125ml (4fl oz) Marsala wine
125ml (4fl oz) reduced-sodium, fat-free chicken stock
500g (8oz) tomatoes, peeled, seeded and chopped
60g (2oz) finely chopped fresh parsley

In a frying pan, melt the margarine over medium heat. Add the chicken and brown on both sides, about 5 minutes. Sprinkle with the salt and pepper, and remove from the skillet.

Add the shallots or spring onions, wine, stock and tomatoes to the skillet. Simmer over medium heat until the liquid is partially reduced, about 10 minutes. Return the chicken to the pan, spooning sauce over it. Cover and simmer over low heat

until the chicken is tender, about 15 to 20 minutes longer. To serve, transfer the chicken to warmed plates and spoon the sauce over the top. Sprinkle with the parsley.

Nutritional Analysis

Calories	195.43	Kcal	Protein	28.66	gm
Fat	4.61	gm	Carbohydrate	8.87	gm
Sodium	266.41	mg	Cholesterol	68.44	mg
Saturated fat	0.88	gm			

Chicken Gumbo

Serves: 8

90g (3oz) plain flour
1 tbsp sunflower oil
250g (8oz) boneless, skinless chicken breasts, cut into thin strips
90g (3oz) chorizo sausage, thinly sliced
1 onion, chopped

1 large green pepper, seeded and diced
1 stalk celery, finely chopped
4 cloves garlic, crushed
750ml (1½pt) reduced-sodium, fat-free chicken stock
500g (1lb) tinned diced tomatoes, undrained
300g (10oz) frozen okra, slightly thawed and sliced
4 jalapeño peppers, pierced all over with a fork
1 bay leaf
½ tsp dried thyme leaves
Tabasco sauce, to taste
Salt and pepper to taste
750g (1lb 4oz) cooked white rice

Heat a heavy cast-iron pan over medium heat. Add flour and cook, stirring constantly with a wooden spoon, until flour turns deep golden, 7 to 10 minutes. (There will be a strong aroma similar to burned toast. Be careful not to let flour burn; reduce the heat if the flour seems to be browning too quickly. Alternatively, you can toast the flour in a pie pan in a 200°C/400°F, gas mark 6 oven for 20 minutes.) Transfer to a plate to cool.

In a Dutch oven or heavy soup pot, heat ½ tablespoon of the oil over high heat. Add the chicken and sausage; cook, stirring, until brown on all sides, about 3 minutes. Remove from pot and drain on paper towels.

Reduce heat to medium; heat the remaining oil. Add onions, peppers, celery and garlic. Cook, stirring, until onions are light brown, about 7 minutes. Stir in the toasted flour. Gradually stir in chicken stock and bring to a simmer.

Add the tomatoes and their juice, okra, jalapeños, bay leaf and thyme. Stir. Reduce heat to low, cover and simmer for 30 minutes.

Add the reserved chicken and sausage and simmer for 5 minutes more. Discard jalapeños and bay leaf. Season with hot sauce, salt and pepper. Serve with rice and optional hot sauce.

Nutritional Analysis

Calories	219.98 Kcal	Protein	12.89 gm
Fat	5.41 gm	Carbohydrate	29.61 gm
Sodium	437.75 mg	Cholesterol	23.57 mg
Saturated fat	1.34 gm		

Yogurt Chicken Paprika

Serves: 6

3 chicken thighs, skinned
3 skinless chicken breast halves
⅛ tsp pepper
60g (2oz) plain flour
1 tbsp olive oil
60g (2oz) diced onion
250ml (8fl oz) hot water
2 tsp lemon juice
2 tbsp cornflour
500ml (1pt) plain low-fat yogurt
2 tsp paprika

Season the chicken pieces with the pepper. Roll the chicken in the flour, coating well. In a large frying pan, heat the oil over medium heat. Add the chicken and brown on both sides, 10 to 15

(continued)

minutes. Add the onion, water and lemon juice. Cover and cook over low heat until tender, about 40 minutes. Remove the chicken from the pan to a warmed platter and keep warm.

In a bowl, stir the cornflour into 2 tablespoons of the yogurt, then mix in the remaining yogurt. Stir into the pan dripping. Simmer over low heat until thickened, about 5 minutes. Add paprika and mix well. Pour the yogurt sauce over the chicken and serve.

Nutritional Analysis

Calories	207.79 Kcal	Protein	25.06 gm
Fat	5.64 gm	Carbohydrate	12.83 gm
Sodium	122.10 mg	Cholesterol	67.38 mg
Saturated fat	1.59 gm		

Raspberry Chicken

Serves: 4

4 chicken leg quarters, skinned
1/2 tsp salt
1/2 tsp black pepper
125g (4oz) seedless raspberry jam
2 tbsp balsamic vinegar
1 tbsp reduced-sodium soy sauce
1/8 tsp crushed red pepper or 1/2 tsp red pepper flakes

Preheat oven to 190°C (375°F), gas mark 5. Spray a 230 x 330mm (9 x 13in) baking dish with nonstick cooking spray. Place the chicken leg quarters in the baking dish and sprinkle with salt and black pepper. Bake for 45 to 50 minutes, or until the chicken is golden and cooked through.

In a small saucepan, combine the remaining ingredients; mix well. Cook over low heat for about 1 minute, until the sauce is smooth, stirring occasionally. Remove the chicken from the baking dish and place on a serving platter. Top with the sauce and serve.

Nutritional Analysis

Calories	259.22 Kcal	Protein	26.71 gm
Fat	5.31 gm	Carbohydrate	26.66 gm
Sodium	567.86 mg	Cholesterol	104.00 mg
Saturated fat	1.27 gm		

Curried Chicken

Serves: 6

125g (4oz) plain flour
1/8 tsp salt
1/2 tsp pepper
1 chicken, about 1.25kg (2lb 8oz), skinned and cut into
    serving pieces
2 tbsp corn oil
1 onion, chopped
1 green pepper, chopped
1 clove garlic, crushed
185g (6oz) tomato puree
500ml (1pt) water
1 1/2 tsp curry powder
1/2 tsp dried thyme, crumbled
1 tsp raisins

In a shallow bowl, combine the flour, salt and pepper, mixing well. Coat the chicken pieces with

the seasoned flour. In a large frying pan, heat the oil over medium heat. Add the chicken pieces and brown on both sides, about 7 minutes a side. Add the onion, pepper and garlic, and cook until soft, about 10 minutes.

Drain the fat. Add the tomato puree, water, curry powder and thyme. Simmer, uncovered, over medium heat, until the juices run clear when the chicken is pierced, about 30 minutes. Add the raisins, heat through for another 5 minutes and serve.

Nutritional Analysis

Calories	218.71	Kcal	Protein	22.10	gm
Fat	6.67	gm	Carbohydrate	17.54	gm
Sodium	344.53	mg	Cholesterol	63.56	mg
Saturated fat	1.18	gm			

Grilled Yogurt-Lemon Chicken

Serves: 10

500ml (1pt) plain low-fat yogurt
80ml (2¹/₂fl oz) vinegar
2 tbsp lemon juice
2 cloves garlic, crushed
2 tsp coriander seeds, crushed
¹/₄ tsp ground cloves
8 drops of Tabasco sauce
¹/₂ tsp pepper
1 tsp dry mustard
¹/₂ tsp ground ginger
2.5kg (5lb) chicken pieces, skinned

(continued)

Bulgur

Bulgur is a crunchy, nutty wheat grain that adds texture to dishes. Similar to cracked wheat, it can be substituted for rice or tiny pasta in many menus. It is also easy to prepare, as all you need to do is pour boiling water over it and then let it sit until the liquid is absorbed. You can create your own recipes by adding onion and garlic, vegetables, chicken or anything else you like.

In a large bowl, mix together all the ingredients except the chicken. Add the chicken, turn to coat, cover and refrigerate overnight.

Preheat oven to 170°C (325°F), gas mark 3. Transfer the chicken to a baking dish. Bake, basting every 30 minutes with pan juices, until the juices run clear when the chicken pieces are pierced, 2 to 2½ hours. (Alternatively, cook over medium-hot coals, turning and basting every 15 minutes, for 2 to 2½ hours.)

Nutritional Analysis

Calories	163.31	Kcal	Protein	25.81	gm
Fat	4.17	gm	Carbohydrate	4.31	gm
Sodium	117.21	mg	Cholesterol	78.99	mg
Saturated fat	1.31	gm			

Poached Chicken

Serves: 4

1 tbsp buttery light, reduced-fat margarine
1 onion, sliced
3 carrots, cut into thin strips
3 celery stalks, cut into strips
1.25kg (2lb 8oz) chicken pieces, skinned
1l (2pt) reduced-sodium, fat-free chicken stock
60ml (2fl oz) dry vermouth or white wine (optional)
1 bay leaf
3 parsley sprigs
½ tsp dried thyme, crumbled
⅛ tsp salt
⅛ tsp pepper

In a heavy saucepan, melt the margarine over medium heat. Add the onion, carrots and celery, and sauté until soft, about 5 minutes. Add the chicken, cover the pan and cook for another 5 minutes.

Add the stock, vermouth or wine, bay leaf, parsley, thyme, salt and pepper. Cook gently until the juices run clear when the chicken is pierced, about 25 minutes. Remove and discard the bay leaf. Serve with poaching liquid in individual bowls.

Nutritional Analysis

Calories	246.51	Kcal	Protein	33.08	gm
Fat	7.27	gm	Carbohydrate	10.63	gm
Sodium	749.38	mg	Cholesterol	95.34	mg
Saturated fat	1.56	gm			

Very Lemony Chicken

Serves: 4

750g (1lb 8oz) chicken pieces, skinned
125ml (4fl oz) lemon juice
2 tbsp distilled white vinegar
60g (2oz) slivered lemon zest
1 tbsp chopped fresh oregano or 1 tsp dried oregano, crumbled
1 onion, sliced
¼ tsp salt
⅛ tsp pepper
½ tsp paprika

Place the chicken pieces in a 230 x 330 x 50mm (9 x 13 x 2in) baking dish. In a small bowl, mix together the lemon juice, vinegar, lemon zest, oregano and onion. Pour over the chicken, cover and marinate in the refrigerator for several hours or as long as overnight, turning occasionally. Sprinkle with salt, pepper and paprika.

Preheat oven to 400°C (200°F), gas mark 6. Cover the baking dish with tin foil and bake for 30 minutes. Uncover and continue to bake until the juices run clear when a chicken piece is pierced, about 30 minutes longer. Serve immediately.

Nutritional Analysis

Calories	131.21	Kcal	Protein	18.34	gm
Fat	2.74	gm	Carbohydrate	8.34	gm
Sodium	214.53	mg	Cholesterol	57.20	mg
Saturated Fat	0.66	gm			

Skillet Chicken and Rice

Serves: 6

1kg (2lb) chicken pieces, skinned
750g (1lb 8oz) sliced mushrooms
4 carrots, cut into 12mm (1/2in) thick slices
185g (6oz) long-grain white rice
60g (2oz) chopped onion
1 tsp low-fat chicken bouillon granules
1 tsp poultry seasoning
1/4 tsp salt
500ml (1pt) water

Spray a 305mm (12in) frying pan with nonstick spray coating and place over medium heat. Brown the chicken pieces on both sides, about 15 minutes. Remove the chicken from the pan. Drain off the fat from the pan, if necessary. Add the mushrooms, carrots, rice, onion, bouillon granules, poultry seasoning, salt and water. Place the chicken on top of the rice mixture. Cover and simmer over low heat until the juices run clear when a chicken piece is pierced and the rice is tender, about 30 minutes. Serve at once.

Nutritional Analysis

Calories	208.77	Kcal	Protein	18.55	gm
Fat	2.80	gm	Carbohydrate	26.41	gm
Sodium	344.75	mg	Cholesterol	50.84	mg
Saturated Fat	0.64	gm			

Strawberry Chicken Salad

Serves: 4

125ml (4fl oz) low-fat mayonnaise
2 tbsp chutney
1 tbsp lemon juice
1 tsp grated lemon zest
1 tsp salt
1 tsp curry powder
500g (1lb) diced cooked chicken
250g (8oz) sliced celery
60g (2oz) chopped red onion
4 lettuce leaves
750g (1lb 8oz) strawberries, destemmed
fresh mint sprigs

In a large bowl, stir together the mayonnaise, chutney, lemon juice and zest, salt and curry

(continued)

powder, mixing well. Add the chicken, celery and onion. Toss well, cover and chill.

Just before serving, slice 500g (1lb) of the strawberries. Add to the chicken mixture and toss gently. Line a platter or individual serving plates with the lettuce leaves. Place the chicken mixture on the lettuce. Garnish with the whole strawberries and mint. Serve at once.

Handling Chicken Safely

Today, with everyone so aware of salmonella and other bacteria that can easily be transmitted through raw chicken, the following standards must be met:

- **Always wash your hands before and after handling raw chicken.**
- **Thoroughly wash all cutting boards and utensils that you've used to prepare raw chicken.**
- **Make sure chicken is thoroughly cooked (to 115°C/180°F) before serving it.**
- **If chicken smells at all odd, throw it away.**

Nutritional Analysis

Calories	252.74 Kcal	Protein	21.61 gm
Fat	7.77 gm	Carbohydrate	24.56 gm
Sodium	969.90 mg	Cholesterol	62.30 mg
Saturated fat	1.45 gm		

Chicken Pizza

Serves: 6

185g (6oz) dry-packed sun-dried tomatoes, cut into thin strips
60ml (2fl oz) olive oil
375g (12oz) skinless chicken meat, diced
1 tsp dried oregano, crumbled
1/2 tsp dried basil, crumbled
1/2 tsp dried thyme, crumbled
1/2 tsp salt
1/2 tsp pepper
1 ready-made pizza crust, 305mm (12in) in diameter
500g (1lb) cooked, peeled and diced prawns
1 avocado, stoned, peeled and diced
1 jalapeño pepper, seeded and finely diced
250g (8oz) redcurrant jelly
250g (8oz) grated low-fat cheddar or low-fat mozzarella cheese

184

Soak the tomatoes in hot water for 30 minutes. Drain and set aside.

In a frying pan, heat 2 tablespoons of the oil over medium heat. Add the chicken, oregano, basil, thyme, salt and pepper, and cook, stirring often, until the chicken is tender, about 15 minutes. Drain off the oil and set aside.

Preheat oven to 230°C (450°F), gas mark 8.

Prepare the pizza crust for topping as directed on the package. Brush with the remaining oil. Spoon the chicken over the dough. Scatter the tomatoes, prawns, avocado and jalapeño over the chicken. Pour the redcurrant jelly over the top, and sprinkle with the cheese.

Bake until the crust is golden brown, 15 to 20 minutes. Cut into wedges to serve.

Nutritional Analysis

Calories	636.22 Kcal	Protein	32.91 gm
Fat	21.89 gm	Carbohydrate	76.52 gm
Sodium	652.85 mg	Cholesterol	133.85 mg
Saturated fat	3.93 gm		

Sweet-and-Sour Chicken

Serves: 8

1 tbsp vegetable oil
1.5kg (3lb) chicken, cut into serving pieces and skinned
600g (1lb 4oz) tinned pineapple chunks, drained, juice reserved
125g (4oz) sliced celery
1 green or red pepper, cut into chunks
60g (2oz) firmly packed brown sugar
125ml (4fl oz) vinegar

2 tbsp soy sauce
1 tbsp tomato ketchup
1½ tsp Worcestershire sauce
¼ tsp ground ginger
2 tbsp cornflour
2 tbsp cold water

In the bottom of a pressure cooker, heat the oil over medium heat. Add the chicken pieces and brown on both sides, about 5 minutes. Measure out 250ml (8fl oz) of the reserved pineapple juice and combine with the celery, pepper, brown sugar, vinegar, soy sauce, ketchup, Worcestershire sauce and ginger. Mix well and pour over the chicken. Secure the lid in place. Bring to high pressure over high heat. Adjust the heat to maintain high pressure and cook for 8 minutes. Reduce the pressure with the quick-release method.

Remove the chicken and vegetables to a warmed platter. In a small bowl, stir together the cornflour and water, then stir into the hot liquid. Place over high heat and cook, stirring, until the mixture boils and thickens, about 5 minutes. Add the pineapple chunks and heat through. Pour the sauce over the chicken and serve.

Nutritional Analysis

Calories	199.22 Kcal	Protein	18.18 gm
Fat	4.28 gm	Carbohydrate	22.33 gm
Sodium	363.05 mg	Cholesterol	57.20 mg
Saturated fat	0.85 gm		

Fiesta Chicken

Serves: 6

250ml (8fl oz) tomato sauce
125ml (4fl oz) orange juice
125g (4oz) finely chopped onion
2 tbsp raisins
2 tbsp chopped pimiento
1/2 tsp dried oregano, crumbled
1/2 tsp chilli powder
1 clove garlic, crushed
several dashes of Tabasco sauce
6 skinless, boneless chicken breast halves
2 tsp cornflour
1 tbsp water
60g (2oz) finely chopped fresh parsley
750g (1lb 8oz) hot cooked white rice

In a large frying pan, combine the tomato sauce, orange juice, onion, raisins, pimiento, oregano, chilli powder, garlic and Tabasco sauce. Bring to the boil, cover, reduce the heat to low and simmer for 5 minutes. Add the chicken to the pan and return to the boil. Cover, reduce the heat to low and simmer until the juices run clear when a chicken breast is pierced, 12 to 15 minutes.

Meanwhile, in a small bowl, combine the cornflour and water. Stir into the pan and cook and stir until thickened and bubbling, about 5 minutes. Cook and stir for 2 minutes longer. Toss the parsley into the hot rice and spoon the rice onto a platter or individual plates. Serve the chicken mixture over rice.

Nutritional Analysis

Calories	274.19	Kcal	Protein	30.39	gm
Fat	1.83	gm	Carbohydrate	32.26	gm
Sodium	311.55	mg	Cholesterol	68.44	mg
Saturated Fat	0.44	gm			

Sesame Chicken Teriyaki

Serves: 2

2 tbsp teriyaki sauce
1 tbsp water
2 cloves garlic, crushed
1/4 tsp round ginger
2 skinless, boneless chicken breast halves, cut into long 19mm (3/4in) wide strips
1/4 tsp sesame seeds, toasted

In a small bowl, combine the teriyaki sauce, water, garlic and ginger, mixing well. Stir in the chicken. Let stand for 20 minutes at room temperature, stirring occasionally.

Preheat grill.

Drain the chicken and thread it onto two 255 to 305mm (10 to 12in) skewers or four 150mm (6in) skewers, weaving it accordion style. Place on a grill pan and slip under the grill 100 to 125mm (4 to 5in) from the heat source. Grill for 3 minutes. Turn the chicken over and continue to grill until the chicken is tender and no longer pink, 2 to 3 minutes longer. Sprinkle with the sesame seeds and serve.

Nutritional Analysis

Calories	152.26 Kcal	Protein	28.57 gm
Fat	1.66 gm	Carbohydrate	4.09 gm
Sodium	767.26 mg	Cholesterol	68.44 mg
Saturated fat	0.40 gm		

Chicken Breasts with Curried Stuffing

Serves: 4

1 tbsp butter
125g (4oz) grated carrot
60g (2oz) sliced spring onions
1 tsp curry powder
125g (4oz) fresh breadcrumbs
2 tbsp raisins
1 tbsp water
4 skinless, boneless chicken breast halves
1/8 tsp salt
1/4 tsp paprika
60ml (4fl oz) plain low-fat yogurt
2 tsp orange marmalade

In a small saucepan, melt the butter over medium heat. Add the carrot, spring onions and curry powder, and cook, stirring, until tender, about 5 minutes. Remove from the heat and stir in the breadcrumbs, raisins and water.

Preheat oven to 180°C (350°F), gas mark 4.

Place 1 chicken breast half, boned side up, between 2 sheets of cling film. Working from the centre to the edges, beat lightly with a meat mallet to 6mm (1/4in) thickness. Remove the cling film.

Repeat with the remaining chicken. Sprinkle the chicken pieces lightly with salt. Place a quarter of the stuffing mixture on half each piece of chicken. Fold the other half of the chicken breast over the filling. Secure with a toothpick. Place chicken in a 200mm (8in) square baking dish with 50mm (2in) sides. Sprinkle with the paprika. Cover with tin foil.

Bake until the chicken is tender and the juices run clear when pierced, about 25 minutes.

Meanwhile, in a small bowl, combine the yogurt and marmalade. Serve with 1 tablespoon of the yogurt mixture on each piece of chicken.

Nutritional Analysis

Calories	211.42 Kcal	Protein	28.99 gm
Fat	4.88 gm	Carbohydrate	11.81 gm
Sodium	225.53 mg	Cholesterol	77.27 mg
Saturated fat	2.34 gm		

Cheesy Chicken Rolls

Serves: 4

125g (4oz) shredded low-fat mozzarella cheese
75g (2 1/2 oz) bottled sliced mushrooms, drained
60ml (2fl oz) plus 1 tbsp plain low-fat yogurt
1 tbsp snipped fresh chives
1 tbsp finely chopped fresh parsley
1 tbsp chopped pimiento
4 skinless, boneless chicken breast halves
salt and pepper to taste
1 tsp fine dried breadcrumbs
1 tbsp paprika

(continued)

Preheat oven to 180°C (350°F), gas mark 4.

In a small bowl, combine the cheese, mushrooms, 60ml (2fl oz)yogurt, chives, parsley and pimiento. Stir well. Place 1 chicken breast half, boned side up, between 2 pieces of cling film. Working from the centre to the edges, beat lightly with a meat mallet to 3mm (1/8in) thickness. Remove the cling film. Repeat with the remaining chicken. Sprinkle lightly with salt and pepper. Spread an equal amount of the filling on each chicken breast half. Fold in the sides and roll up. Secure with toothpicks. Arrange the rolls, seam side down, in a baking dish with 50mm (2in) sides. In a small bowl, combine the breadcrumbs and paprika. Brush the chicken with the tablespoon of yogurt, then sprinkle with the crumb mixture.

Bake until the chicken is tender and the juices run clear when a piece is pierced, 20 to 25 minutes. Serve immediately.

Nutritional Analysis

Calories	176.43	Kcal	Protein	33.40	gm
Fat	2.06	gm	Carbohydrate	4.69	gm
Sodium	251.19	mg	Cholesterol	71.00	mg
Saturated fat	0.60	gm			

Nutty Chicken Fingers

Serves: 6

90g (3oz) crushed cornflakes
60g (2oz) finely chopped pecan nuts
1 tbsp dried parsley flakes
1/8 tsp garlic powder
1/8 tsp salt

---

4 skinless, boneless chicken breast halves, cut into strips
75mm (3in) long by 25mm (1in) wide
2 tbsp nonfat milk

Preheat oven to 200°C (400°F), gas mark 6.

In a shallow dish, stir together the cornflake crumbs, pecans, parsley, garlic powder and salt. Dip the chicken in the milk, then roll in the crumb mixture. Place in a 255 x 380mm (10 x 15in) baking dish with 25mm (1in) sides.

Bake until the chicken is tender and the juices run clear when a piece is pierced, 7 to 9 minutes. Serve at once.

Nutritional Analysis

Calories	214.65	Kcal	Protein	28.81	gm
Fat	6.05	gm	Carbohydrate	9.79	gm
Sodium	270.93	mg	Cholesterol	68.59	mg
Saturated fat	0.74	gm			

Crab-Stuffed Chicken

Serves: 6

125g (4oz) cooked crabmeat, picked over for shells and flaked
60g (2oz) finely chopped water chestnuts
2 tbsp fine dried breadcrumbs
2 tbsp low-fat mayonnaise
1 tbsp finely chopped fresh parsley
1/4 tsp Dijon mustard
6 skinless, boneless chicken breast halves
2 tbsp Worcestershire sauce
2 spring onions, finely chopped

In a bowl, combine the crabmeat, water chestnuts, breadcrumbs, mayonnaise, parsley and mustard. Stir well. Place 1 piece of chicken, boned side up, between 2 pieces of cling film. Working from the centre to the edges, beat lightly with a meat mallet to 3mm (1/8in) thickness. Remove the cling film. Repeat with the remaining chicken. Spoon an equal amount of the filling onto half each chicken piece. Fold in the sides and roll up. Secure with toothpicks. Arrange the chicken, seam side down, in a 180 x 305mm (7 x 12in) baking dish with 50mm (2in) sides. Brush with some of the Worcestershire sauce.

Bake until the chicken is tender and the juices run clear when a piece is pierced, 20 to 25 minutes. Brush with the remaining Worcestershire sauce, sprinkle with the spring onions, then serve.

Nutritional Analysis

Calories	201.29 Kcal	Protein	31.56 gm
Fat	5.54 gm	Carbohydrate	4.13 gm
Sodium	223.59 mg	Cholesterol	90.05 mg
Saturated Fat	0.98 gm		

Chicken-and-Vegetable Casseroles

Serves: 2

500g (1lb) sliced courgettes
1 small onion, chopped
1 small tomato, cut into thin wedges
2 tbsp sliced pitted black olives
2 tbsp finely chopped fresh parsley
1 tbsp finely chopped fresh basil

1/8 tsp garlic powder
2 skinless, boneless chicken breast halves
1 tsp butter, cut into bits
1/8 tsp salt
1/8 tsp pepper

Preheat oven to 180°C (350°F), gas mark 4.

Halve any large courgette slices. In a bowl, stir together the courgette, onion, tomato, olives, parsley, basil and garlic powder. Divide evenly between 2 individual baking dishes or gratin dishes. Top each with a chicken breast half. Dot the tops with the butter. Sprinkle with the salt and pepper. Cover with tin foil. Bake until the chicken is tender and the juices run clear when a piece is pierced, about 40 minutes. Serve at once.

Nutritional Analysis

Calories	205.02 Kcal	Protein	29.70 gm
Fat	4.67 gm	Carbohydrate	11.11 gm
Sodium	327.11 mg	Cholesterol	73.62 mg
Saturated fat	1.73 gm		

Ginger and Peach Chicken

Serves: 4

4 skinless, boneless chicken breast halves
250g (8oz) tinned peach slices in light syrup
1 tsp cornflour
1/2 tsp peeled and grated fresh ginger
1/4 tsp salt
125g (4oz) sliced water chestnuts
500g (1lb) hot cooked white rice
185g (6oz) mangetouts, cooked and kept hot

(continued)

Spray a large frying pan with nonstick cooking spray and heat over medium heat. Add the chicken and cook, turning to brown evenly, until tender and the juices run clear when a piece is pierced, 8 to 10 minutes. Remove from the pan; keep warm.

Meanwhile, drain the peaches, reserving juice. If necessary, add water to the juice to equal 125ml (4fl oz). Stir in the cornflour, ginger and salt. Add to the pan and cook, stirring over medium heat until thickened and bubbling, about 10 minutes. Cook and stir for 1 minute longer. Gently stir in the peaches and water chestnuts and heat through.

On a serving platter or 4 individual plates, arrange the rice, mangetouts and chicken. Spoon the sauce over the chicken and serve.

Nutritional Analysis

Calories	301.86 Kcal	Protein	31.01 gm
Fat	2.07 gm	Carbohydrate	37.89 gm
Sodium	227.29 mg	Cholesterol	68.44 mg
Saturated fat	0.46 gm		

Chicken Medallions

Serves: 4

375g (12oz) sliced mushrooms
2 tbsp grated carrot
2 tbsp sliced spring onions
2 tbsp finely chopped celery
2¹/₂ tsp lemon juice
¹/₄ tsp dried thyme, crumbled
¹/₈ tsp pepper, or more to taste
1 tomato, peeled, seeded and chopped
4 skinless, boneless chicken breast halves

¹/₈ tsp salt
¹/₂ tsp chicken bouillon granules
125ml (4fl oz) water
1 tbsp cornflour
60ml (2fl oz) nonfat milk

In a saucepan, combine the mushrooms, carrot, spring onions and celery, and add water to cover. Bring to the boil, cover and cook until tender, about 5 minutes. Drain and place in a bowl. Stir in 1¹/₂ teaspoons of the lemon juice, half the thyme and ¹/₈ teaspoon pepper. Stir in the tomato. Place 1 chicken breast half, boned side up, between 2 sheets of cling film. Working from the centre to the edges, beat lightly with a meat mallet to 3mm (¹/₈in) thickness. Remove the cling film. Repeat with the remaining chicken. Sprinkle the chicken breasts with the salt and a dash of pepper. Spoon an equal amount of the filling onto half each chicken piece. Fold in the sides and roll up. Secure with toothpicks.

Spray a frying pan with nonstick cooking spray and heat over medium heat. Add the chicken and brown, turning occasionally, for 3 to 4 minutes. Add the remaining lemon juice and thyme, the bouillon granules and the water. Cover and simmer over low heat until the chicken is tender and the juices run clear when a piece is pierced, about 15 minutes. Remove the chicken.

In a small bowl, stir together the cornflour and milk. Add to the pan and cook and stir over medium heat until thickened and bubbling, about 10 minutes. Cook and stir for 2 minutes longer. Remove from the heat. Remove the toothpicks.

Cut the chicken into 12mm (½in) thick slices. Spoon the sauce onto individual plates and arrange the chicken on top. Serve immediately.

Nutritional Analysis

Calories	162.75 Kcal	Protein	28.67 gm
Fat	1.94 gm	Carbohydrate	6.26 gm
Sodium	297.04 mg	Cholesterol	68.74 mg
Saturated fat	0.41 gm		

Marinated Chicken Kebabs

Serves: 4

1 tbsp lemon juice
1 tbsp water
1 tbsp olive oil
½ tsp dried tarragon, crumbled
¼ tsp Tabasco sauce
⅛ tsp salt
1 clove garlic, crushed
4 skinless, boneless chicken breast halves, cut into 25mm (1in) cubes
1 red pepper, cut into 25mm (1in) squares
2 medium courgettes, cut into 25mm (1in) slices

In a small bowl, combine the lemon juice, water, oil, tarragon, Tabasco sauce, salt and garlic. Place the chicken in a resealable plastic bag and set in a deep bowl. Pour the lemon juice mixture into the bag, close the top and let the chicken stand for 20 minutes at room temperature, turning the bag frequently.
Preheat grill.

Drain the chicken, reserving the marinade. Thread the chicken, pepper and courgettes alternately onto 4 255 to 305mm (10 to 12in) long skewers. Arrange the skewers on a grill pan. Slip under the grill 100 to 125mm (4 to 5in) from the heat source. Grill, turning once and brushing occasionally with the reserved marinade, until the chicken is tender and cooked through, about 8 minutes. Serve immediately.

Nutritional Analysis

Calories	179.00 Kcal	Protein	28.47 gm
Fat	4.99 gm	Carbohydrate	4.21 gm
Sodium	155.74 mg	Cholesterol	68.44 mg
Saturated fat	0.85 gm		

Lime-Sauced Chicken

Serves: 4

4 skinless, boneless chicken breast halves
½ medium lime
180ml (6fl oz) apple juice or cider
2 tsp cornflour
½ tsp chicken bouillon granules

Spray a large frying pan with nonstick cooking spray and heat over medium heat. Add the chicken and cook, turning to brown evenly, until tender and the juices run clear when a piece is pierced, 8 to 10 minutes. Remove from the pan and keep warm.
Meanwhile, using a vegetable peeler, remove strips of zest from the lime half. Cut the peel into narrow strips; set aside. Squeeze 1 tablespoon juice

(continued)

191

from the lime half. Combine the lime juice, apple juice, cornflour and bouillon granules in a bowl, stirring well. Add to the pan and cook and stir over medium heat until thickened and bubbling, about 10 minutes. Cook and stir for 2 minutes longer. To serve, cut each chicken breast half on the diagonal into 25mm (1in) pieces. Spoon some of the sauce over each serving. Garnish with the reserved lime zest. Pass around the remaining sauce.

Nutritional Analysis

Calories	160.76	Kcal	Protein	27.27	gm
Fat	1.76	gm	Carbohydrate	7.10	gm
Sodium	207.72	mg	Cholesterol	68.44	mg
Saturated fat	0.38	gm			

Chicken Jerusalem

Serves: 6

6 skinless, boneless chicken breast halves
1 tsp paprika
60g (2oz) butter
2 spring onions, chopped
180ml (6fl oz) dry white wine
180ml (6fl oz) water
250g (8oz) sliced fresh mushrooms
875g (1lb 12oz) tinned artichoke hearts, drained
500g (1lb) egg noodles, cooked and drained
1/2 tsp parsley
2 tbsp grated Parmesan cheese

Dust the chicken with the paprika. In a frying pan, melt the butter over medium heat. Add the chicken and brown on both sides, about 10

Safe Barbecuing

Studies conducted in the last few years have caused some people to forego barbecued chicken and other foods because some cooking techniques – including grilling over a charcoal fire or on a gas grill – may cause carcinogens to form on the meat.

To enjoy the taste of barbecued chicken safely, follow these steps:

- Cook the chicken in a saucepan or frying pan first, then transfer to the grill for the last few minutes of cooking.
- Wrap the chicken in tin foil before grilling.

minutes. Add the spring onions, wine and water, and simmer over medium heat for 45 minutes. Add the mushrooms and artichoke hearts, and cook slowly until the chicken is tender and the juices run clear when a piece is pierced, about 15 minutes longer.

Serve over noodles sprinkled with parsley. Sprinkle the Parmesan cheese over the chicken.

Nutritional Analysis

Calories	530.37	Kcal	Protein	41.02	gm
Fat	12.88	gm	Carbohydrate	61.27	gm
Sodium	462.91	mg	Cholesterol	162.32	mg
Saturated fat	6.13	gm			

Hunter's Chicken

Serves: 8

1 chicken, about 1.5kg (3lb), skinned and cut into 8 pieces
1 tbsp olive oil
125ml (4fl oz) plus 2 tbsp dry white wine
3 spring onions, chopped
60g (2oz) chopped onion
2 large cloves garlic, crushed
250g (8oz) mushrooms, sliced
1 tbsp dried thyme
500g (1lb) tinned chopped tomatoes, drained
salt and pepper to taste
1 tbsp chopped fresh parsley
375g (12oz) egg noodles, cooked, drained and kept hot

Preheat grill.

Place the chicken pieces in a roasting pan. Slip under the grill 75mm (3in) from the heat source and grill for 7 minutes. Turn the chicken over and grill for another 5 minutes. Remove from the grill.

In a frying pan, heat the oil and 2 table-spoons of wine over medium heat. Add the spring onions, onion and garlic, and cook until soft, about 5 minutes. Add the mushrooms and thyme, cover and cook for 5 minutes. Stir in the rest of the wine and tomatoes. Add the chicken, cover and cook over low heat until the chicken is tender, about 25 minutes. Season with salt and pepper, and garnish with the parsley. Serve over the noodles.

Nutritional Analysis

Calories	318.75	Kcal	Protein	24.96	gm
Fat	8.26	gm	Carbohydrate	35.68	gm
Sodium	302.82	mg	Cholesterol	94.65	mg
Saturated fat	1.87	gm			

Spicy Chicken Enchiladas

Serves: 6

5 skinless, boneless chicken breast halves
250ml (8fl oz) reduced-sodium, fat-free chicken stock
2 tbsp olive oil
1 onion, chopped
2 cloves garlic, crushed
2 tbsp plain flour
125g (4oz) tinned diced green chilli peppers, drained
875g (1lb 12oz) tinned chopped tomatoes, drained

(continued)

12 corn tortillas
250g (8oz) grated Parmesan cheese

Preheat oven to 180°C (350°F), gas mark 4. Spray a medium baking dish with nonstick cooking spray.

In a saucepan, combine the chicken breasts and stock. Place over low heat and simmer gently until the chicken is tender and the juices run clear when a piece is pierced, about 15 minutes. Remove the chicken, reserving the stock, and chop into bite-sized pieces. Set the stock and chicken aside.

In a frying pan, heat the oil over medium heat. Add the onion and sauté until soft, about 5 minutes. Add the garlic and flour and cook, stirring, for 1 minute. Stir in 125ml (4fl oz) of the reserved stock and cook, stirring occasionally, until the mixture thickens, about 5 to 8 minutes. Add the chillies and tomatoes and simmer for 10 minutes.

Dip a tortilla in the sauce and place in the prepared baking dish. Place a spoonful each of the cheese, chicken and sauce across the middle of the tortilla and roll it up, folding in the sides as you roll. Place seam side down in the dish. Repeat, using all of the tortillas. Spoon the remaining sauce over the enchiladas and top with the remaining cheese. Bake until the cheese melts completely, about 15 minutes. Serve hot.

Nutritional Analysis

Calories	381.46 Kcal	Protein	33.63 gm
Fat	12.05 gm	Carbohydrate	35.36 gm
Sodium	818.32 mg	Cholesterol	67.56 mg
Saturated fat	3.84 gm		

Szechuan-Style Chicken and Vegetables

Serves: 6

2 tbsp peanut oil
2 cloves garlic, crushed
1 tsp red pepper flakes
1 tsp peeled and grated fresh ginger
3 skinless, boneless chicken breast halves, cut into small chunks
2 tsp black bean sauce
2 tbsp water
1kg (2lb) chopped cauliflower
1kg (2lb) broccoli florets
2 carrots, sliced
1 green or red pepper, chopped
6 spring onions, sliced
500ml (1pt) reduced-sodium, fat-free chicken stock
2 tbsp cornflour
750g (1lb 8oz) hot cooked white rice

In a wok or large, deep frying pan, heat 1 tablespoon of the oil over high heat. Add the garlic, red pepper flakes and ginger, and stir-fry for 3 minutes. Add the chicken and stir-fry until the meat turns white, about 7 minutes. Soften 1 teaspoon of the bean sauce in 1 tablespoon of the

water, add to the pan and stir to coat the chicken. Remove from the pan.

Add the remaining oil to the pan over high heat. Stir in the cauliflower, broccoli, carrots, pepper and spring onions. Soften the remaining bean sauce in the remaining water, add to the pan and stir to coat the vegetables. Reduce the heat to medium, cover the pan and cook for 1 minute. Uncover, raise the heat to high and stir-fry for 2 minutes. Add 375ml (12fl oz) of the chicken stock, cover and bring to the boil.

Meanwhile, in a small bowl, stir the cornflour into the remaining stock and add to the vegetables. Return the chicken to the pan and cook until the sauce thickens slightly, about 5 minutes. Serve over the rice.

Nutritional Analysis

Calories	289.04 Kcal	Protein	21.79 gm
Fat	6.28 gm	Carbohydrate	37.49 gm
Sodium	425.94 mg	Cholesterol	34.22 mg
Saturated fat	1.09 gm		

Jamaican-Style Chicken

Serves: 6

> 1 onion, quartered
> 1 jalapeño pepper, seeded
> 2 cloves garlic, cut
> 1 large onion, coarsely chopped
> 80ml (2¹/₂fl oz) orange juice
> 60ml (2fl oz) soy sauce
> 1 tbsp peanut oil
> 2 tbsp red wine vinegar

> 1 tsp dried thyme, crumbled
> 1 tsp ground allspice
> ¹/₂ tsp ground cinnamon
> ¹/₂ tsp curry powder
> salt and pepper to taste
> 1kg (2lb) boneless, skinless chicken pieces

In a food processor, process the onion, jalapeño, garlic and onion until puréed. Add the orange juice, soy sauce, oil, vinegar, thyme, allspice, cinnamon, curry powder, salt and pepper. Process until smooth. Place the chicken pieces in a shallow dish and pour the puréed ingredients over them. Cover and refrigerate for 2 hours, turning occasionally.

Prepare a fire in a charcoal grill.

Remove the chicken from the marinade. Place on the grill rack over hot coals and grill, turning once, until the chicken is tender and the juices run clear when a piece is pierced, 8 to 10 minutes on each side. (Alternatively, bake in a 170°C, 325°F, gas mark 3 oven until it is done, about 40 minutes.) Serve hot.

Nutritional Analysis

Calories	211.88 Kcal	Protein	33.18 gm
Fat	5.85 gm	Carbohydrate	4.78 gm
Sodium	474.58 mg	Cholesterol	105.93 mg
Saturated fat	1.38 gm		

Easy Barbecued Chicken

Serves: 8

> *125ml (4fl oz) buttermilk*
> *1 tbsp Dijon mustard*
> *1 tbsp honey*
> *2 cloves garlic, crushed*
> *1 tsp dried oregano, crumbled*
> *1 tsp dried basil, crumbled*
> *1 tsp dried thyme, crumbled*
> *1 tsp dried rosemary, crumbled*
> *salt and pepper to taste*
> *1.5kg (3lb) chicken pieces, skinned*

In a large bowl, combine the buttermilk, mustard, honey, garlic, oregano, basil, thyme, rosemary, salt and pepper. Add the chicken, turn to coat, cover and refrigerate for 3 hours.

Prepare a fire in a charcoal grill.

Remove the chicken from the marinade. Place on the grill rack over hot coals and grill, turning once, until the chicken is tender and the juices run clear when a piece is pierced, 8 to 10 minutes on each side. (Alternatively, bake in a 170°C, 325°F, gas mark 3 oven until it tests done, about 40 minutes.) Serve hot.

Nutritional Analysis

Calories	188.54 Kcal	Protein	24.24 gm
Fat	6.20 gm	Carbohydrate	7.22 gm
Sodium	151.82 mg	Cholesterol	73.10 mg
Saturated fat	1.76 gm		

Chicken and Dumpling Stew

Serves: 8

> *4 skinless, boneless chicken breasts, cut into chunks*
> *4 white potatoes, peeled and cut into chunks*
> *2 carrots, cut into chunks*
> *2 onions, cut into chunks*
> *3 celery stalks, finely chopped*
> *2 sweet potatoes, peeled and cubed*
> *1l (2pt) reduced-sodium, fat-free chicken stock*
> *1 tsp dried thyme, crumbled*
> *1 tsp dried sage, crumbled*
> *salt and pepper to taste*
> *250g (8oz) frozen peas*

Dumplings:
> *250g (8oz) unbleached plain flour*
> *3 tbsp chopped fresh parsley*
> *1 tbsp butter*
> *2 tsp baking soda*
> *1/2 tsp salt*
> *125ml (4fl oz) low-fat milk*

In a large soup pot, combine the chicken, potatoes, carrots, onions, celery, sweet potatoes, stock, thyme, sage, salt and pepper. Place over high heat, bring to the boil, cover, reduce the heat to low and cook for 20 minutes.

Meanwhile, make the dumplings: in a food processor, combine the flour, parsley, butter, baking soda and salt. Process with on-off pulses until the mixture has the consistency of coarse crumbs. Add the milk and process for a few seconds. The dough should be stiff. Add the peas

to the soup pot. Then drop the dumpling dough by tablespoonfuls into the soup pot. Cover and cook over low heat until the dumplings are tender and cooked through, about 15 minutes. Ladle into shallow bowls to serve.

Nutritional Analysis

Calories	295.11	Kcal	Protein	21.12	gm
Fat	2.92	gm	Carbohydrate	45.34	gm
Sodium	661.04	mg	Cholesterol	38.71	mg
Saturated fat	1.24	gm			

Jambalaya

Serves: 8

1 tbsp butter
2 large onions, chopped
375g (12oz) finely chopped celery
1 green pepper, chopped
90g (3oz) chorizo sausage, diced
750g (1lb 8oz) skinless, boneless chicken breasts,
    cut into chunks
2 cloves garlic, crushed
2 bay leaves
2 tsp dried oregano, crumbled
1 tsp dried thyme, crumbled
1 tsp salt
1 tsp cayenne pepper
1 tsp black pepper
750g (1lb 8oz) tinned tomatoes, drained
250ml (8fl oz) tomato sauce
1l (2pt) reduced-sodium, fat-free chicken stock
500g (1lb) long-grain white rice

(continued)

Where's the Fat?

Even though it's a pain to remove the skin from chicken, and you feel like you're missing out by not eating that crunchy, satisfying skin, consider these figures:

- **A 250g (8oz) chicken breast – about one serving – without the skin contains 9 grams of fat.**
- **A 250g (8oz) serving from a whole chicken with the skin removed contains 13 grams of fat.**
- **A 250g (8oz) serving from a whole chicken with the skin left on contains 38 grams of fat.**

500g (1lb) medium prawns, peeled and deveined
1 red pepper, chopped
1 onion, finely chopped
125g (4oz) chopped fresh parsley

In a large soup pot, melt the butter over medium heat. Add the chopped onion and celery, and sauté until vegetables begin to soften, about 3 minutes. Add the green pepper, chorizo, chicken, garlic, bay leaves, oregano, thyme, salt, cayenne pepper and black pepper. Cook, stirring, for 5 minutes. Add the tomatoes, tomato sauce, stock and rice. Reduce the heat to low, cover and cook until rice is tender, 20 to 30 minutes.

Add the prawns, stir and cook until the prawns turn pink, another 5 to 10 minutes. Garnish with the chopped onion, red pepper and parsley before serving.

Nutritional Analysis

Calories	488.26 Kcal	Protein	38.46 gm
Fat	8.44 gm	Carbohydrate	62.56 gm
Sodium	1118.77 mg	Cholesterol	130.34 mg
Saturated fat	3.00 gm		

Chicken and Mangetouts with Hoisin Sauce

Serves: 4

180ml (6fl oz) reduced-sodium, fat-free chicken stock
2 tbsp soy sauce
1 tbsp sherry
1 tsp sugar
2 tsp cornflour

1 tsp sesame oil
1 tbsp peanut oil
3 tbsp hoisin sauce
2 cloves garlic, crushed
2 tbsp peeled and finely chopped fresh ginger
1 tsp red pepper flakes
500g (1lb) skinless, boneless chicken breasts, cut into narrow strips
500g (1lb) mangetouts

In a small bowl, stir together the stock, soy sauce, sherry, sugar, cornflour and sesame oil; set aside. In a wok or a large, deep frying pan, heat the peanut oil over high heat. Add the hoisin sauce, garlic, ginger and red pepper flakes. Stir-fry for 1 minute. Add the chicken and stir-fry for 5 minutes. Add the mangetouts and stir-fry until the chicken is tender and the mangetouts are crisp-tender, about 5 minutes. Stir the soy sauce mixture and add to the pan. Stir-fry over medium heat until the sauce thickens slightly, 1 to 2 minutes. Serve immediately.

Nutritional Analysis

Calories	256.55 Kcal	Protein	29.36 gm
Fat	6.13 gm	Carbohydrate	16.83 gm
Sodium	922.49 mg	Cholesterol	65.83 mg
Saturated fat	1.13 gm		

Chicken Simmered in Barbecue Sauce

Serves: 6

1 tbsp olive oil
1 onion, chopped
125ml (4fl oz) tomato ketchup
125ml (4fl oz) water
2 tbsp red wine vinegar
2 tbsp brown sugar
1 tbsp Worcestershire sauce
1 tsp chilli powder
1 chicken, about 1.25kg (2lb 8oz), skinned and cut into serving pieces

In a large frying pan, heat the oil over medium heat. Add the onion and sauté until translucent, about 5 minutes. Add the ketchup, water, vinegar, brown sugar, Worcestershire sauce and chilli powder. Bring to the boil, reduce the heat to low and add the chicken. Spoon the sauce over the chicken pieces, cover and cook for 30 minutes. Uncover, turn the chicken over and cook until the chicken is tender, about 15 minutes longer. Serve immediately.

Nutritional Analysis

Calories	181.21	Kcal	Protein	20.21	gm
Fat	5.21	gm	Carbohydrate	13.22	gm
Sodium	341.45	mg	Cholesterol	63.56	mg
Saturated fat	1.02	gm			

Chicken in Buttermilk

Serves: 6

1 tbsp olive oil
1 chicken, about 1.25kg (2lb 8oz), skinned and cut into serving pieces
6 spring onions, finely chopped
1kg (2lb) tinned tomatoes, drained
500ml (1pt) low-fat buttermilk
1 tsp dried dill, crumbled
1 tsp sugar
salt and pepper to taste
Tabasco sauce to taste
250ml (8fl oz) plain low-fat yogurt
1 tsp cornflour
60g (2oz) grated Parmesan cheese

In a large frying pan, heat the oil over medium heat. Add the chicken and brown on both sides, almost 10 minutes. Add half the spring onions to the pan and cook the chicken for about 2 minutes longer. Remove from the heat.

In a food processor, combine the tomatoes, buttermilk, dill, sugar, salt, pepper and Tabasco. Process until smooth. Pour the sauce over the chicken and return the pan to medium heat. Bring to a boil, cover, reduce the heat to low and cook until the chicken is tender, about 20 minutes. Mix and add the yogurt, cornflour and Parmesan, and heat the chicken for 10 minutes longer. Garnish with the remaining chopped spring onions.

(continued)

Reducing the Fat Even More

Since chicken is naturally low in fat, and even lower once you remove the skin, it's generally necessary to use a little bit of fat when cooking chicken in a frying pan. Choose a nonstick pan, or use a bit of water or chicken stock in place of the usual oil or butter. Alternatively, you may find that you can cut the amount of fat in a traditional recipe by half, without reducing the appeal of the dish. Cooking methods such as grilling, baking, poaching and microwaving also use little fat in cooking.

Nutritional Analysis

Calories	1487.74 Kcal	Protein	165.80 gm
Fat	47.36 gm	Carbohydrate	98.58 gm
Sodium	3284.58 mg	Cholesterol	440.76 mg
Saturated fat	15.62 gm		

Chicken Marsala

Serves: 6

1 tbsp olive oil
4 cloves garlic, crushed
2 onions, sliced
2 tbsp peeled and finely chopped fresh ginger
1 cinnamon stick
2 bay leaves
2 tsp ground cloves
2 tsp ground cardamom
2 tbsp curry powder
salt and pepper to taste
60ml (2fl oz) water
1 chicken, about 1.5kg (3lb), skinned and cut into
*   6 pieces*
1 tomato, chopped

In a large frying pan, heat the oil over medium heat. Add the garlic, onion, ginger, cinnamon, bay leaves, cloves, cardamom and curry powder. Cook until the onion is translucent, about 5 minutes. Stir in the salt, pepper and water, then add the chicken pieces. Cook over low heat for 30 minutes until the chicken is tender. During the last 5 minutes of cooking, stir the tomato into the pan.

Nutritional Analysis

Calories	191.09 Kcal	Protein	24.62 gm
Fat	6.25 gm	Carbohydrate	8.99 gm
Sodium	90.86 mg	Cholesterol	76.27 mg
Saturated fat	1.21 gm		

Garlicky Grilled Chicken

Serves: 8

> 10 cloves garlic, chopped
> 3 tbsp dried oregano, crumbled
> 1 large red onion, chopped
> 125ml (4fl oz) olive oil
> salt and pepper to taste
> 250ml (8fl oz) reduced-sodium, fat-free chicken stock
> 8 skinless, boneless chicken breast halves

In a large shallow dish, combine the garlic, oregano, onion, oil, salt, pepper and stock. Mix well. Add the chicken, turn to coat well, cover and marinate in the refrigerator overnight.

Prepare a fire in a charcoal grill. Remove the chicken from the marinade and place on the grill rack. Grill, turning once, until tender and the juices run clear when a piece is pierced, about 10 minutes on each side. Serve hot or at room temperature.

Nutritional Analysis

Calories	166.83 Kcal	Protein	27.53 gm
Fat	5.01 gm	Carbohydrate	1.23 gm
Sodium	95.19 mg	Cholesterol	68.44 mg
Saturated fat	0.86 gm		

Chicken Chimichanga

Serves: 5

> 3 tbsp olive oil
> 1 skinless, boneless whole chicken breast, diced
> 1 red onion, chopped
> 3 cloves garlic, crushed
> 1 large tomato, chopped
> 2 tbsp chopped fresh coriander
> 1 tbsp chilli powder
> 2 tsp ground cumin
> 1 jalapeño pepper, seeded and chopped
> 250g (8oz) grated low-fat cheddar cheese
> 60ml (2fl oz) low-fat sour cream
> salt and pepper to taste
> 5 flour tortillas, each 305mm (12in) in diameter, heated
> 60ml (2fl oz) tomato salsa

Preheat oven to 180°C (350°F), gas mark 4.

In a large frying pan, heat 2 tablespoons of the oil over medium heat. Add the chicken and sauté for 5 minutes. Add the onion, garlic, tomato, coriander, chilli powder, cumin and jalapeño. Continue to cook over medium heat for 10 more minutes. Remove from the heat.

Stir the cheese, sour cream, salt and pepper into the chicken mixture. Place a couple of spoonfuls of the chicken filling in the middle of each warmed tortilla. Roll up and secure with a toothpick. Place on a baking tray. Repeat with the remaining tortillas and filling. Lightly brush the rolled tortillas with the remaining oil.

(continued)

Bake, uncovered, until crispy brown on the outside, about 10 minutes. Serve with the salsa.

Nutritional Analysis

Calories	468.43 Kcal	Protein	27.56 gm
Fat	15.66 gm	Carbohydrate	55.02 gm
Sodium	739.89 mg	Cholesterol	33.77 mg
Saturated fat	2.72 gm		

Mexican Chicken Roll-ups

Serves: 4

1 tbsp olive oil
1 green pepper, chopped
1 red pepper, chopped
1 onion, chopped
2 cloves garlic, crushed
1 skinless, boneless whole chicken breast, diced
4 flour tortillas, 305mm (12in) in diameter, heated
1 head shredded lettuce
750g (1lb 8oz) chopped tomatoes
60g (2oz) chopped spring onions
60g (2oz) grated low-fat cheddar cheese
60g (2oz) salsa

In a large frying pan, heat the oil over high heat. Add the peppers, onion and garlic, and sauté until soft, about 7 minutes. Add the chicken, cover, reduce the heat to low and cook until the chicken is tender, about 8 minutes.

Transfer the chicken mixture to a serving bowl. Set out the warmed tortillas. Place the lettuce, tomato, spring onions, cheese and salsa in separate small bowls. Let diners make their own roll-ups.

Nutritional Analysis

Calories	397.24 Kcal	Protein	23.98 gm
Fat	9.82 gm	Carbohydrate	52.21 gm
Sodium	630.49 mg	Cholesterol	34.97 mg
Saturated Fat	1.51 gm		

Quick Chicken Parmesan

Serves: 2

1 skinless, boneless whole chicken breast, split
60g (2oz) seasoned dried breadcrumbs
1 tbsp olive oil
2 slices low-fat mozzarella cheese
2 thick tomato slices
1/2 tsp dried basil, crumbled

Place 1 piece of chicken, boned side up, between 2 pieces of cling film. Working from the centre to the edges, beat lightly with a meat mallet to 3mm (1/8in) thickness. Remove the cling film. Repeat with the other piece of chicken. Place the breadcrumbs in a shallow dish. Dip the chicken cutlets into the breadcrumbs, coating thoroughly. In a frying pan, heat the oil over medium heat. Add the chicken and sauté, turning once, until golden and tender, about 8 minutes.

Reduce the heat to low and place the cheese, tomato and basil on top of the chicken cutlets. Cover for 1 minute, then serve.

Nutritional Analysis

Calories	288.59 Kcal	Protein	38.54 gm
Fat	8.65 gm	Carbohydrate	12.47 gm
Sodium	685.66 mg	Cholesterol	71.43 mg
Saturated fat	1.39 gm		

Chicken with Couscous

Serves: 2

250g (8oz) instant couscous
¹/₂ tsp ground cinnamon
125g (4oz) diced cooked chicken breast
250g (8oz) tinned chick peas, drained and rinsed
60g (2oz) raisins
80ml (2¹/₂fl oz) low-fat plain yogurt

Cook the couscous according to the directions on the packet, adding the cinnamon at the start of cooking. Remove from heat and place in a serving bowl. Stir in the chicken, chick peas, raisins and yogurt. Serve immediately.

Nutritional Analysis

Calories	641.37 Kcal	Protein	32.03 gm
Fat	4.41 gm	Carbohydrate	116.49 gm
Sodium	191.28 mg	Cholesterol	32.36 mg
Saturated fat	0.95 gm		

Grilled Chicken with Yogurt and Spices

Serves: 6

1 tsp ground cumin
1 tsp ground coriander
1 tsp cayenne pepper
¹/₄ tsp ground allspice
250ml (8fl oz) plain low-fat yogurt
1 tsp grated lemon zest
2 tbsp lemon juice
3 cloves garlic, chopped
salt to taste
6 skinless, boneless chicken breast halves

In a shallow dish, combine the cumin, coriander, cayenne and allspice. Stir well. Add the yogurt, lemon zest and juice, garlic and salt. Stir well again. Add the chicken and spoon the sauce over the chicken to coat. Cover and refrigerate overnight.

Preheat grill. Remove the chicken from the marinade and drain well. Place the chicken on a grill pan. Slip under the grill about 75mm (3in) from the heat source. Grill, turning once, until nicely browned and cooked through, about 5 minutes. Serve immediately.

Nutritional Analysis

Calories	144.71 Kcal	Protein	28.31 gm
Fat	1.80 gm	Carbohydrate	1.94 gm
Sodium	90.97 mg	Cholesterol	69.57 mg
Saturated fat	0.56 gm		

Turkey Tetrazzini

Serves: 4

1 tbsp butter
250g (8oz) mushrooms, sliced
2 tbsp plain flour
salt and pepper to taste
500ml (1 pint) low-fat milk
1 tsp Worcestershire sauce
125g (4oz) grated low-fat Swiss cheese
1 green pepper, sliced
4 spring onions, finely chopped
500g (1lb) diced cooked turkey
250g (8oz) spaghetti, cooked and drained
90g (3oz) grated Parmesan cheese

Preheat oven to 180°C (350°F), gas mark 4. Spray a medium baking dish with nonstick cooking spray.

In a frying pan, melt the butter over medium heat. Add the mushrooms and sauté, stirring occasionally, until tender, about 5 to 7 minutes. Add the flour, salt and pepper, and stir until well blended. Slowly pour in the milk, stirring constantly. Add the Worcestershire sauce and simmer, stirring occasionally, until the sauce thickens, about 5 minutes. Add the Swiss cheese, pepper and spring onions, and mix well. Add the turkey and spaghetti, mixing well. Transfer to the prepared baking dish and sprinkle with the Parmesan cheese.

Bake, uncovered, until the flavours have blended, about 20 minutes. Serve immediately.

Nutritional Analysis

Calories	537.07 Kcal	Protein	40.68 gm
Fat	15.57 gm	Carbohydrate	57.06 gm
Sodium	518.46 mg	Cholesterol	84.79 mg
Saturated fat	7.84 gm		

Turkey Cutlets, Indian Style

Serves: 6

2 large limes
80ml (2½fl oz) plain low-fat yogurt
1 tbsp vegetable oil
2 tsp peeled ginger, finely chopped
1 tsp ground cumin
1 tsp ground coriander
1 tsp salt
1 garlic clove, crushed
750g (1lb 8oz) turkey cutlets
fresh coriander sprigs for garnish

Prepare a fire in a charcoal grill.

Grate the peel and extract the juice from 1 lime. Place 1 teaspoon of grated peel and 1 tablespoon juice in large bowl. Cut the other lime into wedges and set aside. Add the yogurt, vegetable oil, ginger, cumin, ground coriander, salt and garlic to the lime peel and juice, and mix until blended.

Just before grilling, add the turkey cutlets to the bowl with the yogurt mixture, stirring to coat the cutlets. Do not let the cutlets marinate in the

yogurt mixture, otherwise their texture will become mealy.

Place turkey cutlets on the grill over medium-hot coals. Cook for 5 to 7 minutes until they just lose their pink colour throughout. Serve with lime wedges. Garnish with coriander sprigs.

Nutritional Analysis

Calories	160.77 Kcal	Protein	28.75 gm
Fat	3.28 gm	Carbohydrate	2.74 gm
Sodium	453.78 mg	Cholesterol	71.11 mg
Saturated fat	0.63 gm		

Turkey Shish Kebab

Serves: 6

750g (1lb 4oz.) turkey breast steaks
80ml (2½fl oz) bottled chilli sauce
2 tbsp lemon juice
1 tbsp sugar
8 mushrooms
8 cherry tomatoes
1 medium courgette, cut into 12mm (½in) thick slices
½ green pepper, cut into 12mm (½in) squares
2 onions, quartered
2 tbsp olive oil

Cut the turkey steaks into 38mm (1½in) cubes and place in a bowl. In a small bowl, stir together the chilli sauce, lemon juice and sugar. Pour over the turkey cubes. Toss to coat. Cover and refrig-

(continued)

Turkey Year-Round

Turkey isn't just for Christmas anymore. Its popularity has risen dramatically, and now it is a common sight on dinner tables, tucked into sandwiches or tossed in stir-fries.

And if you enjoy turkey all year round, why not ring the changes for a big Christmas meal by serving capon or even goose, which was the favourite Christmas dinner in Victorian times. It was a goose that Scrooge bought for the Cratchit family after his miraculous conversion in Charles Dickens' *A Christmas Carol*.

erate for at least 4 hours or overnight, stirring occasionally.

Prepare a fire in a charcoal grill. Remove the turkey from the marinade. Thread the turkey onto skewers alternately with the mushrooms, cherry tomatoes, courgette, pepper and onions. Brush lightly with the oil and place on the grill rack about 150mm (6in) above medium-hot coals. Grill, turning as needed, and basting occasionally with the marinade, until the turkey is cooked through and the vegetables are tender, about 10 minutes. (Alternatively, cook in a preheated broiler about 150mm/6in from the heat source for the same amount of time.) Serve hot.

Nutritional Analysis

Calories	206.49 Kcal	Protein	25.30 gm
Fat	5.45 gm	Carbohydrate	14.18 gm
Sodium	253.24 mg	Cholesterol	58.64 mg
Saturated fat	0.81 gm		

Pistachio-Turkey Taco Salad

Serves: 6

1 head iceberg lettuce
8 prepared taco shells
500g (1lb) cooked turkey breast meat, minced
500g (1lb) tomatoes, chopped
1 large green pepper, chopped
60ml (2fl oz) low-fat sour cream
60g (2oz) pistachios, chopped
250ml (8fl oz) bottled salsa, mild or hot

1 tsp grated lime zest
2 tbsp lime juice

Shred the lettuce and divide among 4 plates. Stand 2 taco shells upright in the centre of each bed of lettuce. Fill the shells with the turkey, tomatoes and pepper, dividing evenly. Top with the sour cream and pistachios, again dividing evenly.

In a bowl, stir together the salsa, lime zest and lime juice. Spoon over the tacos and serve.

Nutritional Analysis

Calories	271.52 Kcal	Protein	27.01 gm
Fat	8.79 gm	Carbohydrate	21.44 gm
Sodium	550.27 mg	Cholesterol	66.13 mg
Saturated fat	1.72 gm		

Vegetarian Dishes

CHAPTER ELEVEN

Amount Per Chapter

28 Recipes

	% Daily Value
Easy to Prepare	**100%**
Low Fat/High Flavour	**100%**
Simple to Understand	**100%**

DELICIOUS, EASY, LOW-FAT RECIPES

Even if you grew up eating meat at least once a day, there are times when all you crave is a lunch or dinner rich in carbohydrates – rice or pasta – and vegetables, with no meat in sight.

The following recipes have many influences – Chinese, Indian, Jewish – and each of them delivers a hearty, satisfying meal. Some families have adopted the practice of eating a vegetarian dinner on the same night every week, focusing on a different culture each time. Everyone takes a turn researching a cuisine and preparing a dish. This is a great way to introduce your family to a variety of cultures and at the same time provide them with low-fat meals.

Italian Vegetable Bake

Serves: 8

> 875g (1lb 12oz) tinned chopped tomatoes, juices reserved
> 1 onion, sliced
> 250g (8oz) green beans, sliced
> 250g (8oz) okra, cut into 12mm (1/2in) lengths
> 185g (6oz) finely chopped green peppers
> 2 tbsp lemon juice
> 1 tbsp chopped fresh basil
> 1 1/2 tsp fresh oregano leaves, chopped
> 3 medium courgettes, cut into 25mm (1in) cubes
> 1 aubergine, peeled and cut into 25mm (1in) chunks
> 2 tbsp grated Parmesan cheese

Preheat oven to 170°C (325°F), gas mark 3.

In a baking dish, combine the tomatoes and their liquid, onion, green beans, okra, peppers, lemon juice, basil and oregano. Cover with tin foil or a lid.

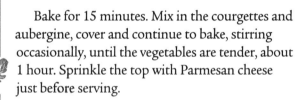

Bake for 15 minutes. Mix in the courgettes and aubergine, cover and continue to bake, stirring occasionally, until the vegetables are tender, about 1 hour. Sprinkle the top with Parmesan cheese just before serving.

Nutritional Analysis

Calories	82.48 Kcal	Protein	4.27 gm
Fat	0.84 gm	Carbohydrate	17.05 gm
Sodium	195.07 mg	Cholesterol	0.98 mg
Saturated fat	0.28 gm		

Winter Chilli
Serves: 6

> 1 green pepper, cut into 25mm (1in) pieces, seeds reserved
> 1 red pepper, cut into 25mm (1in) pieces, seed reserved
> 250g (8oz) very coarsely chopped onion
> 3 cloves garlic, crushed

1 tsp ground cumin
1¹/₂ to 3 tbsp chili powder, to taste
*¹/₄ tsp finely chopped habañero pepper (very hot) or
    jalapeño pepper (medium-hot) or 2 tbsp dried
    chopped ancho pepper (mild)*
¹/₂ tsp cocoa powder
¹/₂ tsp brown sugar
250ml (8fl oz) tomato sauce
1kg (2lb) tinned dark kidney beans, drained
375ml (12fl oz) water or tomato juice
salt and pepper to taste

In a large nonstick saucepan, combine all the ingredients, including the pepper seeds. Bring to the boil, cover, reduce the heat to low and simmer, stirring to loosen the bottom occasionally, until heated through, 35 to 50 minutes. Adjust the seasoning and serve piping hot.

Nutritional Analysis

Calories	122.28	Kcal	Protein	7.35	gm
Fat	1.33	gm	Carbohydrate	21.94	gm
Sodium	400.28	mg	Cholesterol	0.00	mg
Saturated Fat	0.05	gm			

Welsh Rarebit with Vegetables
Serves: 2

60g (2oz) finely chopped cabbage
60g (2oz) finely chopped carrot
2 tbsp finely chopped green pepper
2 tbsp finely chopped celery
2 tbsp finely chopped onion

2 tbsp finely chopped radishes
2 slices wholemeal bread, toasted
125g (4oz) grated low-fat cheddar cheese
dash of red pepper flakes
2 tbsp water
60g (2oz) alfalfa sprouts

Preheat grill.

In a bowl, combine the cabbage, carrot, pepper, celery, onion and radishes. Top each slice of toast with an equal amount of the vegetable mixture. Place the slices on a baking tray. In a small saucepan, combine the cheese, red pepper flakes and water. Place over low heat and stir until the cheese melts. Spoon over the sandwiches, dividing evenly. Slip the baking tray under the grill about 100mm (4in) from the heat source and grill until the cheese is bubbling, about 5 minutes. Transfer to serving plates. Top with the sprouts.

Nutritional Analysis

Calories	132.01	Kcal	Protein	13.39	gm
Fat	1.30	gm	Carbohydrate	18.86	gm
Sodium	374.76	mg	Cholesterol	3.00	mg
Saturated fat	0.26	gm			

Stuffed Courgettes

Serves: 4

2 medium courgettes
250g (8oz) frozen sweetcorn kernels
125g (4oz) low-fat small-curd cottage cheese

(continued)

¹⁄₈ tsp salt
¹⁄₈ tsp pepper
2 tbsp chopped spring onions
60g (2oz) grated Parmesan cheese

Preheat oven to 200°C (400°F), gas mark 6. Spray a 200mm (8in) square baking dish with nonstick cooking spray. Cut each courgette in half lengthways. Scoop out the seeds from each half.

In a bowl, mix together the sweetcorn, cottage cheese, salt, pepper and spring onions. Spoon the mixture into the courgette halves, mounding it slightly. Top with the Parmesan cheese. Place the courgettes in the prepared baking dish.

Bake, uncovered, until the courgettes are tender and the cheese topping has melted, about 15 minutes. Serve immediately.

Nutritional Analysis

Calories	100.77	Kcal	Protein	7.84	gm
Fat	3.15	gm	Carbohydrate	12.18	gm
Sodium	295.11	mg	Cholesterol	7.67	mg
Saturated fat	1.78	gm			

Pizza Crust

Makes: two 230mm (9in) crusts

1 tsp active dry yeast
125ml (4fl oz) plus 1 tbsp lukewarm water
375g (12oz) bread flour or plain flour
2 tsp sugar
1 tsp salt
1 tbsp extra-virgin olive oil
1 tsp olive oil for coating

In a small bowl, sprinkle the yeast over the lukewarm water and set aside until bubbles appear on the surface, 5 to 10 minutes. Place the flour, sugar and salt in a large bowl. Make a well in the centre and pour the yeast mixture and extra-virgin olive oil into it. Using a wooden spoon, gradually combine the wet and dry ingredients. When a dough has formed, lightly oil your hands and knead the dough for 5 minutes. It should be slightly tacky. Lightly oil the dough ball.

Rub the surface of a 1l (2 pint) bowl with the oil and place the dough ball in it. Cover the bowl with cling film, sealing it airtight. Set aside at room temperature to rise until doubled in size, 1¹⁄₂ to 2 hours.

To obtain a wonderfully chewy, tasty dough, punch it down, reform a nice round ball and return it to the same bowl. Cover again so it is airtight with cling film, and place in the refrigerator overnight.

About 2 hours before you are ready to make the pizza, remove the dough from the refrigerator and, using a sharp knife, divide it into 2 equal portions. Roll each portion into a round, smooth ball; seal any holes by pinching them closed. Place the dough balls in a glass dish, spaced far enough apart to allow room for rising, and let rise at room temperature until doubled in size, about 2 hours. The balls should be smooth and puffy.

Place a pizza stone in an oven and preheat to 240°C (500°F), gas mark 10.

To stretch the dough to shape the pizza, sprinkle flour onto a work surface. Using a spatula, carefully transfer 1 dough ball to the

surface. Be very careful to preserve its round shape. Sprinkle the dough liberally with flour. Using your hand or a rolling pin, press down the dough to form a flat round about 12mm (1/2in) thick. Pinch the dough between your fingers around the edge, forming a 6mm (1/4in) high rim. Continue this outward stretching until you have formed a dough round 230mm (9in) in diameter.

Top the pizza rounds as directed in individual recipes, then bake until cheese is bubbling, 8 to 10 minutes.

Nutritional Analysis

Calories	473.00 Kcal	Protein	13.07 gm
Fat	11.04 gm	Carbohydrate	79.47 gm
Sodium	1168.19 mg	Cholesterol	0.00 mg
Saturated fat	1.55 gm		

California French Bread Pizza

Serves: 8

1 French loaf
1 onion, thinly sliced into rings
1 green pepper, thinly sliced into rings
250g (8oz) sliced mushrooms
1 clove garlic, crushed
325ml (12fl oz) tomato sauce
125g (4oz) grated low-fat mozzarella cheese
2 tbsp grated sharp romano cheese
salt and pepper to taste
dried oregano and basil, crumbled, to taste
red pepper flakes to taste

Preheat oven to 210°C (425°F), gas mark 7. Spray a baking tray with nonstick cooking spray.

Cut the bread in half lengthways. Pull out the doughy centre from each half, leaving only the crust. Layer the onion, pepper and mushrooms inside the hollowed-out halves. Sprinkle with the garlic and spoon on the tomato sauce. Sprinkle with the mozzarella and romano cheeses and seasonings. Place both bread halves on the prepared baking tray.

Bake, uncovered, until cheese is slightly browned and bubbling, about 20 minutes. To serve, slice each half into 4 pieces.

Nutritional Analysis

Calories	159.22 Kcal	Protein	7.50 gm
Fat	1.86 gm	Carbohydrate	28.58 gm
Sodium	604.48 mg	Cholesterol	2.05 mg
Saturated fat	0.48 gm		

Rosie's Pizza Dough

Makes: 8 individual pizza crusts

180ml (6fl oz) lukewarm water
1 tsp honey
1 tbsp active dried yeast
375g (12oz) semolina flour
1/2 tsp salt
1 tsp olive oil
125g (4oz) cornmeal

In a medium bowl, combine the water and honey. Sprinkle the yeast on top and set aside

(continued)

until bubbles form on the surface, about 5 to 10 minutes.

In a food processor, combine the flour and salt. Turn the machine on and slowly add the yeast mixture through the feed tube. Process for about 1 minute, or until the dough forms a ball, drizzling a little additional water into the feed tube if necessary. Continue to process for another 2 minutes.

Rub the surface of a large bowl with the olive oil. Transfer the dough ball to the bowl and turn to coat the surface with oil. Cover the bowl with a towel and let stand in a warm place until the dough doubles in size, about 1 hour.

Preheat oven to 200°C (400°F), gas mark 6.

Spread a work surface with the cornmeal. Place the dough on the work surface and roll out 6mm (1/4in) thick. Using a sharp knife and a saucer as a template, cut out eight 138mm (5 1/2in) rounds.

Spray a baking tray 3 times with nonstick cooking spray. Transfer the pizza rounds to the prepared tray. Bake until golden, 3 to 5 minutes. Remove from the oven and top as desired.

Nutritional Analysis

Calories	159.01	Kcal	Protein	5.27	gm
Fat	1.45	gm	Carbohydrate	30.79	gm
Sodium	146.13	mg	Cholesterol	0.00	mg
Saturated fat	0.12	gm			

Rosie's Pizza Sauce

Makes: 325ml (12fl oz) sauce

1 tbsp tomato paste
250ml (8fl oz) tomato purée
1/4 tsp red pepper flakes
2 tsp dried oregano, crumbled
2 tsp dried basil, crumbled
2 tsp dried thyme, crumbled

In a small saucepan, combine all the ingredients and cook over low heat until the sauce thickens, about 15 minutes.

Nutritional Analysis

Calories	24.17	Kcal	Protein	0.97	gm
Fat	0.19	gm	Carbohydrate	5.72	gm
Sodium	188.37	mg	Cholesterol	0.00	mg
Saturated fat	0.02	gm			

California Vegetable Pizza Topping

Makes: one 305mm (12in) pizza (serves: 8)

1 batch Rosie's Pizza Dough (see page 211)
125ml (4fl oz) Rosie's Pizza Sauce (see above)
125g (4oz) lightly steamed tiny broccoli florets
125g (4oz) chopped artichoke hearts
60g (2oz) sliced black olives
1 tomato, sliced
6 green pepper rings

Preheat oven to 240°C (500°F), gas mark 10. Oil a 305mm (12in) pizza pan.

Place the dough on a lightly floured work surface and press to flatten. Lightly roll out the dough into a 305mm (12in) round, transfer to the prepared pizza pan, and pinch the edge to form a rim.

Spread the sauce on the dough to within 25mm (1in) of the rim. Arrange all the vegetables in layers on the sauce, ending with the peppers.

Bake until the crust is brown and crisp, about 15 minutes. Remove from the oven and let cool for 5 minutes, then cut into wedges to serve.

Nutritional Analysis

Calories	1511.69 Kcal	Protein	51.33 gm.
Fat	23.69 gm	Carbohydrate	275.53 gm
Sodium	2057.89 mg	Cholesterol	0.00 mg
Saturated Fat	2.21 gm		

Olives

Olives are a great way to add a bit of texture and saltiness to a dish. But be careful, as they are also high in fat and sodium. As a rule of thumb, black olives contain less fat and sodium than green olives. To cut down further on the fat content, select olives that have been packed in brine, not oil, and be sure to rinse them thoroughly before cooking with them.

Top-Hat Pizza

Makes: one 305mm (12in) pizza (serves: 8)

1 batch Rosie's Pizza Dough (see page 211)
500g (1lb) grated low-fat mozzarella cheese
60g (2oz) red peppers, cut into thin strips
60g (2oz) green peppers, cut into thin strips
125g (4oz) tinned diced mild green chilli peppers, drained
2 tbsp pitted black olives, sliced

(continued)

2 spring onions, sliced
2 avocados
1 tbsp lemon juice
1 tsp garlic salt
1/2 tsp seasoned salt
5 drops of Tabasco sauce
60g (2oz) finely crushed tortilla crisps
12 plum tomatoes, sliced

Preheat oven to 240°C (500°F), gas mark 10. Oil a 305mm (12in) pizza pan.

Place the dough on a lightly floured work surface and press to flatten. Lightly roll out the dough into a 305mm (12in) round and transfer to the prepared pan. Sprinkle with the mozzarella cheese, red and green peppers, chillies, olives and spring onions. Bake until the cheese is melted, 10 to 12 minutes.

Meanwhile, stone and peel the avocados. Cut, place in a bowl and mash with a fork. Add the lemon juice, garlic salt, seasoned salt, Tabasco sauce and crushed crisps. Mix well to form a guacamole.

Remove the pizza from the oven. Arrange the tomato slices on top. Place a generous mound of the guacamole in the centre of each tomato slice. Serve at once. Pass round the remaining guacamole at the table.

Nutritional Analysis

Calories	315.06 Kcal	Protein	16.18 gm
Fat	10.25 gm	Carbohydrate	41.73 gm
Sodium	745.92 mg	Cholesterol	3.00 mg
Saturated fat	1.52 gm		

Sweet Potato Tart

Serves: 12

Crust:
125g (4oz) crushed cream crackers
1 tsp ground cinnamon
1 egg white

Filling:
4 medium sweet potatoes, baked until tender and
*   peeled*
6 egg whites
1/4 tsp ground nutmeg
1/4 tsp ground cloves
1/4 tsp ground allspice
1/4 tsp ground ginger
2 tsp pure vanilla extract
5 tbsp pure maple syrup
1 tbsp honey
185g (6oz) light cream cheese
60ml (2fl oz) orange juice

Preheat oven to 180°C (350°F), gas mark 4.

Spray a 305mm (12in) tart pan 3 times with nonstick cooking spray. To make the crust, combine the crackers, cinnamon and egg white in a food processor. Pulse 5 times. Transfer the

mixture to the prepared tart pan and pat to cover the bottom evenly.

To make the filling, put the baked sweet potatoes in a large bowl and mash with a fork. Add the egg whites, nutmeg, cloves, allspice and ginger. Whisk to blend. Add all the remaining filling ingredients and continue to whisk until smooth. Pour the filing into the crust.

Bake until the centre of the tart is firm and not sticky to the touch, 30 to 45 minutes. Transfer to a rack and let cool for 30 minutes, then refrigerate for 1 hour before serving.

Nutritional Analysis

Calories	146.79	Kcal	Protein	4.71	gm
Fat	3.48	gm	Carbohydrate	23.24	gm
Sodium	127.83	mg	Cholesterol	10.00	mg
Saturated fat	2.01	gm			

Caribbean Rice and Beans

Serves: 6

1 tbsp olive oil
2 tsp crushed garlic
250g (8oz) coarsely chopped onions
1 hot red chilli pepper, seeded and chopped, or 1 generous pinch of red pepper flakes
250g (8oz) diced red pepper
250g (8oz) coarsely chopped plum tomatoes
500ml (1pt) boiling water
500g (1lb) long-grain brown rice
125g (4oz) unsweetened grated dried coconut
1/2 tsp dried thyme or oregano, crumbled

1 tsp salt, or to taste
250g (8oz) cooked black-eyed peas
60g (2oz) finely chopped fresh coriander
2 very ripe plantains, peeled, cut on the diagonal into thin slices

Heat the oil in a pressure cooker over medium-high heat. Add the garlic, onions and chilli pepper or pepper flakes, and cook, stirring frequently, for 1 minute. Add the pepper, tomatoes, boiling water, rice, coconut, oregano or thyme and salt.

Secure the lid in place. Adjust the heat to maintain high pressure and cook for 25 minutes. Allow the pressure to reduce naturally, which will take 10 minutes. (If after 10 minutes the pressure is not released, use the quick-release method.)

Remove the lid, tilting away from you to allow excess pressure to escape. Add the cooked peas and coriander. Stir well to distribute all the ingredients. Serve topped with the plantains.

Nutritional Analysis

Calories	358.95	Kcal	Protein	7.62	gm
Fat	7.53	gm	Carbohydrate	68.42	gm
Sodium	402.10	mg	Cholesterol	0.00	mg
Saturated fat	3.64	gm			

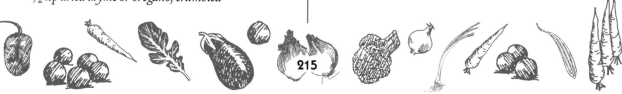

Legumes

Legumes – dried beans, peas and lentils – were largely regarded as peasant food for many years in this country. Now they have caught on in many circles as an efficient and delicious way to add fibre and nutrients to a low-fat diet. Legumes are high in protein, as well as being rich in iron and calcium.

My favourite quick meal is to cook some spaghetti and top it with some spaghetti sauce, chick peas, spring onions and Parmesan cheese. Even my cats like legumes – chick peas in particular.

St Tropez Vegetables

Serves: 6

> 1kg (2lb) summer squash, cut into 6mm (¼in) thick slices
> 1kg (2lb) tomatoes, cut into wedges
> 1 onion, very thinly sliced
> 2 tsp dried basil
> ¼ tsp pepper
> 4 tsp crushed garlic
> 3 tbsp pistachio nuts, chopped

Preheat oven to 200°C (400°F), gas mark 6.

Cut six 380mm (15in) squares of greaseproof paper or tin foil. Place on a work surface. Divide the squash, tomatoes and onion evenly among the squares, stacking the ingredients. Sprinkle with the basil, pepper and garlic. Bring together the opposite sides of the square and fold down tightly. Fold the ends under to seal in any juices. Place in a shallow baking pan. Bake until the vegetables are tender, about 40 minutes. To test, open 1 packet and check for firmness and temperature. (Be careful of steam.) Sprinkle the vegetables with the pistachios just before serving.

Nutritional Analysis

Calories	100.67	Kcal	Protein	4.41	gm
Fat	2.79	gm	Carbohydrate	18.11	gm
Sodium	18.30	mg	Cholesterol	0.00	mg
Saturated fat	0.37	gm			

Summer Vegetable Paella

Serves: 6

1 tsp olive oil
750g (1lb 8oz) broccoli florets
2 courgettes, sliced on the diagonal
1 tomato, diced
2 nectarines, stoned and sliced

In a large nonstick frying pan, heat the oil over high heat. Add the broccoli and courgettes, and cook, stirring often, for 5 minutes. Add the tomato and nectarines, cover, lower heat to medium and cook until the vegetables are crisp-tender, 2 to 3 minutes longer.

Nutritional Analysis

Calories	61.04 Kcal	Protein	3.43 gm
Fat	1.43 gm	Carbohydrate	11.19 gm
Sodium	31.18 mg	Cholesterol	0.00 mg
Saturated fat	0.16 gm		

Vegetable Egg Scramble

Serves: 6

1 tsp olive oil
3 spring onions, finely chopped
2 cloves garlic, crushed
250g (8oz) mushrooms, sliced
1 green pepper, chopped
250g (8oz) tinned sweetcorn kernels, drained
2 whole eggs
6 egg whites
salt and pepper to taste

In a large frying pan, heat the oil over medium heat. Add the spring onions, garlic, mushrooms, pepper and sweetcorn, and sauté, stirring occasionally, until the vegetables are tender, about 5 minutes. Meanwhile, beat the whole eggs and egg whites in a medium bowl. Add the eggs to the vegetables, season with salt and pepper and scramble until thoroughly cooked. Serve at once.

Nutritional Analysis

Calories	85.66 Kcal	Protein	7.34 gm
Fat	2.85 gm	Carbohydrate	8.73 gm
Sodium	133.89 mg	Cholesterol	70.83 mg
Saturated fat	0.66 gm		

Vegetable Casserole with Mozzarella

Serves: 6

500g (1lb) sliced carrots
1 onion, sliced
300g (10oz) chopped frozen spinach
325ml (12fl oz) water
1 tbsp butter
3 tbsp plain flour
325ml (12fl oz) nonfat milk
250g (8oz) grated low-fat mozzarella cheese
1/4 tsp salt
pepper to taste

Place carrots, onion and spinach on a rack in a pressure cooker. Add a third of the water. Secure the lid in place. Place over high heat, and as soon

(continued)

as the pressure regulator begins to rock, reduce the pressure with the quick-release method.

In a small saucepan, melt the butter over low heat. Add the flour and cook, stirring, until well blended, 1 to 2 minutes. Gradually add the milk, stirring constantly. Continue to cook, stirring, until the sauce thickens, about 4 minutes. Remove from the heat and stir in the cheese, salt and pepper. Stir until the cheese is melted.

Place half the spinach in a 1.5l (3 pint) metal bowl that will fit loosely in the pressure cooker. Top with half the carrots and onions. Cover with half of the cheese sauce. Repeat the layers, ending with the sauce. Cover the bowl tightly with tin foil. Pour the remaining water into the cooker, place the cooking rack in place and place the bowl on the rack. Secure the lid in place. Bring to high pressure over high heat. Adjust the heat to maintain high pressure and cook for 7 minutes. Allow the pressure to reduce naturally, 10 minutes.

Remove the lid, tilting it away from you to allow excess steam to escape. Serve directly from the bowl.

Nutritional Analysis

Calories	121.68	Kcal	Protein	10.67	gm
Fat	2.31	gm	Carbohydrate	15.73	gm
Sodium	339.15	mg	Cholesterol	8.39	mg
Saturated fat	1.29	gm			

Vegetable Tamale Pie

Serves: 8

Vegetable Filling:
425g (14oz) tinned pinto beans, drained
1 white onion, chopped
1/2 green pepper, diced
2 jalapeño peppers, seeded and chopped
500g (1lb) tinned chopped tomatoes, drained
1/2 red pepper, diced
375g (12oz) grated low-fat sharp cheddar cheese
8 pitted black olives, sliced
3/4 tsp crushed garlic
3/4 tsp ground cumin
3/4 tsp chilli powder

Tamale Topping:
125g (4oz) plus 1 tbsp plain flour
250g (8oz) yellow cornmeal
1 1/2 tsp baking powder
1/2 tsp bicarbonate of soda
1/8 tsp salt
125ml (4fl oz) plain low-fat yogurt
1 egg, at room temperature
2 tsp butter, melted and cooled
1 tbsp snipped fresh chives (optional)

Preheat oven to 190°C (375°F), gas mark 5.

Spray a 200mm (8in) square baking pan with nonstick cooking spray. Combine all the filling ingredients in the prepared pan. Toss until well mixed; set aside.

To make the topping, in a medium bowl, combine the flour, cornmeal, baking powder, bicarbonate of soda and salt; stir until evenly mixed. In a small bowl, beat together the yogurt, egg and butter. Add to the flour mixture and stir just until the dry ingredients are moistened. Spoon the mixture evenly on top of the vegetable filling. If desired, sprinkle evenly with the chives.

Bake until the filling is hot and bubbling, the topping is lightly browned and a toothpick inserted into the centre of the topping comes out clean, 35 to 40 minutes. Let stand for 5 minutes before cutting into slices.

Nutritional Analysis

Calories	214.69 Kcal	Protein	14.31 gm
Fat	3.11 gm	Carbohydrate	33.28 gm
Sodium	608.45 mg	Cholesterol	32.25 mg
Saturated fat	1.05 gm		

Stuffed Onions

Serves: 6

6 large onions
2 stalks celery
1 sprig fresh rosemary
5 sprigs fresh parsley
1 sprig fresh thyme
2 garlic cloves
2 tbsp vegetable oil
500g (1lb) long-grain rice

60g (2oz) toasted pine nuts
1 tbsp olive oil
2 tbsp balsamic vinegar
Salt and pepper to taste

Peel the onions. Slice off both ends of the onions, so they are able to stand upright. Place the onions in a saucepan with enough water to cover them. Bring to the boil, then reduce the heat, cover and let simmer for 10–15 minutes depending on the size and type of onion, until they are tender.

Using a slotted spoon, gently remove the onions and drain. When cool, gently push out the cores of the onions with your fingers, leaving the onion shell intact. Reserve the shells and cores.

To prepare the filling, trim and finely chop the celery, onion cores and herbs. Peel and chop the garlic. Heat the vegetable oil in a saucepan. Add the chopped onion, celery, garlic and herbs. Cook until the vegetables are soft but not brown, stirring frequently. Add the rice and fry it with the vegetables for 3 to 4 minutes. Pour in 1l (2 pints) boiling water, cover and simmer for 15 to 20 minutes, until the rice is soft and the water has been absorbed. Add the pine nuts and salt and pepper to taste.

To prepare the vinaigrette, combine the olive oil and balsamic vinegar with some salt and pepper in a bowl. Beat with a whisk.

Preheat the oven to 170°C (325°F), gas mark 3. Pour the vinaigrette into the baking dish. Using a teaspoon, stuff the onions with the rice

(continued)

filling. Arrange the onions upright in the baking dish and cover with tin foil. Place in the oven and bake for 30 minutes.

Nutritional Analysis

Calories	453.10	Kcal	Protein	10.00	gm
Fat	12.40	gm	Carbohydrate	77.48	gm
Sodium	23.04	mg	Cholesterol	0.00	mg
Saturated fat	1.78	gm			

Stuffed Tomatoes

Serves: 2

2 large tomatoes
2 tbsp chopped fresh parsley
2 tbsp chopped onion
2 cloves garlic, crushed
1/4 tsp dried thyme, crumbled
1 tbsp dried basil
60g (2oz) seasoned dried breadcrumbs
salt and pepper to taste
1 tsp olive oil

Preheat oven to 180°C (350°F), gas mark 4. Slice the top off each tomato, reserving the 'lids'. Scoop out the pulp and reserve in a bowl. To the tomato pulp, add the parsley, onion, garlic, thyme and basil, and blend. Add the breadcrumbs, salt, pepper and oil, and mix well. Fill the tomato shells with this mixture. Replace the lids.

Bake until the mixture is heated through. Serve immediately.

Nutritional Analysis

Calories	138.21	Kcal	Protein	4.76	gm
Fat	3.50	gm	Carbohydrate	24.66	gm
Sodium	421.03	mg	Cholesterol	0.00	mg
Saturated fat	0.51	gm			

Dal

Serves: 4

250g (8oz) dried lentils
500ml (1pt) water
1 tsp salt
1/2 tsp ground turmeric
1/4 tsp cayenne pepper
2 tbsp sesame oil
1 medium onion, thinly sliced
1 tsp ground cumin
1 tsp ground coriander

In a saucepan, combine the lentils, water, salt, turmeric and cayenne pepper. Bring to the boil. Meanwhile, in a large saucepan, heat the sesame oil over medium heat. Add the onion and sauté until soft, about 5 minutes. Add the cumin and coriander, and cook for 5 minutes longer. Add the onion mixture to the lentils, cover and cook over medium heat until the lentils are tender, about 30 minutes.

Nutritional Analysis

Calories	242.04 Kcal	Protein	14.07 gm
Fat	7.47 gm	Carbohydrate	31.56 gm
Sodium	589.74 mg	Cholesterol	0.00 mg
Saturated fat	1.03 gm		

Potato Pancakes

Serves: 8

1kg (2lb) potatoes, peeled and coarsely grated
1 large onion, coarsely grated
1 egg white
1 whole egg
60ml (2fl oz) low-fat milk
1 carrot, grated
60g (2oz) matzo meal or 125g (4oz) unbleached
  plain flour
1 tsp salt
pepper to taste
1 to 2 tbsp vegetable oil

Put the potatoes and onion in a colander, and press against the vegetables to extract the extra water. Let the mixture stand for a few minutes, then press them again. Transfer to a bowl. In a small bowl, beat together the egg white and whole egg until blended. Add to the potato mixture along with the milk, carrot, matzo meal or flour, salt and pepper. Stir to combine thoroughly.

In a large frying pan, heat 1 to 2 tablespoons of oil – just enough to cover the bottom of the pan – over medium heat. Measure out 60ml (2fl oz) batter for each pancake, and add to the pan.

(continued)

Perfect Potato Pancakes

Potato pancakes are traditionally fried in oil, and so they can be very greasy if not cooked properly. First, start by using just a thin layer of oil, only enough to coat the pan with a film. Next, make sure that the oil is hot before you spoon the batter into the pan. After the pancakes have finished cooking, place them on paper towels and blot as much of the oil out of them as you can.

Lo Mein Noodles

Although you can use the packaged dried lo mein noodles found in most supermarkets, you'll come much closer to creating the lo mein you're familiar with in Chinese restaurants if you purchase fresh Chinese wheat noodles, which are now available in many supermarkets, usually in the produce section. The noodles, sold in 250g (8oz) or 500g (1lb) bags, can be kept in the refrigerator for a week or in the freezer for a month. Whenever I find them, I stock up.

Do not overfill the pan. Fry, turning once, until golden brown on both sides, about 4 minutes on each side. Using a slotted spatula, transfer to paper towels to drain. Keep warm while you cook the remaining pancakes. Serve hot.

Nutritional Analysis

Calories	135.24 Kcal	Protein	4.03 gm
Fat	3.42 gm	Carbohydrate	22.54 gm
Sodium	318.96 mg	Cholesterol	26.86 mg
Saturated fat	0.58 gm		

Vegetable Lo Mein

Serves: 6

3 tbsp soy sauce
2 tbsp oyster sauce
1 tbsp sesame oil
¹/₂ tsp sugar
2l (4pt) water
250g (8oz) fresh Chinese wheat noodles
1 tbsp peanut oil
8 cloves garlic, chopped
250g (8oz) chopped celery
185g (6oz) tinned bamboo shoots, drained
250g (8oz) grated white cabbage
250g (8oz) chopped pak choi
250g (8oz) beansprouts
500g (1lb) loosely packed, coarsely chopped spinach

In a small bowl, combine the soy sauce, oyster sauce, sesame oil and sugar; stir well. Set aside. In a large saucepan, bring the water to the boil. Add the noodles, boil for 3 minutes and drain. Rinse

under cold water and drain again. Set aside. In a wok or large, deep frying pan, heat the peanut oil over high heat. Add the garlic, celery, bamboo shoots, cabbage, pak choi and beansprouts. Stir-fry for 1 minute. Add the cooked noodles, mix well and then add the spinach. Stir-fry to mix. Add the sauce and stir and toss to mix well and heat through. Serve immediately.

Nutritional Analysis

Calories	194.75 Kcal	Protein	8.43 gm
Fat	5.75 gm	Carbohydrate	28.99 gm
Sodium	835.41 mg	Cholesterol	27.61 mg
Saturated fat	0.86 gm		

Rice with Black Beans and Ginger

Serves: 4

1 tbsp olive oil
2 cloves garlic, crushed
2 tbsp chopped onion
1 tbsp peeled and finely chopped fresh ginger
250g (8oz) washed white rice
500ml (1pt) reduced-sodium, fat-free vegetable stock
250g (8oz) cooked black beans
salt and pepper to taste

In a frying pan, heat the oil over medium heat. Add the garlic, onion and ginger, and cook, stirring, for 1 minute. Add the rice and stock. Lower heat, cover and cook until the rice is tender and the liquid has been absorbed, about 20 minutes.

Add the black beans and salt and pepper and stir to heat through, then serve.

Nutritional Analysis

Calories	268.09 Kcal	Protein	8.75 gm
Fat	3.91 gm	Carbohydrate	48.31 gm
Sodium	283.96 mg	Cholesterol	0.00 mg
Saturated fat	0.59 gm		

John Barleycorn Casserole

Serves: 4

1 tbsp olive oil
1 onion, chopped
2 cloves garlic, crushed
250g (8oz) grated carrots
250g (8oz) pearl barley
750ml (1¹/₂pt) reduced-sodium, fat-free vegetable stock
500g (1lb) fresh or tinned sweetcorn kernels
60g (2oz) chopped fresh parsley
salt and pepper to taste

Preheat oven to 180°C (350°F), gas mark 4.

In a flameproof baking dish, heat the oil over medium-high heat. Add the onion, garlic and carrots, and sauté until the onion is translucent, 5 to 7 minutes. Add the barley and broth, and cover with tin foil or a lid.

Bake until the barley is tender, about 1 hour. Uncover and add the sweetcorn, parsley, salt and pepper, mixing well. Cover and continue to bake until heated through, about 5 minutes, then serve.

(continued)

Nutritional Analysis

Calories	314.73 Kcal	Protein	10.61 gm
Fat	4.97 gm	Carbohydrate	60.68 gm
Sodium	449.75 mg	Cholesterol	0.00 mg
Saturated fat	0.71 gm		

Potato and Chick Pea Stew

Serves: 4

1 tbsp olive oil
1 onion, chopped
2 cloves garlic, crushed
1 tsp paprika
3 tomatoes, coarsely chopped
1 tsp dried oregano, crumbled
2 large white potatoes, peeled and diced
250ml (8fl oz) reduced-sodium, fat-free vegetable stock
500g (1lb) tinned chick peas, drained and rinsed
90g (3oz) chopped fresh basil
salt and pepper to taste
60g (2oz) chopped fresh parsley

In a large, heavy saucepan, heat the oil over medium heat. Add the onion and sauté until translucent, about 5 minutes. Add the garlic, paprika, oregano and two-thirds of the tomatoes. Reduce the heat to low and cook, stirring occasionally, for 5 minutes. Add the potatoes and stock, cover and bring to the boil. Boil for 5 minutes, stirring occasionally. Add the chick peas, reduce the heat to low and cook until the potatoes are tender, about 5 minutes.

Add the remaining tomato, the basil, salt and pepper; heat for 3 minutes to heat through. Garnish with the parsley just before serving.

Nutritional Analysis

Calories	252.49 Kcal	Protein	9.29 gm
Fat	6.17 gm	Carbohydrate	41.51 gm
Sodium	310.11 mg	Cholesterol	0.00 mg
Saturated fat	0.61 gm		

Stuffed Baked Potatoes

Serves: 4

4 large potatoes
125ml (4fl oz) low-fat milk
250g (8oz) semi-skimmed ricotta cheese
3 cloves garlic, chopped
salt and pepper to taste
500g (1lb) chopped cooked broccoli
60g (2oz) grated Parmesan cheese

Preheat oven to 200°C (400°F), gas mark 6. Pierce potato skins with a fork. Bake for 1 hour. Remove from oven and reduce oven temperature to 190°C (375°F), gas mark 5. Cut a slice off the top of each potato. Scoop out the potato flesh into a bowl, being careful not to tear the skins. Set both aside.

Add the milk to the potato flesh and mash thoroughly with a fork. Add the ricotta cheese, garlic, salt, pepper, broccoli and Parmesan cheese. Mix well. Spoon the potato mixture into the potato skins and replace the tops. Place the potatoes on a baking tray. Bake until heated through, about 30 minutes.

Nutritional Analysis

Calories	311.44 Kcal	Protein	16.02 gm
Fat	7.11 gm	Carbohydrate	47.84 gm
Sodium	218.04 mg	Cholesterol	24.23 mg
Saturated fat	4.25 gm		

Cheese-Egg Casserole

Serves: 4

> 5 slices stale French bread
> 2 whole eggs
> 8 egg whites
> 250ml (8fl oz) low-fat milk
> dash of dry mustard
> 150g (5oz) sausage meat
> 250ml (8fl oz) grated low-fat cheddar cheese
> salt and pepper to taste

Arrange the bread slices in a single layer in the bottom of a baking dish. In a bowl, stir together the whole eggs, egg whites, milk and mustard. Pour over the bread.

In a frying pan, cook the sausage, breaking it up, until brown, about 5 minutes. Pour into a sieve to drain well. Sprinkle the sausage, cheddar cheese, salt and pepper on top of the bread. Cover and refrigerate overnight.

The next day, bake in an oven preheated to 180°C (350°F), gas mark 4 until a knife inserted in the centre comes out clean, about 30 minutes.

Cut into squares and serve immediately.

Nutritional Analysis

Calories	294.04 Kcal	Protein	28.45 gm
Fat	9.72 gm	Carbohydrate	22.27 gm
Sodium	806.92 mg	Cholesterol	126.76 mg
Saturated fat	3.33 gm		

Spicy Chilli

Serves: 4

> 1 tbsp olive oil
> 2 large onions, chopped
> 5 cloves garlic, crushed
> 1 green pepper, chopped
> 2 jalapeño peppers, seeded and finely chopped
> 1kg (2lb) tinned chopped tomatoes, drained
> 1 tsp ground coriander
> pinch of ground cloves
> pinch of ground allspice
> 2 tsp dried oregano, crumbled
> 1 tbsp brown sugar
> 2 tbsp chilli powder
> 2 tbsp ground cumin
> 500g (1lb) cooked kidney beans
> 500ml (1pt) water
> 250g (8oz) washed white rice

In a large frying pan, heat the oil over medium heat. Add the onions, garlic, pepper and jalapeño pepper, and sauté until the vegetables are tender, about 10 minutes. Add the tomatoes, coriander, cloves, allspice, oregano, brown sugar, chilli

(continued)

Combining Proteins for Best Results

Most of us get our protein requirements from eating animal meat that also has lots of saturated fat. But you can get plenty of protein from vegetable sources without saturated fat if you know how to combine foods such as grains, legumes, nuts and seeds. Combining foods from complementary protein groups provides you with all the protein you need. An example of complementary combinations is rice and kidney beans.

To prepare dried kidney beans, soak them overnight in water in the refrigerator. Drain the water and add fresh water to cover. Bring to the boil and boil for 10 minutes, then reduce the heat and simmer for about 2 1/2 hours.

powder, cumin and beans. Bring to the boil, cover, reduce the heat to low and cook until the flavours are blended, about 30 minutes.

Meanwhile, in a saucepan, bring the water to the boil. Add the rice, reduce the heat to low, cover and cook until the rice is tender and the liquid is absorbed, 20 to 30 minutes. To serve, spoon the rice onto individual plates. Serve the chilli over the rice.

Nutritional Analysis

Calories	471.99 Kcal	Protein	16.06 gm
Fat	5.69 gm	Carbohydrate	92.63 gm
Sodium	447.28 mg	Cholesterol	0.00 mg
Saturated fat	0.63 gm		

Desserts

CHAPTER TWELVE

Amount Per Chapter

42 Recipes

	% Daily Value
Easy to Prepare	**100%**
Low Fat/High Flavour	**100%**
Simple to Understand	**100%**

DELICIOUS, EASY, LOW-FAT RECIPES

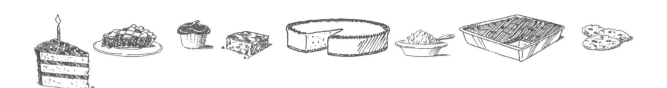

When I was growing up in the 1960s and 1970s, I would regularly have a piece of chocolate cake and a glass of milk for breakfast. Nobody was alarmed, and I made it all the way through to lunch. Perhaps the fact that we have created a systematic categorization of 'good' foods and 'bad' foods (including dessert) has made us obsessed about the sweet things we do and don't allow ourselves to eat.

Today, in many circles, dessert gets a bad deal. To true dessert lovers, this is an unfortunate maligning of what often turns out to be the best part of a meal. All too often, we connect being virtuous with eating foods that require too much chewing and that have a taste that makes all that jaw action not worth much. If you forego having dessert too often, the world indeed does seem like a harsher place, no matter what your circumstances are or where you live.

Indeed, dessert is a way you can feel better about your life, as well as being an easy way to make other people happy, too. Have you ever noticed how people brighten up whenever someone walks into a room carrying a box tied with bakery string? And how can your best friend stay cross with you after an argument when you knock on her door bearing a freshly baked low-fat lemon meringue pie?

Buttermilk Pops

Makes: 10 pops

*185g (6oz) frozen orange juice concentrate, thawed
  and undiluted*
250ml (8fl oz) nonfat buttermilk
250ml (8fl oz) evaporated skim milk

In a large bowl, combine all the ingredients. Using an electric mixer, beat until blended. Pour into 125ml (4fl oz) paper cups or ice-lolly moulds and freeze until hardened. If you are using cups, freeze for about 15 minutes until thick and then insert the stick and continue to freeze until solid. Then, when ready to serve, just tear off the paper cup.

Nutritional Analysis

Calories	63.56 Kcal	Protein	3.23 gm
Fat	0.30 gm	Carbohydrate	12.19 gm
Sodium	55.69 mg	Cholesterol	2.00 mg
Saturated fat	0.16 gm		

Light Lemon Pudding

Serves: 6

1 envelope (1 tbsp) unflavoured gelatin
250ml (8fl oz) plus 1 tbsp cold water
250ml (8fl oz) boiling water
125g (4oz) sugar
60ml (2fl oz) plus ¼ tsp lemon juice
1 tsp grated lemon zest
125g (4oz) regular nonfat dry milk powder
125ml (4fl oz) iced water

In a small bowl, soften the gelatin in 1 tablespoon of cold water. Add the boiling water to dissolve. Add the sugar, the remaining cold water, the 60ml (2fl oz) lemon juice and the lemon zest. Chill until very thick, about 90 minutes.

Chill a deep mixing bowl and beaters. Add the dry milk, iced water and remaining lemon juice to the chilled bowl. Beat until fluffy, then cover and chill.

Break up the lemon mixture with a fork. Add to the whipped milk mixture. Using an electric mixer, beat until fluffy but not too soft. Cover and chill until firm before serving, about ½ hour.

Nutritional Analysis

Calories	91.17	Kcal	Protein	3.03	gm
Fat	0.07	gm	Carbohydrate	20.33	gm
Sodium	35.81	mg	Cholesterol	1.02	mg
Saturated fat	0.02	gm			

Strawberry Sorbet

Serves: 8

500ml (1pt) strawberries, stemmed
180ml (6fl oz) orange juice
125ml (4fl oz) low-fat milk
125ml (4fl oz) plus 1 tbsp honey
2 egg whites

In a blender, combine the berries, orange juice, milk and 125ml (4fl oz) honey. Blend until smooth, about 1 minute. Pour into a 230mm (9in) square baking pan. Cover and freeze until almost firm, 2 to 3 hours.

In an electric mixer bowl, beat the egg whites at medium speed until soft peaks form. Increase the speed to high and gradually add the remaining honey, beating until stiff peaks form.

Break the frozen mixture into chunks. Transfer the pieces to a chilled large bowl. Beat with an electric mixer until smooth. Fold in the egg whites with a rubber spatula. Return the mixer to the baking pan. Cover tightly and freeze until firm, 6 to 8 hours. To serve, scrape across the surface of the frozen mixture with a spoon, and place in mounds in dessert dishes.

Nutritional Analysis

Calories	73.32	Kcal	Protein	1.79	gm
Fat	0.31	gm	Carbohydrate	17.02	gm
Sodium	22.46	mg	Cholesterol	0.61	mg
Saturated fat	0.10	gm			

A Low-Fat Crust

The Tangy Lime Pie (page 233) has a crumb crust that is deliberately crumbly. If you prefer a firmer baked crust, bake the unfilled crust at 180°C (350°F), gas mark 4 for 10 to 12 minutes, then let it cool completely before filling it. You can, of course, substitute a regular baked pie crust, but keep in mind that the fat content will be considerably higher.

Applesauce Pound Cake

Makes: 1 loaf cake (serves: 8)

250ml (8fl oz) nonfat milk
250g (8oz) raisins
250g (8oz) apple sauce
90g (3oz) firmly packed brown sugar
60ml (2fl oz) sunflower oil
1/2 tsp ground cinnamon
1/2 tsp ground allspice
salt (optional)
1/8 tsp ground nutmeg
500g (1lb) plain flour
1 tsp baking powder
1 tsp bicarbonate of soda
250g (8oz) chopped peeled apples or pitted dates
125g (4oz) chopped walnuts (optional)

Preheat oven to 170°C (325°F), gas mark 3. Spray a 230 x 100mm (9 x 4in) loaf pan with nonstick cooking spray.

In a large bowl, combine the milk, raisins, apple sauce, sugar, oil and spices. Beat until thoroughly mixed. In another bowl, stir together the flour, baking powder and bicarbonate of soda. Add the flour mixture to the milk mixture, stirring until just combined. Fold in the apples or dates and the walnuts, if using.

Bake until a cake tester comes out clean, about 1¼ hours. Cool on a rack, then slice and serve.

Nutritional Analysis

Calories	292.22 Kcal	Protein	3.92 gm
Fat	7.40 gm	Carbohydrate	54.64 gm
Sodium	241.91 mg	Cholesterol	0.61 mg
Saturated fat	0.56 gm		

Pear Pudding Cake

Serves: 8

185g (6oz) wholewheat pastry flour
185g (6oz) plain flour
1 tsp bicarbonate of soda
1¹/₂ tsp ground ginger
¹/₄ tsp ground cardamom
¹/₈ tsp salt
90g (3oz) dried currants or raisins
90g (3oz) slivered blanched almonds, toasted
500g (1lb) peeled and diced pears (about 2 large)
180ml (6fl oz) pear or other noncitrus fruit juice
80ml (2¹/₂fl oz) pure maple syrup
750ml (1.5pt) boiling water

Spray a 1kg (2lb) baking pan or heatproof baking dish with nonstick cooking spray.

In a large bowl, combine the flours, bicarbonate of soda, ginger, cardamom, salt, currants or raisins and almonds. Stir in the pears. In a measuring cup, combine the juice and syrup. Stir the juice mixture into the flour mixture just until combined. Pour the batter into the prepared baking pan. Cover tightly with a sheet of tin foil large enough to tuck the ends under the bottom of the pan.

Place a rack in the bottom of a pressure cooker. Pour in the boiling water. Lower the filled baking pan into the cooker, resting it on the rack. (Make sure there's a 12mm (¹/₂in) space between the sides of the pressure cooker and the edges of the baking pan.) Secure the lid in place. Bring to high pressure over high heat. Adjust the heat to maintain high pressure and cook for 25 minutes (30 minutes if you're using a baking dish instead of

a baking pan.) Allow the pressure to come down naturally for 15 minutes. If after 15 minutes the pressure is not released, use a quick-release method. Remove the lid, tilting it away from you to allow any steam to escape.

Lift the baking pan out of the cooker. Remove the tin foil and set the pan on a rack to cool. Unmould the cake or serve directly from the pan. Serve warm or at room temperature.

Helpful hint: to lift the baking pan or dish in and out of the cooker, cut a piece of tin foil 610mm (24in) long by 305mm (12in) wide. Fold it twice lengthways. Centre the pan on the strip, and use the ends of the strip to lower the pan into the cooker. Fold the ends of the strip over the top of the pan. Use the ends of the strip to lift the pan out of the cooker.

Nutritional Analysis

Calories	211.10	Kcal	Protein	4.44	gm
Fat	4.01	gm	Carbohydrate	41.80	gm
Sodium	198.17	mg	Cholesterol	0.00	mg
Saturated fat	0.45	gm			

Buttermilk Fruit Sherbet

Serves: 4

500g (1lb) frozen unsweetened blueberries
125ml (4fl oz) nonfat buttermilk
2 or 3 drops of honey (optional)

In a food processor, combine the frozen berries with half the buttermilk. Process until the berries are coarsely chopped. Cover and process, adding

(continued)

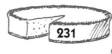

the remaining buttermilk a little at a time through the cover opening. Uncover and redistribute the berries. Cover and process again until the mixture is smooth and has the texture of frozen custard or soft-serve ice cream. Don't overprocess. If desired, sweeten to taste with a few drops of honey. Serve immediately.

Nutritional Analysis

Calories	50.78 Kcal	Protein	1.44 gm
Fat	0.49 gm	Carbohydrate	11.05 gm
Sodium	37.01 mg	Cholesterol	0.62 mg
Saturated fat	0.00 gm		

Minted Middle Eastern Buttermilk Shake

Serves: 1

a handful of ice cubes
250ml (8fl oz) nonfat buttermilk
pinch of salt
a small handful of fresh mint leaves

Combine all the ingredients in a blender. Cover and blend until the ice becomes blended. Pour into a tall mug and garnish with more mint leaves.

Nutritional Analysis

Calories	100.51 Kcal	Protein	8.29 gm
Fat	2.19 gm	Carbohydrate	12.20 gm
Sodium	398.52 mg	Cholesterol	9.80 mg
Saturated fat	1.35 gm		

Margarita Pie

Serves: 8

1 envelope unflavoured gelatin
185g (6oz) sugar
1/4 tsp salt
125g (4oz) egg substitute
125ml (4fl oz) lime juice
1 tsp grated lime zest
125ml (4fl oz) tequila
325ml (12fl oz) nonfat whipped low-fat cream
230mm (9in) prebaked pie shell
4 lime slices

In a small saucepan, combine the gelatin, sugar and salt. In a bowl, beat together the egg substitute and lime juice until blended.

Add to the gelatin mixture. Cook over medium heat, stirring, until the gelatin dissolves, 5 to 7 minutes. Remove from the heat.

Stir in the lime zest and tequila. Cover and chill until the mixture thickens to a pudding consistency. Fold the whipped cream into the tequila mixture. Spoon into the pie shell and chill well. Garnish with lime slices just before serving.

Nutritional Analysis

Calories	239.51 Kcal	Protein	3.74 gm
Fat	7.81 gm	Carbohydrate	33.66 gm
Sodium	230.44 mg	Cholesterol	0.00 mg
Saturated fat	1.93 gm		

Tangy Lime Pie

Serves: 8

Crust:
15 Rich Tea or other plain biscuits, crushed
2 tbsp butter, melted

Filling:
80ml (2¹/₂fl oz) frozen apple juice concentrate, thawed
1 envelope unflavoured gelatin
125g (4oz) sugar
1 tbsp grated lime zest
80ml (2¹/₂fl oz) lime juice
1 tsp pure vanilla extract
325ml (12fl oz) plain low-fat yogurt

To make the crust, mix together the crumbs and butter in a bowl. Grease a 230mm (9in) pie pan. Transfer the crumb mixture to the prepared pan and pat onto the bottom and sides, forming an even layer. Place in the freezer.

To make the filling, pour the apple juice concentrate into a saucepan, add the gelatin and let the mixture stand for a few minutes to allow the gelatin to soften. Stir in the sugar and heat the mixture over low heat until the gelatin and sugar dissolve. Pour into a bowl and add 2 teaspoons of the lime zest, all the lime juice and the vanilla. Place the mixture in the refrigerator until partially set (the consistency of unbeaten egg whites), about 30 minutes.

Using a rotary beater, whip the lime mixture until fluffy. Add the yogurt and whip again. Remove the crust from the freezer and pour the lime mixture into it. Sprinkle the remaining lime

(continued)

Egg Whites and Yolks

Frequently, a recipe will call for a number of egg whites or yolks – and you are left with the unused other halves. If you're stuck with extra egg whites, they can be whipped up with a bit of sugar for some meringues, or, used unwhipped, for a great face mask. With extra yolks, stir them lightly and then freeze in ice cube trays to be defrosted later to brush on bread as a glaze for baking. Alternatively, you can always mix them into the dog's food for a shiny coat.

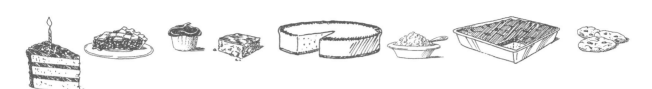

zest over the top. Chill the pie until firm before serving.

Nutritional Analysis

Calories	182.50	Kcal	Protein	3.99	gm
Fat	4.90	gm	Carbohydrate	31.15	gm
Sodium	144.88	mg	Cholesterol	10.31	mg
Saturated fat	2.53	gm			

Balancing Your Menu

If you're leafing through this book in order to find the perfect dessert to balance a particular menu, keep in mind that opposites attract. In other words, if your main course is rich, go for a light fruit-based dessert. Or if you are serving a light salad or sandwiches, choose a calories-be-damned chocolate dessert.

Baked Apple Pancake

Serves: 6

1 tbsp butter
4 medium apples, peeled, cored and thinly sliced
3 tbsp granulated sugar
2 tsp pure vanilla extract
1/4 tsp ground cinnamon
185g (6oz) plain flour
250ml (8fl oz) low-fat milk
2 egg whites
2 whole eggs
3 tbsp icing sugar

Preheat oven to 210°C (425°F), gas mark 7.

In an ovenproof pan, melt the butter over medium heat. Add the apple slices to the pan, and sprinkle 2 tablespoons of the granulated sugar over them. Cook over medium heat until the apples have softened, about 15 minutes. Sprinkle the apples with the vanilla and cinnamon. Remove from the heat.

In a bowl, stir together the flour, milk, egg whites, whole eggs and the remaining granulated

sugar until blended. Pour the batter over the apples.

Bake the pancake for 20 minutes. Reduce the heat to 180°C (350°F), gas mark 4, and continue to bake until the top browns, about 15 minutes longer. Remove from the oven, sprinkle with icing sugar and cut into wedges. Serve immediately.

Nutritional Analysis

Calories	232.05 Kcal	Protein	6.87 gm
Fat	4.47 gm	Carbohydrate	41.03 gm
Sodium	79.74 mg	Cholesterol	77.62 mg
Saturated fat	2.03 gm		

Lemony Cheesecake

Serves: 8

Crust:
12 Rich Tea or other plain biscuits, crushed
2 tbsp butter, melted

Filling:
500g (1lb) low-fat small curd cottage cheese
2 egg whites
2 whole eggs
125ml (4fl oz) evaporated skim milk
125g (4oz) sugar
1 tbsp grated lemon zest
80ml (2½fl oz) lemon juice
60g (2oz) plain flour
lemon slices

To make the crust, mix together the crumbs and butter in a bowl. Grease a 230mm (9in) loose-bottom cake tin. Transfer the crumb mixture to

the prepared tin and press the mixture onto the bottom. Place in the freezer.

Preheat oven to 150°C (300°F), gas mark 2.

To make the filling, in a food processor combine the cottage cheese, egg whites, whole eggs, evaporated milk, sugar, lemon zest and lemon juice. Process until smooth. Add the flour and process a few seconds longer. Remove the crust from the freezer and pour the cottage cheese mixture into it.

Bake until the filling has set, about 1 hour. Cool on a rack. Release the tin sides and slide the cheesecake onto a serving plate. Decorate with the lemon slices.

Nutritional Analysis

Calories	215.83 Kcal	Protein	11.86 gm
Fat	6.36 gm	Carbohydrate	27.87 gm
Sodium	373.30 mg	Cholesterol	63.78 mg
Saturated fat	2.92 gm		

Spicy Cold Pears
Serves: 4

4 pears, peeled, cored and halved lengthways
500ml (1pt) cranberry juice
2 tbsp sugar
½ tsp ground cinnamon
½ tsp ground cloves
1 tsp grated orange zest
1 tsp grated lemon zest

In a saucepan, combine all the ingredients. Bring to the boil, cover, reduce the heat to low and

(continued)

simmer until tender, about 15 minutes. Serve the pears warm or chilled.

Nutritional Analysis

Calories	196.66 Kcal	Protein	0.66 gm
Fat	0.83 gm	Carbohydrate	50.10 gm
Sodium	3.35 mg	Cholesterol	0.00 mg
Saturated fat	0.04 gm		

Pineapple Milk Sherbet

Serves: 4

430ml (14fl oz) low-fat milk
125g (4oz) sugar
250g (8oz) tinned crushed pineapple
2 tbsp lemon juice
60ml (2fl oz) orange juice

Combine the milk and sugar. Add the remaining ingredients and stir until the sugar is dissolved. Pour into a loaf tin and freeze. Stir twice during freezing to break up the sugar crystals.

Nutritional Analysis

Calories	204.46 Kcal	Protein	3.87 gm
Fat	3.62 gm	Carbohydrate	41.00 gm
Sodium	54.85 mg	Cholesterol	14.94 mg
Saturated fat	2.22 gm		

Cranberry Sherbet

Serves: 4

1¹/₂ tsp unflavoured gelatin
500ml (1pt) cranberry juice
125g (4oz) sugar
pinch of salt
2 tbsp skimmed milk powder
125ml (4fl oz) corn syrup
3 tbsp lemon juice

In a small saucepan, sprinkle the gelatin over 125ml (4fl oz) of the juice. Let stand for a few minutes to allow the gelatin to soften. Place over low heat and heat, stirring, until dissolved. Stir in the sugar and salt until dissolved. Pour the remaining juice into a bowl. Sprinkle the milk powder over the top and beat with a fork to dissolve. Add the gelatin mixture to the milk-juice mixture, then mix with all the remaining ingredients. Stir until well mixed. Pour into a metal ice cube tray (if you have one – I found one at a garage sale, the old-fashioned kind where you remove the insert that divides the tray into cubes), or a loaf tin and freeze until almost firm. Beat until fluffy. Refreeze until firm, then serve.

Nutritional Analysis

Calories	297.33 Kcal	Protein	1.52 gm
Fat	0.16 gm	Carbohydrate	76.40 gm
Sodium	103.02 mg	Cholesterol	0.38 mg
Saturated fat	0.00 gm		

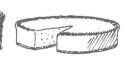

Low-Calorie Orange Sherbet

Serves: 2

250g (8oz) skimmed milk powder
125ml (4fl oz) water
3 tbsp frozen orange juice concentrate, thawed

In a blender, combine all the ingredients. Process until blended. Pour into an ice cube tray. Freeze. When almost solid, turn out of the tray into a bowl and beat with a fork. Return to the tray. Refreeze until firm, then serve.

Nutritional Analysis

Calories	164.05 Kcal	Protein	12.56 gm
Fat	0.29 gm	Carbohydrate	27.90 gm
Sodium	187.45 mg	Cholesterol	6.12 mg
Saturated Fat	0.15 gm		

Quick Fruit Leather

If you're want to make your own fruit leather in bad weather, you can dry it indoors. Let the prepared fruit sit under a lamp or in the sun for 2 hours, then place the baking trays in an oven set at 100°C (140°F). Leave the door open a few centimetres. The leather will be completely dried in 4 to 5 hours.

Peach or Apricot Leather

Serves: 6

10 peaches or apricots, about 1.5kg (3lb)
250g (8oz) sugar

Bring a saucepan of water to the boil. Slip the peaches or apricots into the water for 30 seconds. Using a slotted spoon, transfer to cold water and slip off the skins. Slice the fruit, discarding the stones. You should have 1kg (2lb). Transfer to a large saucepan. Add the sugar and bring to the boil, stirring until the sugar is dissolved. Boil for 3 minutes. Pour into a blender and process until smooth. Cool to lukewarm.

(continued)

Meanwhile, prepare a smooth, level drying surface in full sunlight. Cover baking trays or baking tins with cling film. Spread the purée 6mm (¼in) thick on the prepared surfaces. You can make 4 sheets, each 305 x 380mm (12 x 15in). Let dry outdoors in the sunlight. (Drying may take up to 3 days, depending on the temperature and humidity.) Bring the tins inside at the end of the day, and then return them to the outdoors the next day. The fruit is fully dried when the purée can easily be peeled off the cling film.

To store, roll up the leather in cling film. Wrap in more cling film and seal tightly. The leather will keep at room temperature for 1 month, in the refrigerator for 4 months or in the freezer for 1 month.

Nutritional Analysis

Calories	197.00 Kcal	Protein	1.10 gm
Fat	0.14 gm	Carbohydrate	50.85 gm
Sodium	0.33 mg	Cholesterol	0.00 mg
Saturated fat	0.01 gm		

Spice Cake

Serves: 6

1 tbsp butter
250g (8oz) sugar
2 eggs, well beaten
1 tsp bicarbonate of soda
250ml (8fl oz) nonfat buttermilk
500g (1lb) plain flour
pinch of salt

1 tsp ground nutmeg
1 tsp ground cinnamon
1 tsp ground allspice
1 tsp ground cloves
250g (8oz) raisins

Preheat oven to 180°C (350°F), gas mark 4.

In a bowl, cream together the butter and sugar. Add the eggs and mix thoroughly. Dissolve the bicarbonate of soda in the buttermilk, and stir into the sugar-egg mixture. In a bowl, sift together the flour, salt and spices. Beat the flour mixture into the sugar mixture. Fold in the raisins. Pour the batter into a 200mm (8in) square or round pan. Bake until a knife comes out clean, about 1 hour. Cool on a rack.

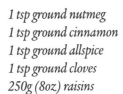

Nutritional Analysis

Calories	415.06 Kcal	Protein	8.74 gm
Fat	4.33 gm	Carbohydrate	87.53 gm
Sodium	327.61 mg	Cholesterol	76.83 mg
Saturated fat	1.90 gm		

Angel Food Cake

Serves: 8

12 egg whites
½ tsp cream of tartar
185g (6oz) caster sugar
1½ tsp pure vanilla extract
½ tsp pure almond extract
250g (8oz) sifted plain flour
300g (10oz) icing sugar
¼ tsp salt

Preheat oven to 180°C (350°F), gas mark 4

In a large bowl, using an electric mixer set on high speed, beat the egg whites and cream of tartar until foamy. Add the caster sugar, 1 tablespoon at a time, beating constantly until the sugar is dissolved and whites are glossy and stand in soft peaks. Beat in the vanilla and almond extracts.

In a bowl, sift together the flour, icing sugar and salt. Sift again. Sift about 125g (4oz) of the flour mixture over the egg whites and, using a rubber spatula, fold in gently just until the flour disappears. Repeat, folding in the remaining flour mixture 125g (4oz) at a time. Turn into an ungreased 255mm (10in) cake tin.

Bake until the top springs back when touched lightly with a finger, 30 to 40 minutes. Invert the cake in the tin onto a funnel or bottle neck to cool, then remove from the tin.

Nutritional Analysis

Calories	217.64	Kcal	Protein	6.25	gm
Fat	0.11	gm	Carbohydrate	47.46	gm
Sodium	154.42	mg	Cholesterol	0.00	mg
Saturated fat	0.01	gm			

Orange-Peach Angel Cake

Serves: 8

1 angel food cake – use recipe above
250g (8oz) tinned sliced peaches
125g (4oz) orange-flavoured jelly
80ml (2¹/₂fl oz) iced water

Angel Food Cake Secrets

Angel food cakes are leavened with just air: no bicarbonate of soda and no baking powder in sight. Whether or not you get a light, tender cake will depend on how much you beat the egg whites, the lightness with which you fold in the sugar-and-flour mixture and the temperature at which you bake the cake. You should beat the egg whites until they are stiff enough to hold up in soft peaks but remain moist and glossy.

(continued)

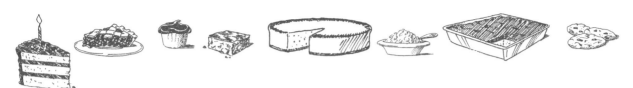

125g (4oz) skimmed milk powder
2 tbsp lemon juice
250g (8oz) tinned mandarin oranges, drained

Cut a 12mm (1/2in) thick slice off the top of the cake and set aside. With the point of the knife, cut a ring 12mm (1/2in) in from the edge of the base and 12mm (1/2in) in from the centre hole. Pull out soft cake to form a trough 38mm (11/2in) deep.

Drain the peaches, capturing the juice in a measuring cup. Add water to measure 125ml (4fl oz). Pour into a saucepan and heat to boiling. Place the jelly in a bowl and pour in the boiling liquid, stirring to dissolve the jelly. Chill until slightly thickened. Mix the iced water and milk powder in a small mixing bowl, and beat until thick. Add the lemon juice. Beat until stiff.

Beat the thickened jelly until smooth, and fold in the whipped milk. Divide the mixture in half. Add the peaches to one half of the mixture and transfer to the cake shell, spreading evenly. Replace the top of the cake. Chill the remaining jelly mixture until it is of a spreading consistency, about 1 hour. Frost the top and sides of the cake. Decorate with the mandarin orange segments.

Nutritional Analysis

Calories	320.23 Kcal	Protein	9.09 gm
Fat	0.17 gm	Carbohydrate	71.43 gm
Sodium	217.65 mg	Cholesterol	0.76 mg
Saturated fat	0.02 gm		

Rhubarb Muffins

Makes: 12 muffins

500g (1lb) finely chopped rhubarb
185g (6oz) sugar
1 tsp grated orange zest
625g (1lb 4oz) plain flour
1/2 tsp baking powder
1 tsp bicarbonate of soda
1 tsp salt
2 eggs, beaten
180ml (6fl oz) nonfat buttermilk
3 tbsp butter or buttery light, reduced-fat margarine, melted

Preheat oven to 190° (375°F), gas mark 5. Grease a 12-cup muffin tin.

In a bowl, combine the rhubarb, 60g (2oz) of the sugar and the orange zest. Stir well and let stand for 5 minutes.

Meanwhile, in another bowl, stir together the flour, the remaining sugar, the baking powder, bicarbonate of soda and salt. Make a well in the centre. In yet another bowl, stir together the eggs, buttermilk and butter or margarine. Add all at once to the flour mixture, stirring just until moistened. The batter should be lumpy. Gently fold in the rhubarb mixture. Spoon into the prepared muffin tin, filling each cup two-thirds full.

Bake until a knife comes out clean, 20 to 25 minutes. Remove from the oven and cool on a rack for 15 minutes before serving.

Nutritional Analysis

Calories	197.47 Kcal	Protein	4.50 gm
Fat	4.70 gm	Carbohydrate	34.27 gm
Sodium	378.81 mg	Cholesterol	43.48 mg
Saturated fat	2.24 gm		

Apple Date Bread

Serves: 8

Topping:
185g (6oz) firmly packed light brown sugar
185g (6oz) nuts, chopped
2 tbsp butter, softened
60g (2oz) plain flour
1/4 tsp ground cinnamon
1/4 tsp salt

370g (12oz) plain flour
370g (12oz) wholemeal flour
250g (8oz) sugar
1 tbsp baking powder
1 1/2 tsp salt
250g (8oz) flaked dried coconut
325ml (12fl oz) low-fat milk
1 egg, lightly beaten
250g (8oz) dates, stoned and diced
250g (8oz) apples, peeled, cored and finely chopped

Preheat oven to 180°C (350°F), gas mark 4. Spray a 230 x 75mm (9 x 3in) loaf tin with nonstick cooking spray.

To make the topping, combine all the ingredients in a bowl, mixing well. Set aside.

In a bowl, stir together the flours, sugar, baking powder and salt. Stir in the coconut. In another bowl, stir together the milk and egg. Add the milk mixture to the flour mixture, blending well. Stir in the apples and dates, mixing well. Turn into the prepared loaf tin. Sprinkle with the topping. Bake until a knife comes out clean, about 1 1/4 hours. Cool on a rack, then turn out of the tin and slice to serve.

Nutritional Analysis

Calories	598.47 Kcal	Protein	10.66 gm
Fat	15.24 gm	Carbohydrate	110.58gm
Sodium	785.80 mg	Cholesterol	36.15 mg
Saturated fat	5.75 gm		

Pear Tea Bread with Lemon Glaze

Serves: 8

500g (1lb) tinned pear halves
625g (1lb 4oz) plain flour
125g (4oz) caster sugar
1 tbsp baking powder
1 tsp salt
1/8 tsp ground cardamom
60ml (2fl oz) corn oil
1 egg, lightly beaten
2 tsp grated lemon zest

Lemon Glaze:
1 tbsp lemon juice
60g (2oz) icing sugar

(continued)

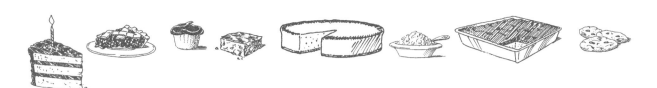

Reducing Fat in Cakes

Fruit purées, such as pear or apple-sauce, add sweetness and moistness to baked goods without adding fat. For a tasty, moist cake, use only a quarter of the oil called for in a recipe, and substitute a fruit purée for the rest.

Preheat oven to 180°C (350°F), gas mark 4. Spray a 230 x 100mm (9 x 4in) loaf tin with nonstick cooking spray.

Drain the pears, reserving the syrup. Set aside 1 pear half for garnish.

In a blender or food processor, purée the remaining pear halves. Add enough of the reserved pear syrup to the puréed pears to measure 250ml (8fl oz).

In a bowl, stir together the flour, caster sugar, baking powder, salt and cardamom. In another bowl, combine the puréed pear mixture with the oil, egg and lemon zest. Stir the pear mixture into the flour mixture just until combined. Pour into the prepared loaf tin. Slice the reserved pear half into sixths. Arrange the slices on top of the batter. Bake until the bread tests done, when a knife inserted comes out clean, 50 to 55 minutes.

While the bread is baking, make the glaze: in a bowl, stir together the lemon juice and icing sugar to form a thin glaze.

When the bread is done, remove from the oven and let cool in the pan for 5 minutes. Turn onto a rack and spoon the lemon glaze over the top. Let cool completely. Wrap in tin foil and let stand overnight at room temperature before serving.

Nutritional Analysis

Calories	427.02 Kcal	Protein	6.69 gm
Fat	10.64 gm	Carbohydrate	77.14 gm
Sodium	647.54 mg	Cholesterol	35.41 mg
Saturated fat	1.48 gm		

Sherried Egg-White Custard with Spiced Cherry Sauce

Serves: 4

2 tbsp sugar
1/8 tsp salt
310ml (10fl oz) milk
1/4 tsp pure vanilla extract
2 to 3 tsp sherry or rum flavouring
3 egg whites, lightly beaten

Spiced Cherry Sauce:
250g (8oz) tinned cherries, unsweetened
3 drops of red food colouring
1 tsp cornflour
2 tsp water or lemon juice
pinch of ground cloves
pinch of ground cinnamon
pinch of ground ginger

Preheat oven to 170°C (325°F), gas mark 3.

In a saucepan, combine the sugar, salt and milk. Place over medium heat and stir until the sugar dissolves. Cool. Add the vanilla, flavouring and egg whites. Stir well and pour through a sieve into a 500ml (1 pint) baking dish. Place in a baking tin, and pour hot water into the pan to reach halfway up the sides of the dish. Bake until a knife comes out clean, about 1 hour.

Meanwhile, make the sauce: in a saucepan, combine the cherries and food colouring. Place over medium heat and bring to a simmer. In a small bowl, stir together the cornflour and water or lemon juice. Add to the pan and cook, stirring, until the sauce is clear, about 5 minutes. Stir in the spices.

Remove the custard from the oven. Serve warm with the warm cherry sauce drizzled over the top.

Nutritional Analysis

Calories	121.10	Kcal	Protein	5.72	gm
Fat	2.75	gm	Carbohydrate	16.01	gm
Sodium	158.26	mg	Cholesterol	11.35	mg
Saturated fat	1.69	gm			

Sweet Potato Pudding

Serves: 8

425g (14oz) plain flour
330g (11oz) sugar
1 tsp bicarbonate of soda
1/4 tsp baking powder
1/2 tsp salt
1/2 tsp ground cinnamon
1/2 tsp ground allspice
1/4 tsp ground cloves
250g (8oz) mashed cooked sweet potato
60g (2oz) butter, at room temperature
80ml (2 1/2 fl oz) water
1 egg

Preheat oven to 180°C (350°F), gas mark 4. Grease a 200mm (8in) square cake tin.

In a bowl, sift together the flour, sugar, bicarbonate of soda, baking powder, salt, cinnamon, allspice and cloves. Add the sweet potato, butter and water to the flour mixture. Using an electric mixer, beat the mixture for 2 minutes. Add the egg

(continued)

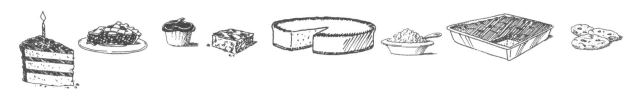

and beat for another 2 minutes. Pour the batter into the prepared cake pan.

Bake for about 40 minutes. Serve warm.

Nutritional Analysis

Calories	332.53 Kcal	Protein	4.20 gm
Fat	7.28 gm	Carbohydrate	63.40 gm
Sodium	390.23 mg	Cholesterol	42.08 mg
Saturated fat	3.95 gm		

Fresh Peach Pie

Serves: 8

pastry dough for double-crust 230mm (9in) pie
185g (6oz) firmly packed light brown sugar
425g (14oz) plain flour
1/2 tsp ground cinnamon
1/4 tsp ground ginger
1/2 tsp ground nutmeg
8 peaches, peeled, stoned and quartered

Preheat oven to 200°C (400°F), gas mark 6.

Roll out half the pastry dough on a floured work surface into a 255mm (10in) round. Transfer the round to a 230mm (9in) pie plate.

In a medium bowl, combine the brown sugar, flour and spices, mixing well. Add the peaches to the sugar-flour mixture, tossing gently. Pour the peach mixture into the pie shell. Roll out the remaining dough into a 255mm (10in) round and drape over the peach filling. Trim and flute the edges of the pastry. Prick the top crust with a fork.

Bake for 10 minutes, reduce the heat to 190°C (375°F), gas mark 5, and continue to bake until

the crust is golden brown, 50 to 55 minutes. Cool on a rack. Serve warm or at room temperature.

Nutritional Analysis

Calories	461.04 Kcal	Protein	6.69 gm
Fat	15.36 gm	Carbohydrate	75.54 gm
Sodium	241.58 mg	Cholesterol	0.00 mg
Saturated fat	3.79 gm		

Lemon Meringue Pie

Serves: 6

375g (12oz) plus 6 tbsp sugar
3 tbsp cornflour
3 tbsp plain flour
pinch of salt
125ml (4fl oz) hot water
3 eggs, separated
1/2 tsp grated lemon zest
2 tbsp butter or buttery light, reduced-fat margarine
80ml (2 1/2 fl oz) plus 1 tsp lemon juice
230mm (9in) prebaked pie shell

In a saucepan, combine the 375g (12oz) sugar, cornflour, flour and salt. Stir in hot water until smooth. Bring to the boil over high heat, stirring constantly. Reduce the heat to medium. Cook, stirring, until slightly thickened, about 8 minutes. Remove from the heat. In a bowl, lightly beat the egg yolks. Stir a small amount of the hot mixture into the egg yolks and return to the hot mixture. Bring to the boil over high heat, stirring constantly. Reduce the heat to low and cook, stirring, 4 minutes longer. Remove from the heat. Add the lemon zest and butter or

margarine. Stir in the 80ml (2¹/₂fl oz) lemon juice. Cover with cling film, pressing it directly onto the surface, and cool for 10 minutes. Pour into prebaked pie shell. Cool completely.

Preheat oven to 180°C (350°F), gas mark 4.

In a bowl, using an electric mixer set on high speed, beat the egg whites with the remaining lemon juice until soft peaks form. Gradually add the remaining sugar, beating until stiff peaks form and the sugar is dissolved. Spread over the cooled filling, sealing to the edges of the pastry.

Bake until the egg whites brown, about 12 to 15 minutes. Cool completely on a rack before serving.

Nutritional Analysis

Calories	504.51	Kcal	Protein	5.60	gm
Fat	16.90	gm	Carbohydrate	84.60	gm
Sodium	259.92	mg	Cholesterol	116.70	mg
Saturated fat	5.80	gm			

Strawberry Whip

Serves: 2

1 egg white
300g (10oz) strawberries, sliced
60g (2oz) sugar
a few drops of lemon juice

In a bowl, using an electric mixer, whip together the egg white and strawberries. When the mixture begins to thicken, gradually add the sugar. Continue to beat until the mixture holds soft peaks. Stir in a few drops of lemon juice. Chill before serving.

Happy Meringue

When I was growing up and watched my mother make lemon meringue pie, I always thought that the meringue part of the process – beating the egg whites and then spooning it onto the lemon part – was fascinating. I was especially intrigued when the peaks of meringue began to lean gently to one side, under their own weight. After the pie was baked and cooled, I always ate the meringue but not the lemon custard, which was never sweet enough for me.

For your own happy meringue, use a copper bowl if you have one to beat the whites, and don't even bother if the humidity is above 80 per cent.

(continued)

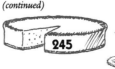

Nutritional Analysis

Calories	133.66 Kcal	Protein	2.32 gm
Fat	0.35 gm	Carbohydrate	31.82 gm
Sodium	28.64 mg	Cholesterol	0.00 mg
Saturated fat	0.01 gm		

Baked Pears

Serves: 6

2 tbsp lemon juice
6 pears, peeled and cored
2 to 4 tbsp sugar
125ml (4fl oz) whipped low-fat cream

Preheat oven to 190°C (375°F), gas mark 5.

Put the lemon juice in a 1l (2 pint) baking dish and add just enough water to cover the bottom. Add the pears, cover and bake until tender when pierced with a knife, 20 to 25 minutes.

Remove from the oven. Sprinkle each pear with 1 to 2 teaspoons sugar. Bake uncovered for 10 minutes longer to glaze. Serve warm or chilled. Top with whipped cream, if desired.

Nutritional Analysis

Calories	136.51 Kcal	Protein	0.66 gm
Fat	1.33 gm	Carbohydrate	32.97 gm
Sodium	1.12 mg	Cholesterol	0.00 mg
Saturated fat	0.69 gm		

Low-Fat Pumpkin Pie

Serves: 8

185g (6oz) sugar
1/8 tsp salt
1/2 tsp ground cinnamon
1/2 tsp ground ginger
1/2 tsp ground nutmeg
pinch of ground cloves
375g (12oz) tinned unsweetened pumpkin
1 tsp pure vanilla extract
325ml (12fl oz) evaporated skim milk
1/2 tsp grated orange zest
3 egg whites, lightly beaten
230mm (9in) unbaked pie shell

Preheat oven to 220°C (450°F), gas mark 8.

In a bowl, stir together the sugar, salt, cinnamon, ginger, nutmeg and cloves. Stir in the pumpkin. Add the vanilla, evaporated milk, orange zest and egg whites. Beat with an electric mixer until smooth. Pour into the unbaked pie shell. Bake for 10 minutes. Reduce the heat to 170°C (325°F), gas mark 3, and continue to bake until a knife inserted in the filling comes out clean, about 45 minutes. Cool on a rack.

Nutritional Analysis

Calories	240.92 Kcal	Protein	6.81 gm
Fat	7.72 gm	Carbohydrate	36.57 gm
Sodium	231.66 mg	Cholesterol	1.91 mg
Saturated fat	1.99 gm		

Couscous with Yogurt and Fruit

Serves: 4

> 250ml (8fl oz) milk
> 1 tbsp butter
> 1/4 tsp salt
> 185g (6oz) instant couscous
> 125ml (4fl oz) low-fat vanilla yogurt
> 2 tbsp sugar
> 125g (4oz) berries or diced fresh fruit in season

In a medium saucepan, combine the milk, butter and salt and bring to the boil. Stir in the couscous, cover, remove from the heat and let stand for 5 minutes.

Fluff the couscous with a fork to separate the grains. Stir in the yogurt and sugar, and fold in the fruit.

Nutritional Analysis

Calories	232.49 Kcal	Protein	7.46 gm
Fat	5.51 gm	Carbohydrate	38.18 gm
Sodium	224.23 mg	Cholesterol	17.71 mg
Saturated fat	3.29 gm		

Coffee Almond Float

Serves: 1

> 1 tsp brown sugar
> 60ml (2fl oz) brewed cold coffee
> splash of orgeat (almond) syrup
> ice cubes
> 125g (4oz) low-fat milk
> 125g (4oz) coffee or chocolate low-fat, frozen ice-cream
> (dairy-free glacé has no fat)

In a parfait glass, dissolve the sugar in the coffee. Add the syrup, stirring to mix well. Add the ice and milk and stir well. Top with the ice-cream.

Nutritional Analysis

Calories	171.34 Kcal	Protein	7.05 gm
Fat	2.79 gm	Carbohydrate	30.52 gm
Sodium	123.97 mg	Cholesterol	9.87 mg
Saturated fat	1.79 gm		

Pears in Orange Sauce
Serves: 4

> 250ml (8fl oz) water
> 2 William or comice pears, halved lengthways and
>   cored
> 180ml (6fl oz) orange juice
> 2 tbsp lemon juice
> 1 tbsp cornflour
> 3 tbsp honey
> 1/4 tsp finely shredded orange zest
> 1/4 tsp salt
> fresh mint leaves

In a 255mm (10in) pan, bring the water to the boil. Add the pear halves, cover and simmer gently over low heat until tender when pierced with a knife, about 10 minutes. Set aside.

In a small saucepan, mix together the orange juice, lemon juice and cornflour. Stir until the cornflour is dissolved. Add the honey, orange zest and salt, and mix well. Place over medium heat and cook until thickened and bubbling, about 10 minutes. To serve, spoon the sauce over the pears and garnish with mint leaves.

(continued)

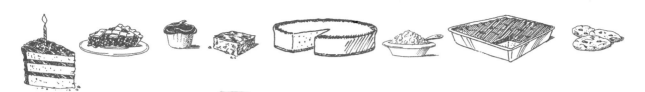

Nutritional Analysis

Calories	125.59 Kcal	Protein	0.68 gm
Fat	0.37 gm	Carbohydrate	32.50 gm
Sodium	145.97 mg	Cholesterol	0.00 mg
Saturated fat	0.01 gm		

Bread Pudding

Serves: 8

1kg (2lb) coarsely crumbled stale bread
3 to 4 apples, peeled and grated
125g (4oz) raisins
125g (4oz) chopped nuts
750ml (1½pt) milk
3 eggs
2 tsp pure vanilla extract
6 tbsp honey
1 tsp ground cinnamon
½ tsp ground nutmeg
juice of ½ lemon

Preheat oven to 180°C (350°F), gas mark 4.

In a 200mm (8in) square baking tin, stir together the breadcrumbs, grated apple, raisins and nuts. In a blender or food processor, combine all the remaining ingredients. Process until blended. Pour over the breadcrumb mixture. Make sure the bread is saturated.

Bake until the bread on top starts to turn slightly brown, about 35 minutes. Serve hot.

Tinned vs Fresh Fruit

A dessert that combines fruit and cake is one of the few sweets for which tinned fruit can be easily substituted for fresh fruit. Such desserts are particularly welcome during the cold weather months. Just make sure you drain the fruit thoroughly – if specified – before using it in the recipe, otherwise you could end up with a mushy mess. You can mix two different types of fruit in the same recipe with ease.

Nutritional Analysis

Calories	273.74 Kcal	Protein	8.27 gm
Fat	8.36 gm	Carbohydrate	43.77 gm
Sodium	166.17 mg	Cholesterol	83.51 mg
Saturated fat	1.79 gm		

Pumpkin Pudding

Serves: 4

500g (1lb) low-fat cottage cheese
¼ tsp salt
500g (1lb) tinned unsweetened pumpkin
4 eggs
60ml (2fl oz) honey
ground nutmeg

Preheat oven to 180°C (350°F), gas mark 4.

In a blender or food processor, combine all the ingredients. Process until smooth. Pour into individual custard cups. Place the cups in a baking tin. Pour hot water into the tin to reach halfway up the sides of the custard cups. Bake until a knife inserted into the centre comes out clean, about 40 minutes. Cool before serving.

Nutritional Analysis

Calories	262.29 Kcal	Protein	21.70 gm
Fat	6.51 gm	Carbohydrate	31.01 gm
Sodium	673.76 mg	Cholesterol	217.04 mg
Saturated fat	2.45 gm		

Peach Sorbet

Serves: 4

500g (1lb) tinned sliced peaches in water, drained and liquid reserved
1 tsp lemon juice
2 tbsp honey
1 envelope unflavoured gelatin
1 tsp pure almond extract

Pour the liquid from the peaches into a measuring jug. Add water to make 375ml (12fl oz). Pour into a small saucepan. Add the lemon juice, honey and gelatin. Let stand for about 5 minutes to allow the gelatin to soften. Place the pan over medium heat and heat, stirring constantly, until the gelatin dissolves. Remove from the heat and add the almond extract. Set aside for 30 minutes.

In a food processor, purée the peaches until smooth. Add the gelatin mixture and process until thoroughly combined. Pour into a 230 x 330mm (9 x 13in) metal pan, and place in the freezer for 2 hours.

Transfer to a chilled bowl, and beat with a rotary beater or an electric mixer until the mixture is fluffy. Return to the metal pan, and then return the pan to the freezer for 2 hours. Scoop into individual dishes to serve.

Nutritional Analysis

Calories	69.00 Kcal	Protein	2.03 gm
Fat	0.06 gm	Carbohydrate	15.73 gm
Sodium	7.55 mg	Cholesterol	0.00 mg
Saturated fat	0.01 gm		

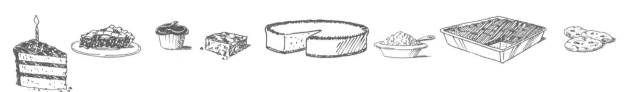

Lemony Blueberry Ice-'Cream'

Serves: 4

500g (1lb) blueberries
125g (4oz) sugar
1 tbsp cornflour
375ml (12fl oz) tinned evaporated skimmed milk
2 egg whites
1 tsp grated lemon zest
2 tbsp lemon juice
1 tsp pure vanilla extract

In a saucepan, combine the blueberries with 60ml (2fl oz) of the sugar. Place over medium heat and heat, stirring constantly, until the sugar dissolves, about 5 minutes. Remove from the heat. Place a colander over a bowl and pour the blueberry mixture into the colander. Press the berries through the colander with the back of a spoon. Scrape the mashed berries from the outside of the colander into the bowl with the blueberry juice. Place the bowl in the refrigerator.

Add the remaining sugar and the cornflour to the saucepan. Stir in about two-thirds of the evaporated milk. Place over medium heat and bring to the boil, stirring constantly. Cook the mixture until it is as thick as pudding.

Remove from the heat and add the egg whites and the remaining evaporated milk, mixing well. Stir the milk mixture into the blueberry purée. Add the lemon zest, lemon juice and vanilla. Stir until blended. Chill for 20 minutes.

Pour into an ice-cream maker and freeze according to the manufacturer's instructions.

Nutritional Analysis

Calories	233.03	Kcal	Protein	9.48	gm
Fat	0.48	gm	Carbohydrate	48.76	gm
Sodium	143.92	mg	Cholesterol	3.82	mg
Saturated fat	0.11	gm			

Chocolatey Ice-'Cream'

Serves: 4

125g (4oz) instant chocolate pudding
60g (2oz) sugar
375ml (12fl oz) tinned evaporated skimmed milk
250ml (8fl oz) low-fat milk

In a medium bowl, stir together the instant pudding and sugar. Add the evaporated milk and low-fat milk, and stir until blended. Pour into an ice-cream maker and freeze according to the manufacturer's instructions.

Nutritional Analysis

Calories	180.09	Kcal	Protein	10.09	gm
Fat	1.70	gm	Carbohydrate	31.57	gm
Sodium	221.18	mg	Cholesterol	9.37	mg
Saturated fat	1.02	gm			

Frozen Yogurt with Berry Sauce

Serves: 4

300g (10oz) frozen strawberries, thawed
1/2 tsp pure vanilla extract
500ml (1pt) low-fat vanilla frozen yogurt

Place the strawberries and vanilla extract in a food processor. Purée until smooth. Spoon the yogurt into individual dishes and drizzle the strawberry sauce over the top. Serve immediately.

Nutritional Analysis

Calories	159.58 Kcal	Protein	3.36 gm
Fat	1.59 gm	Carbohydrate	35.43 gm
Sodium	62.16 mg	Cholesterol	4.99 mg
Saturated Fat	0.99 gm		

Sweet Cocoa Sauce

Yield: 1 cup

125g (4oz) cocoa powder
125g (4oz) sugar
125ml (4fl oz) water
1 tsp pure vanilla extract

In a saucepan, stir together the cocoa powder and sugar. Stir in the water and place over high heat. Bring to the boil, stirring constantly. Remove from the heat and stir in the vanilla. Refrigerate.

(continued)

The Still-Freeze Method

If you don't have an ice-cream maker, you can still make delicious, creamy ice-cream in your freezer using the still-freeze method:

1. Pour the ice-cream mixture into a metal loaf tin or a 200mm (8in) square baking pan.
2. Cover with cling film and place in the freezer.
3. Freeze for at least 1 hour until solid.
4. Break up the frozen mixture with a fork and place in a food processor.
5. Process until soft but not melted.
6. Serve.

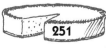

Nutritional Analysis

Calories	31.11	Kcal	Protein	0.52	gm
Fat	0.36	gm	Carbohydrate	7.72	gm
Sodium	0.64	mg	Cholesterol	0.00	mg
Saturated fat	0.21	gm			

Sweet Vanilla Sauce

Makes: 310ml (10fl oz)

60ml (2fl oz) nonfat buttermilk
2 tsp sugar
250ml (8fl oz) vanilla low-fat yogurt

In a small bowl, mix together the buttermilk and sugar. Add the yogurt and mix well. Serve over fruit.

Nutritional Analysis

Calories	12.37	Kcal	Protein	0.66	gm
Fat	0.14	gm	Carbohydrate	2.13	gm
Sodium	11.11	mg	Cholesterol	0.62	mg
Saturated fat	0.09	gm			

Angelic Strawberry Cake

Serves: 8

1 angel food cake – use recipe on page 238
*500ml (1pt) strawberry low-fat frozen yogurt, thawed
   slightly*
500g (1lb) strawberries, destemmed and sliced

Cut the cake in half horizontally. Spread the strawberry yogurt onto the bottom half of the cake. Place half the strawberry slices on top of the yogurt. Replace the top half of the cake. Place more strawberry slices on top of the cake. Freeze for 15 minutes before serving.

Nutritional Analysis

Calories	274.63	Kcal	Protein	7.98	gm
Fat	1.00	gm	Carbohydrate	58.76	gm
Sodium	184.82	mg	Cholesterol	2.49	mg
Saturated fat	0.50	gm			

Salsa Fruit Salad

Serves: 8

500g (1lb) chopped watermelon
1 orange, peeled and diced
500g (1lb) strawberries, destemmed and sliced
2 tbsp lemon juice
1 tbsp honey

In a medium bowl, combine the watermelon, orange and strawberries. Drizzle with the lemon juice and honey, and toss well. Cover and chill for at least 1 hour before serving.

Nutritional Analysis

Calories	42.32	Kcal	Protein	0.62	gm
Fat	0.35	gm	Carbohydrate	10.26	gm
Sodium	2.09	mg	Cholesterol	0.00	mg
Saturated fat	0.00	gm			

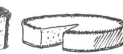

INDEX